T0319985

Economic Theories of International Environmental Cooperation

NEW HORIZONS IN ENVIRONMENTAL ECONOMICS

General Editors: Wallace E. Oates, *Professor of Economics, University of Maryland, USA* and Henk Folmer, *Professor of General Economics, Wageningen University and Professor of Environmental Economics, Tilburg University, The Netherlands*

This important series is designed to make a significant contribution to the development of the principles and practices of environmental economics. It includes both theoretical and empirical work. International in scope, it addresses issues of current and future concern in both East and West and in developed and developing countries.

The main purpose of the series is to create a forum for the publication of high quality work and to show how economic analysis can make a contribution to understanding and resolving the environmental problems confronting the world in the twenty-first century.

Recent titles in the series include:

Economic Growth and Environmental Policy
A Theoretical Approach
Frank Hettich

The Political Economy of Environmental Protectionism
Achim Körber

Principles of Environmental and Resource Economics
A Guide for Students and Decision-Makers
Second Edition
Edited by Henk Folmer and H. Landis Gabel

Designing International Environmental Agreements
Incentive Compatible Strategies for Cost-Effective Cooperation
Carsten Schmidt

Spatial Environmental and Resource Economics
The Selected Essays of Charles D. Kolstad
Charles D. Kolstad

Economic Theories of International Environmental Cooperation
Carsten Helm

Negotiating Environmental Quality
Policy Implementation in Germany and the United States
Markus A. Lehmann

Game Theory and International Environmental Cooperation
Michael Finus

Sustainable Small-Scale Forestry
Socio-Economic Analysis and Policy
Edited by S.R. Harrison, J.L. Herbohn and K.F. Herbohn

Environmental Economics and Public Policy
Selected Papers of Robert N. Stavins
Robert N. Stavins

International Environmental Externalities and the Double Dividend
Sebastian Killinger

Economic Theories of International Environmental Cooperation

Carsten Helm

Otto-von-Guericke University Magdeburg, Germany

NEW HORIZONS IN ENVIRONMENTAL ECONOMICS

Edward Elgar

Cheltenham, UK • Northampton, MA, USA

Published by
Edward Elgar Publishing Limited
Glensanda House
Montpellier Parade
Cheltenham
Glos GL50 1UA
UK

Edward Elgar Publishing, Inc.
136 West Street
Suite 202
Northampton
Massachusetts 01060
USA

A catalogue record for this book
is available from the British Library

Library of Congress Cataloguing in Publication Data

Helm, Carsten, 1966–
    Economic theories of international environmental cooperation /
Carsten Helm
    (New horizons in environmental economics)
    Includes bibliographical references and index.
    1. Environmental policy—International cooperation—Economic aspects.
    2. Environmental economics. I. Series.
    HC79.E5 H455   2000
    333.7'01'5193—dc21   00–037611

ISBN 1 84064 342 0

Printed and bound in Great Britain by Biddles Ltd, *www.biddles.co.uk*

Contents

I International Policy in the Fairness Mode

II International Policy in the Cooperative Mode

III International Policy in the Non-Cooperative Mode

List of Figures

List of Tables

Preface

This book is a revised version of my Ph.D. thesis, which was approved in July 1999 by the Department of Economics and Business Administration of the Humboldt University of Berlin. Most of it originates from my work within two research projects in which I was involved at the Potsdam Institute for Climate Impact Research (PIK).

A number of people have played an important role in the process that led to this book. They helped to arouse my interest in international environmental politics and economic theory, they discussed various topics with me, they read parts or even all of the text, and they gave me the moral support that helped me to enjoy this project. Even though I cannot name all persons to whom I owe a debt of gratitude in one way or another, at least some of them should be mentioned explicitly.

First of all, I would like to thank the two supervisors of my Ph.D. thesis, Bengt-Arne Wickström of the Humboldt University of Berlin and Udo E. Simonis of the Science Center Berlin. Over the years, they have made a tremendous effort in reading through my drafts and offering their suggestions.

Bengt-Arne Wickström accepted me as his Ph.D. student at a time when we hardly knew each other. This quickly changed, and his research colloquium, at which I regularly had the chance to discuss my work, not only fostered my progress, but also taught me to admire his quick grasp of problems that had taken me a long time to think about. (It goes without saying that I also enjoyed the pizza which always completed the colloquium.)

Udo Ernst Simonis has accompanied me since I was a student. He introduced me to the problems of international environmental politics, and I admire his energy and enthusiasm for this topic. It was in particular his encouragement – together with that of Michael Bolle of the Free University Berlin – that was crucial to my decision to enter academia.

I wrote the Ph.D. thesis while I was employed at the Potsdam Institute for Climate Impact Research. Not only its unique location in the beautiful 'Wissenschaftspark Albert Einstein' on the Telegrafenberg, but also my colleagues and project leaders made it a stimulating environment. Thanks go to Ferenc Tóth, Detlef Sprinz, Thomas Bruckner,

xiii

Hans-Martin Füssel, Marian Leimbach, Ina Meyer, Gerhard Petschel-Held, Kirsten Zickfeld and all the other members of the institute whom I cannot mention because it has grown so fast. I am particularly grateful to Hans-Joachim Schellnhuber, director of PIK, for his support which I received on several occasions.

In autumn 1998, I spent three months at the Department of Economics at Stockholm University. I am very grateful for the hospitality which I received there, especially to Peter Bohm, Martin Dufwenberg, Michael Lundholm and Björn Carlén. It was a perfect setting in which to finalize the thesis.

In August 1999 I started my new job as assistant professor at the Faculty of Economics and Management of the Otto-von-Guericke University Magdeburg. Most of the revision of the Ph.D. thesis for publication as a book took place here. I am grateful to Dominique Demougin and my new colleagues Bertrand Köbel and Lutz Weinert, who made me feel comfortable at my new workplace from the very first moment.

Special thanks go to Frank Biermann. He has not only been a good friend for a long time; since the first semester at university, he has read most of the texts that I have written. As he is a political scientist and lawyer, I am sure that this wasn't always fun for him. Nevertheless, I have learned a lot from his critical comments.

I am also grateful to Henry Tulkens and Parkash Chander for their detailed comments on a draft of Chapter 4 of this book, and to Victoria Büsch, Jens Barthel and Wolfgang Hildebrand for their comments at various seminars.

Last but certainly not least I would like to thank my parents for the support and encouragement that I received from them, and Nila – for a multitude of reasons.

Carsten Helm
Magdeburg, December 1999

1. Introduction

The last thing that we find out
in writing a book is to know
what we must put first.

Blaise Pascal (1623–1662)

There are different opinions on whether one should write the introduction before or after the main body of the text. Personally, I agree with the French mathematician Blaise Pascal, and I find the problem mentioned in his statement above to be of the more difficult type.

There is certainly no need to give reasons why transboundary environmental problems are an important subject of study, both theoretically and politically. Although climate change, acid rain and ozone depletion – to name but a few of them – are relatively recent phenomena, they are now widely discussed and heavily researched, not least in the field of economics. Indeed, given that the number of publications has increased rapidly during the last ten years or so, the question is rather whether we need yet another extensive treatise on this topic. Here, my answer is a clear 'yes', which goes beyond the self-serving 'yes' of justifying why this text has been written.

From a positive perspective, the strategic interactions involved in the international decision-making process are only poorly understood; and from a normative perspective, what is a 'good' or 'fair' international environmental policy remains highly controversial.

This book relies heavily on game theory and axiomatic methods to address these issues. The appropriateness of these tool kits, however, and the use of the mathematics they involve for gaining insights into international environmental politics probably need some justification. By its very nature, mathematics is reductionist. In particular non-economists often regard this approach not so much as a useful tool to structure one's ideas and track their implications in a precise way, but rather as an alienation from real-world phenomena.[1]

---

[1] For a discussion of the role of mathematics in economics see Mirkowski (1991) and Streeten (1997).

One might easily put this perspective aside and argue that other disciplines like political science also rely heavily on simplifying assumptions in their analysis. The fact that they are often less explicit about them can hardly be interpreted as a methodological strength. Nevertheless, one should be aware of the limitations of game theory and axiomatic methods, and exercise a substantial modesty in deriving policy conclusions from abstract models. As Summers (1991, 145) put it, 'it is all too easy to confuse what is tractable with what is right'.

In most of this book, the analysis is motivated by a particular political problem, usually related to climate change. Accordingly, theory has been assigned the role of the servant to investigate critical issues of international environmental cooperation; it is *not* the master that drives the analysis. This should not, of course, be understood as an argument against 'pure theory', but it simply reflects the chosen focus. Thus, I will give relatively more space to elaborate on the political problems that underlie the analysis, while still emphasizing the need for rigorous reasoning.

Let me then turn to the structure of the book. If one takes pictures of a house, one can photograph it from the front, from the back, from the side, and in principle also from above. The impressions one gets may be completely different, and one would be ill advised to buy the house after having seen it from one perspective only.

Similarly, the following text contains a collection of snapshots of the same motif – international environmental cooperation – taken from different perspectives and using different techniques. Thus, the basic object of investigation remains very much the same throughout the text: there is a finite set of agents (or countries) that are characterized by a production function with polluting emissions as the only input good, and a damage cost function that depends on domestic and foreign emissions. Sometimes, tradable endowments with emission rights are specified and utility is transferable via a single output good. In a nutshell, we have an economy with multilateral externalities and transferable utility. While this setup is relatively simple, it suffices as a common starting point to systematically analyze various important aspects of international environmental politics.

The book is separated into three parts which relate to different analytical concepts to describe or prescribe states' behavior in regard to international environmental problems. Each part then contains a number of individual chapters, which are largely self-contained.

Part I of this book tells the story about international politics in the fairness mode. Thus, the analysis is purely normative, even though aspects of political feasibility are addressed as well. The empirical focus is on fair burden sharing in the climate change regime.

Chapter 2 addresses this question from the 'local justice' perspective of fair division theory. It starts by setting out some well-known principles for the fair division of common property resources. These are Pareto efficiency, individual rationality, population monotonicity, resource monotonicity and envy-freeness, where the last criterion has to be adapted to the transferable utility context. In the next step, the WESA mechanism (WESA = Walrasian Equilibrium with the Stand-Alone upper bound) is introduced, which comes very close to satisfying all criteria simultaneously. In particular, it compares favorably to the widely advocated Walrasian mechanism, that is the competitive market allocation. The chapter ends with a quantitative illustration using a computable general equilibrium model.

The main objection to applying fair division theory to burden sharing in the climate change regime is its neglect of differences in income levels across countries. Therefore, Chapter 3 explores a more holistic 'global justice' approach based on welfare theory. The main conclusion in this framework is that a fair burden-sharing rule should favor poorer countries, but there is considerable dispute about the 'how much'. A further reason why I devoted a chapter to welfare theory is the assumption throughout the text that actors respectively countries have well-defined payoff functions. It is worthwhile to give at least some thought to the difficulties of determining such a national payoff function.

Part II and Part III of the book use positive theories of international environmental policy. The primary focus is no longer the search for 'fair' agreements, but for those that may arise from the strategic interaction of sovereign states.

In Chapter 4, a stability concept from cooperative game theory – the core – is applied to show that a potential for agreement on Pareto-efficient emission reductions exists even if states are assumed to be selfish. Furthermore, because the core often contains different solutions, there is some scope for picking the one that is most appealing from a normative point of view. The proposed candidate is in the spirit of egalitarian equivalence, and it gives all agents the same individual benefits measured in terms of free environmental protection relative to a reference point.

Turning to non-cooperative game theory, Chapter 5 analyzes some effects that arise if emission allowances are tradable at the international level. It is generally argued that trading leads to lower abatement costs and as such entails the potential to reach agreement on more ambitious reduction targets. It will be shown that this is not necessarily the case; trading may have the perverse effect of resulting in higher rather than lower overall emission levels. The reason is that an international trading system not only increases efficiency, but by introducing the possibility to sell surplus allowances, it changes the incentive structure of the game. This provides a rational explanation for the phenomenon of 'hot air', which refers to the fact that some countries' emission targets in the Kyoto Protocol even exceed their emission projections without any abatement measures.

Chapter 6 introduces aspects of uncertainty into the analysis because the complexities of international environmental problems are often only poorly understood. If there exists a plurality of legitimate perspectives, it is argued that countries can use this veil of uncertainty to hide their distributional interests. Another new theoretical aspect is that international cooperation will be modeled as a repeated game, which allows the possibility to punish other players for non-cooperative behavior in previous rounds. In contrast to much of the text, the empirical focus in this chapter is on the European regime on transboundary acidification and, in particular, on the role of scientific uncertainties in the negotiations of the first Sulphur Protocol signed in 1985.

In Chapter 7, the analysis is enriched by two further aspects of international environmental politics. First, the fact that damages are often caused by the stock, rather than the flow, of pollutants adds dynamics to the problem. This relates to the accumulation process of pollutants over time, and to the additional strategic considerations which arise from the fact that past behavior now influences current payoffs via the pollution stock. Second, natural scientists have pointed out that the responses of ecological systems to pollution are often characterized by discontinuities. It will therefore be analyzed how such thresholds may influence the extent and allocation of emission reductions.

Finally, Chapter 8 summarizes the main findings and outlines some questions for further research.

Regarding terminology, I try to be precise but not overly strict, at least when I believe that the danger of confusion is low. For example, the notions 'fairness', 'justice' and 'equity' will be used interchangeably, even though some authors have offered precise definitions for each of them.[2] But these definitions do not receive widespread recognition, at

---

[2]The Collins Cobuild dictionary defines *justice* as 'fairness in your behavior or the way that people are treated', *equity* as 'the quality of being fair and reasonable in

least if one transcends the borders of a particular scientific discipline. Choosing one notion and sticking to it throughout the text would have been an alternative. However, because I use 'fair' division theory to analyze the demand for 'equity' in the Framework Convention on Climate Change and relate that to Rawls's theory of 'justice', this would have required lengthy explanations, which I did not regard as fruitful in the context of this text. Similarly, I sometimes speak of 'emission allowances', 'emission rights' and, if those are tradable, of 'permits', while meaning essentially the same thing. On those occasions when I lay more weight on terminological precision or confusion might arise, things are stated as an explicit definition.

Finally, in line with the applied character of the analysis, I largely abstract from mathematical technicalities. In particular, I usually assume interior solutions to maximization problems, compactness of sets as well as convexity respectively concavity and differentiability of functions.

---

a way that gives equal treatment to everyone', and *fairness* as 'the quality of being reasonable according to generally accepted ideas about what is right'.

PART I

International Policy in the Fairness Mode

2. An Axiomatic Approach to Fair Burden Sharing

> Act only on that maxim through which
> you can at the same time will that
> it should become a universal law.
>
> Immanuel Kant (1724–1804)

2.1 Introduction

Nowhere has the importance of fairness concerns for international environmental politics become more apparent than in the negotiations of a regime for the protection of the climate system. On the occasion of the 1992 United Nations Conference on Environment and Development (UNCED) in Rio de Janeiro, the UN Framework Convention on Climate Change (UNFCCC) was adopted and ratified (up until September 1999) by 180 states. The principal objective of the Convention is the 'stabilization of greenhouse gas concentrations in the atmosphere at a level that would prevent dangerous anthropogenic interference with the climate system' (Article 2).

Despite its lack of specific prescriptions on how to achieve this objective, the Climate Convention provides some general principles on which climate change protection strategies should be based. In particular, Article 3 states that 'Parties should protect the climate system for the benefit of present and future generations of humankind, on the basis of equity and in accordance with their common but differentiated responsibilities and respective capabilities' (para 1). Furthermore, 'policies and measures to deal with climate change should be cost-effective so as to ensure global benefits at the lowest possible cost' (para 3).

Economists have a fairly precise understanding of 'cost-effectiveness', even though one should note carefully that this need not be shared by all signatories of the Climate Convention. On the other hand, the meaning of 'equity' is much more controversial, both inside and outside the economics profession.

As the Climate Convention fails to specify the criteria according to which the fairness of different policy proposals on the negotiation table should be judged, the demand for equity has provided little guidance so far. In particular, the negotiations of the Kyoto Protocol, which was adopted in December 1997 in Kyoto (Japan), and the process since then have demonstrated the two sides of the equity requirement quite clearly. On the one hand, the individual states tended to refuse any proposals which they perceived as inequitable, but on the other hand the perception of whether a proposal is equitable or not remained highly controversial.

This already indicates why arguments based on equity considerations are generally treated with great suspicion. Two popular reservations, which are also common among economists, go as follows: 'Equity is merely a word that hypocritical people use to cloak self-interest'; and 'it is so hopelessly subjective that it cannot be analyzed scientifically' (Young 1994a, xi; see also Zajac 1995). In many respects, negotiations about climate change seem to confirm those reservations because nearly every actor – ranging from low-lying island states to oil exporters – has defended its policy proposal as the truly equitable one.

In the Kyoto Protocol, the so-called Annex I countries (the group of industrialized countries including the economies in transition) finally agreed to reduce their 1990 emissions of greenhouse gases by an average of 5.2 per cent until the period 2008–2012.[1] Following a relatively recent development in international environmental politics, they chose country-specific rather than uniform reduction targets, as shown in Table 2.1.[2] Although these differ by as much as 18 percentage points, targets for the main CO_2 emitters – the USA, the EC and Japan – are quite similar, ranging from 6 to 8 per cent reductions.

Despite these achievements, there exists a widespread consensus that the Kyoto targets cannot be the end of the story and much higher emission reductions will be required in the long run (see IPCC 1996c and, on climate skeptics, Helm and Schellnhuber 1998). Furthermore, as Rose

---

[1]There are some exceptions to the base year 1990 for economies in transition, in particular for Hungary (average of 1985–1987), Poland and Slovakia (1988) and Romania (1989). For an evaluation of the Kyoto Protocol see Cooper (1998), Simonis (1998) and Ott (1998).

[2]Prior to the Kyoto Protocol, the first real example of country-specific reduction targets was the 1994 Oslo Protocol for the reduction of transboundary sulfur emissions in Europe (see Chapter 6). However, simpler differentiation schemes had already been agreed earlier. For example, the Protocols to combat atmospheric ozone depletion distinguish between developed and developing Parties' obligations, but do not further differentiate the emission prescriptions within those two groups (see Biermann 1998).

Table 2.1: Emission commitments under the Kyoto Protocol

Party	Percentage of 1990 emissions
EC and its member countries, Bulgaria, Czech Republic, Estonia, Latvia, Lithuania, Monaco, Romania, Slovakia, Slovenia, Switzerland	92
United States of America	93
Canada, Hungary, Japan, Poland	94
Croatia	95
New Zealand, Russian Federation, Ukraine	100
Norway	101
Australia	108
Iceland	110
Average of all Parties	94.8

(1998, 1) has pointed out: 'The hesitancy to make a major commitment to control greenhouse gases has often been ascribed to the lack of sufficient scientific information to support the global warming hypothesis. But future action may be less about solid evidence and more about stakeholders and perceptions of fairness'.

Indeed, disputes about the participation of developing countries, referred to as non-Annex I countries in the context of climate change, are already seriously hampering negotiations. For example, the Byrd–Hagel Resolution, passed 95 to 0 in the US Senate in 1997, states that 'the United States should not be a signatory to any protocol that excludes developing countries from legally binding commitments'.[3] Although the USA signed the Kyoto Protocol during the fourth Conference of the Parties (COP4) to the Climate Convention in Buenos Aires (November 1998), ratification will require approval by the US Senate, which seems rather unlikely at the moment. But without ratification by the USA, enforcement of the Protocol moves into the distant future because it requires not only ratification by 55 Parties to the Convention, but also that those account for 55 per cent of Annex I countries' emissions.

Developing countries for their part have argued that they carry only minor historical responsibility for the increase in global CO_2 concentrations. Therefore, industrialized countries should go ahead with climate protection measures.

---

[3] The Byrd–Hagel Resolution, US Senate, 12 June 1997, 105th Congress, 1st Session, Senate Resolution 98.

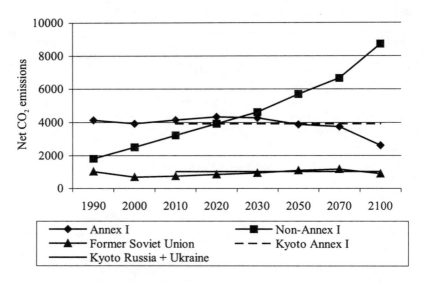

Source: Own calculations based on medium scenario in Victor et al. (1998).

Figure 2.1: CO_2 emission projections and the Kyoto targets

Figure 2.1 depicts CO_2 emission projections for developing (non-Annex I) countries, industrialized (Annex I) countries, and the Former Soviet Union together with the Kyoto targets for the latter two groups.[4] Current CO_2 emission levels are indeed considerably lower in developing countries as compared to industrialized countries. However, despite the uncertainties of emission projections, it is clear from Figure 2.1 that this picture will change within the not too distant future. Even though per capita emissions will remain higher in the industrialized countries during the whole period projected, stabilization of greenhouse gas concentrations at a safe level will require quite substantial reductions of CO_2 emissions in developing countries as well.

How then should emission reduction burdens be allocated? In the following, I shall address this question from a normative point of view and try to put some substance on the notion of an equitable climate change policy – or, more generally, on the fair division of common property

---

[4]The Kyoto emission targets relate only to the budget period 2008–2012. In Figure 2.1 they have simply been extrapolated into the future.

resources.[5]

Based on four general fair division criteria – individual rationality, envy-freeness, resource monotonicity, and population monotonicity – I will develop an allocation rule for emission reductions and associated costs. Through the restriction of the analysis to a limited class of utility function profiles and by allowing compensatory payments, I will avoid most of the inconsistency results generally found in the literature (for a survey see Moulin 1990). Although the empirical focus is on climate change, the proposed allocation rule is applicable to a much larger range of environmental problems. By framing them as problems of fairly dividing common property resources, a highly relevant field of application arises for the theory of fair division, which has until now been largely confined to theoretical contributions with very few applications to real-world problems.

The chapter is structured as follows. In Sections 2.2 and 2.3, I briefly discuss some prerequisites for the application of the theory of fair division, show its relevance for environmental problems and introduce the notation. In Section 2.4, the criterion of individual rationality and the stand-alone utility are shown to constitute lower and upper bounds for fair division. This leads to the formulation of the WESA mechanism for the fair division of common property resources (Section 2.5). Next, I will analyze the consistency of the WESA mechanism with the criterion of envy-freeness (Section 2.6) and with the monotonicity axioms (Section 2.7). The chapter concludes with a quantitative application of the WESA mechanism to burden sharing in the emerging climate change regime (Section 2.8).

2.2 Fair Division Theory and Environmental Problems

Most studies on fair burden sharing in the climate change regime can be subsumed under two approaches. The first focuses on a 'fair initial allocation' of property rights to greenhouse gas emissions. These authors usually assume that property rights will then be traded internationally to achieve Pareto efficiency (for example Edmonds, Wise, and Barns

---

[5]There are, of course, other important equity issues raised by climate change, among them international equity in coping with the impacts of climate change, equity and social considerations within countries, equity in international processes, and equity among generations (IPCC 1996a, 85; see also Tóth 1999).

1995). Sometimes, mixed criteria have been proposed and it is also common to weigh them such that indicators expressing the status quo are emphasized initially, while those being perceived as more fair become increasingly important in the course of time. A much discussed example for this is a proposal by Cline (1992, 353) who uses GDP, historical emissions and population as criteria such that the latter receive more weight in the long run (see also Simonis 1996a). Thereby, equity considerations are mixed with those of political feasibility.

The second class of studies focuses on end-state justice, that is a 'fair outcome' of climate protection strategies. A common criterion for this is the equalization of net cost per GDP (see Bohm and Larsen 1994). Another example is the requirement that developing countries should not be harmed by mitigation efforts (see Edmonds, Wise, and Barns 1995; Bohm 1997).[6]

The approach adopted in the following, which is based on fair division theory, does not really fit into either of these two categories. Although entitlements to the common property resource have to be defined in the first place, the main focus is on the fair division of the gains from their exchange, which arise from differences in marginal abatement costs across countries. A priori it is not obvious why the allocation of those gains should be governed by the market, as most of the writers on climate change seem to assume.

In particular, it will be shown that the application of fairness criteria to the allocation of the gains from emissions trading can have as important implications for burden sharing in the climate change regime as the specification of the entitlements themselves. Before elaborating on this in more detail, it is important to note that not only is the formulation of fairness criteria a normative decision, but also the choice of the perspective or starting position for their application involves some fundamental ethical judgments (see Wickström 1992). These are not captured by the criteria themselves and therefore deserve some discussion.

First, I shall treat the fair division of emission reductions of greenhouse gases and associated abatement costs as a *local* justice problem. I thereby assume that it can be analyzed in isolation from aspects of *social* justice like the global welfare distribution.[7] In contrast to this, some authors have explicitly argued that climate change protection strategies

---

[6]For a more extensive discussion of the different proposals and other fairness concerns of climate change see Grubb, Sebenius, Magalhaes, and Subak (1992); UNCTAD (1992); Beckerman and Pasek (1995); Shue (1995); Rayner, Malone, and Thompson (1999); Rose, Stevens, Edmonds, and Wise (1998).

[7]On the distinction between local and social justice see Young (1994a).

should be designed such that they are to the advantage of developing countries (for example Simonis 1996a). I do not deny the legitimacy of such claims, and the welfarist approach discussed in the next chapter offers indeed some support for them. Nevertheless, in the present chapter I strictly distinguish whether the justification for monetary transfers rests on the injustice of the current global welfare distribution or on the characteristics of climate change. It should be noted, however, that ignoring superordinate aspects of social justice becomes questionable if the proposed solution for a local fair division problem significantly accentuates existing injustices.

Second, in concentrating exclusively on justice in efforts to limit polluting emissions, I abstract from other important ethical aspects, in particular the negative impacts of environmental pollution and associated risks. In some cases, emission reduction targets might actually be chosen such that no environmental damages occur. For example, the critical loads concept agreed to in the European regime to combat transboundary acidification seeks to reduce emissions to a level below which significant harmful effects on specified sensitive elements of the environment do not occur (see Chapter 6 on acid rain). However, in many cases there will be significant damages. My intention is not to deny the importance of justice in coping with those impacts, but I assume that this and other issues can be treated separately from the fair division of emission reductions and associated costs.

Third, I require that the allocation is fair in every period. This excludes situations where the unfair treatment of agents in one period is compensated by preferential treatment in other periods, although the issue of historical emission rights will be addressed briefly in the concluding remarks to this chapter. Nevertheless, intertemporal equity trading might be reasonable if the transition from an unfair to a fair allocation involves a sharp increase in the efforts of some agents.

Finally, the application of fair division criteria requires the preceding specification of entitlements to a common property resource, for example to a particular service of the environment like its absorptive capacity for greenhouse gases. In inheritance problems, which are sometimes used to illustrate the theory of fair division, entitlements may indeed be exogenously given through the will of the deceased. However, for many other problems this is not the case and the specification of entitlements involves fundamental ethical judgments. Most of the general results derived in this chapter do not depend on the distribution of entitlements, but to put flesh on them in a particular fair division problem like climate change they have to be defined, of course.

In this respect, equal per capita entitlements, which correspond to the justice principle of 'equality of resources', have received particular attention. This is especially so in the case of climate change, where the environment's absorptive capacity for greenhouse gases is often regarded as a global common, as it were 'manna fallen from heaven'. Accordingly, equal per capita entitlements is the proposal mentioned most often in the literature (see Bertram 1992; Kverndokk 1995). In fact, convergence towards equal per capita emission rights in the course of time was explicitly mentioned in an early draft of the Climate Convention, but later this provision was replaced by the weaker formulations of Article 3 para 1 as quoted on page 9 above (Beckerman and Pasek 1995, 408).

Some idea of equality has been the starting point of most theories of justice and historically it has guided the imagination and action of many people. As Tocqueville (1969) has put it: 'The passion of mankind for equality is burning, unsatiable, eternal, invincible.' And the Universal Declaration of Human Rights, adopted in 1948, states in its first article: 'All human beings are born free and equal in dignity and rights.' However, Aristotle had already restricted the force of equality in his 'formal principle of justice', according to which 'equals should be treated equally and unequals unequally, in proportion to relevant similarities and differences'. Nevertheless, even here equal treatment is the starting point and unequal treatment requires the presence of relevant similarities and differences.

A first question that arises from the formal principle of justice is 'equality of what?' Indeed, the dispute whether to equalize resources or welfare, that is opportunities or outcomes, has a long tradition in social choice theory (Dworkin 1981a; Dworkin 1981b; Sen 1987; Roemer 1986). In this section, I will elaborate on the 'equality of resources' approach. However, it should be noted that an equal allocation of greenhouse gas entitlements is quite a different thing from the equal allocation of *all* resources as demanded by the advocates of resourcism. This means that the principle of equal resources is applied to a single commodity, while other resources are divided quite unequally, leading possibly to second-best problems (Lipsey and Lancaster 1956).

The other question initiated by Aristotle's principle of justice concerns the presence of relevant similarities and differences, which would limit the appeal of an egalitarian allocation of emission entitlements. Obviously, quite substantial differences exist with respect to climate change. Most widely cited are the much lower income level in developing countries and the much higher emission level in industrialized countries, which would lead to considerable North South transfers in the case of tradable equal per capita permits (see Grubb, Sebenius, Magalhaes, and Subak 1992). However, from a local fair division perspective those differences are not relevant because they relate to social welfare considerations, which are purposely excluded from the analysis in this chapter.

Thus, within the local fair division framework I find it very hard to argue against an equal per capita allocation of entitlements. Some leeway for discussion remains, for example whether entitlements should relate to greenhouse gas emissions or rather to net emissions, which take countries' different endowment with biotic sinks (like forests) into account. Also the question whether to take account of historical emissions remains. But these are relatively minor issues compared to the choice of equal per capita entitlements as the ruling principle. Still, as mentioned above, one might object that the very choice of a local justice perspective is inappropriate for the problem at hand, but I will postpone a more detailed discussion of this point to Chapter 3.

2.3   The Model and Notation

While it is helpful to have climate change as an empirical example in the back of one's head, the following setting is considerably more general. Many environmental problems arise from an overuse of ecosystems' natural absorptive capacity for a particular pollutant or class of pollutants. This capacity is assumed to be given exogenously by nationally or internationally agreed targets, independently of whether they are the result of a negotiation process, cost benefit analysis, threshold effects in the environment or something else. Often, property rights are not defined and the absorptive capacity can be regarded as a continuously divisible common resource which has to be divided fairly among a group of agents.

If an agent does not use his full share of the absorptive capacity for pollutants in the 'business-as-usual' path without abatement measures, the marginal utility of a further increase of his share is zero so that there is satiation beyond a certain level of consumption of the common property resource. If all agents are satiated, the environmental problem does not exist.

Another issue is the feasibility of monetary compensations, which are excluded in most of the literature on fair division problems (for an exception see Moulin 1992b). However, monetary compensations become an increasingly common element of policies to tackle environmental problems. For example, in the international ozone regime developing countries are being compensated for their incremental costs of reducing the emissions of ozone-depleting substances (see Biermann 1997).

Similarly, Article 17 of the Kyoto Protocol introduced for the first time a system of emissions trading at the international level. To take account of those political developments, I assume that compensatory payments are feasible via a single good (money), in which utility is linear. This representation of preferences by a quasilinear utility function can be justified by the assumption that the absorptive capacity is given exogenously, and each agent's demand for a share of it depends only on its relative price – that is whether, at the margin, compensatory payments are cheaper than the emission reductions otherwise required – but not on the available income.

Finally, if more than one pollutant is responsible for the same environmental problem, it is assumed that these pollutants can be expressed in a common unit, which can also be used to define the environment's absorptive capacity for these pollutants. For example, it is common to express carbon dioxide, methane, CFCs and some other gases which have an effect on climate change in CO_2 equivalents, or respectively, their global warming potential. This leads to the following specification of the fair division problem.

In each period t, an infinitely divisible common property resource $\omega \in \mathbb{R}^1_+$ has to be allocated among a set $N = \{1, ..., n\}$ agents, indexed by i.[8] Monetary compensation received (positive sign) or paid (negative sign) by agent i is denoted $m_i \in \mathbb{R}^1$. Each agent i is characterized by a non-negative entitlement ω_i to the common resource, where $\sum_{i \in N} \omega_i = \omega$, and by a continuous, monotone increasing and concave utility function defined on his consumption set in $\mathbb{R}^1_+ \times \mathbb{R}^1$, which consists of his share of the common property resource e_i and monetary compensations m_i.

In particular, utility is strongly monotone increasing in monetary compensations, but as argued previously there exists a level e^s_i beyond which an agent i is satiated in the consumption of the common property resource, that is for all $i \in N : e_i \geq e^s_i \Rightarrow e_i \sim e^s_i$, assuming free disposal. Furthermore, preferences are additive separable between e_i and m_i and linear with respect to m_i. Accordingly, agent i's final utility in a period t is $u_i = u_i(e_i) + m_i$, and the set of all possible utility function profiles

---

[8] As the possibility of intertemporal equity transfers has been excluded by requiring the allocation to be fair in every period, time indices t can be suppressed for ease of notation.

is denoted $U = \{u_1, u_2, \ldots, u_n\}$. Without loss of generality, I normalize $u_i(0) = 0$.

An allocation problem is a triple $(n, U, (\omega_i)_{i \in N})$, and an allocation criterion $F(n, U, (\omega_i)_{i \in N})$ is a correspondence that assigns each agent one or more vectors (e_i, m_i) such that $\sum_{i \in N} e_i \leq \omega$ and $\sum_{i \in N} m_i = 0$.

In applications to environmental problems, a particular share e_i of the common property resource, or its absorptive capacity respectively, entitles an agent i to emit pollutants in the size of this share. Accordingly, an agent's utility from e_i – his willingness to pay for e_i – is the additional abatement costs he would have to undergo without these pollution rights:

$$u_i(e_i) = \int\limits_0^{e_i} -c_i'(e_i)\, de_i = c_i(0) - c_i(e_i), \qquad (2.1)$$

where $c_i(e_i)$ is a decreasing convex function that gives agent i's minimum costs of reducing its emissions to e_i.

2.4 Upper and Lower Bounds for the Fair Division of Common Resources

Fair division theory takes entitlements to the common property resource as given and searches for an allocation mechanism which is compatible with different axiomatic fairness criteria. Hence, the approach does not explicitly look for the 'most equitable solution', but successively excludes from the set of all feasible solutions the obviously inequitable ones. The solution set satisfying the individual fair division criteria is often large, but their intersection can be quite small. Indeed, a common problem is that no solution satisfying all desirable criteria simultaneously exists (Moulin 1990).

Turning to those criteria, an allocation is said to be Pareto-efficient, if no individual can be made better off without making another individual worse off. Sometimes this has been termed the criterion of unanimity. This already shows that Pareto efficiency is not more than a lowest common denominator, the only normative argument on which there exists widespread agreement, at least within the economics profession.

If lump-sum transfers are feasible, Pareto efficiency is equivalent to the maximization of aggregate utility.

Definition 1 *With transferable utility an allocation $(e_i, m_i)_{i \in N}$ is Pareto-efficient if there exists no $(e_i', m_i')_{i \in N}$ such that*

$$\sum_{i \in N} (u_i(e_i') + m_i') > \sum_{i \in N} (u_i(e_i) + m_i). \tag{2.2}$$

Accordingly, emission reductions have to be allocated such that corresponding marginal abatement costs are equalized in all countries. This is a far-reaching result because it determines the allocation of emission reductions. However, it does not say who should bear the costs of them. After the cake has been maximized, it now has to be shared – as equitably as possible.

The first axiom of fair division is individual rationality.[9] This principle was introduced by Steinhaus (1948) and expresses the idea that each agent should be guaranteed at least the utility from consuming his fair share, that is his entitlement to a common property resource. If there are overall gains from a reallocation of the initial shares, this implies that everyone should be weakly better off after the reallocation has taken place. Thus, individual rationality puts a lower bound on each agent's utility.

Definition 2 *With transferable utility an allocation criterion F is individually rational if*

$$for\ all\ \omega \in \mathbb{R}^1_+,\ all\ i \in N : u_i(e_i) + m_i \geq u_i(\omega_i). \tag{2.3}$$

The following two axioms of resource monotonicity (Roemer 1986; Moulin and Thomson 1988) and population monotonicity (Thomson 1983a; Chichilnisky and Thomson 1987) are of more recent origin, but they have received considerable attention, especially as a critique of the Walrasian mechanism to solve fair division problems. Both axioms set limits on how agents' individual utilities should respond to changes of the allocation problem with respect to the size of the common property resource and to the number of claimants.

Resource monotonicity requires that if the common resource to be divided grows, each agent should be at least as well off as from the fair division of the smaller resource.

Definition 3 *With transferable utility an allocation criterion F is resource monotonic if*

$$for\ all\ \omega, \omega' \in \mathbb{R}^1_+,\ all\ i \in N : \omega' \geq \omega \Rightarrow u_i(e_i') + m_i' \geq u_i(e_i) + m_i. \tag{2.4}$$

---

[9]Other names for this criterion are acceptability (Young 1994a), fair share guaranteed (Moulin 1995), and equal split lower bound (Moulin 1991).

For climate change and other environmental problems, this criterion may indeed have high practical relevance. Our best assessment of the environment's absorptive capacity is only preliminary and likely to change as scientific knowledge improves. Furthermore, reduction targets will often be approached stepwise. In both cases, the size of the common resource to be divided changes and due to the commonality of ownership this should affect the welfare of all agents in the same direction.

The criterion of population monotonicity states that if the number of agents entitled to the common resource increases, no agent should be better off than before.

Definition 4 *With transferable utility an allocation criterion F is population monotonic if*

$$for\ all\ \omega \in \mathbb{R}_+^1,\ all\ i \in N : N \subset N' \Rightarrow u_i(e_i') + m_i' \leq u_i(e_i) + m_i. \quad (2.5)$$

Similar to resource monotonicity, the criterion of population monotonicity is based on the ethical argument that common ownership implies a minimum degree of solidarity, namely that everyone should contribute to satisfy the legitimate claims of newcomers.

The monotonicity axioms can be used to deduce the stand-alone utility $u_i(\omega)$, that is an agent's utility from the consumption of the whole common resource, as an upper bound on the utility an agent i may receive from fair division. This stand-alone criterion is more commonly used for cost-sharing problems (see Moulin 1995), but it has been applied by Moulin (1992b) to the fair division of unproduced commodities. Obviously, the bite of the stand-alone criterion for the latter type of problems depends on the assumption that monetary compensations are feasible, because otherwise no agent could do better than using the whole resource for himself.

Lemma 1 *If an allocation mechanism for the fair division of one good and monetary compensations is either population monotonic or resource monotonic or both, then for all $i \in N : u_i(e_i) + m_i \leq u_i(\omega)$, where $u_i(\omega)$ is called agent i's stand-alone utility.*

Proof. If there is only one agent, he receives his stand-alone utility by definition. Population monotonicity requires that the utility of this agent does not increase as the population increases, because the same common resource has to be divided among more agents. This implies that he may not receive more than his stand-alone utility. Similarly, assume that in contradiction to Lemma 1 there is an agent who receives more than his stand-alone utility. By resource monotonicity, this agent's utility must not decrease as the common resource increases. With satiation in e_i, this step can be repeated until all agents are indifferent towards a further increase in the consumption of e_i and, therefore, receive exactly their stand-alone utility, a contradiction.[10]   □

Accordingly, the criteria of resource and population monotonicity require that no agent should be better off when the environment's absorptive capacity for polluting emissions is a scarce resource compared to the case where the environmental problem does not exist. Moulin (1992b, 1333) justifies the stand-alone test by arguing that 'fair division conveys the idea of no subsidization: the presence of other agents who are willing to pay higher monetary transfers than me for consuming the resources should not turn to my advantage'. This argument seems particularly justified if the willingness to pay higher monetary transfers is related to efforts to reduce a problem which affects all agents – like climate change. In this context, one could state the stand-alone test bluntly as: 'no-one should benefit from the emission abatement burdens of others', reflecting the solidarity ideal behind the monotonicity axioms.

Combining the criterion of individual rationality as a lower bound, the stand-alone utility as an upper bound and Pareto efficiency determines a unique allocation for the group of agents whose entitlements ω_i are higher than their satiation level e_i^s.

Proposition 1 *Let $D = \{i \in N : \omega_i \geq e_i^s\}$. An allocation satisfying individual rationality as well as population or resource monotonicity or both for agents $i \in D$ gives them exactly their stand-alone utility.*

Proof. By definition of set D, $u_i(\omega_i) = u_i(\omega)$ for all $i \in D$ so that individual rationality establishes the stand-alone value as a lower utility bound. Similarly, by Lemma 1 population and/or resource monotonicity establish the stand-alone value as an upper utility bound.   □

Figure 2.2 depicts this in an Edgeworth box. Emissions and compensations for the agent $i \in D$, called 'South', are measured in the usual way with the southwest corner as the origin. In contrast, emissions and compensations for the other agent, called 'North', are measured using

---

[10]Obviously, the converse of Lemma 1 is not true: if no agent is better off than with his stand-alone utility, this neither implies population nor resource monotonicity. This follows immediately from the fact that the stand-alone criterion only sets an upper bound to each agent's utility, but says nothing about allocations below this upper bound.

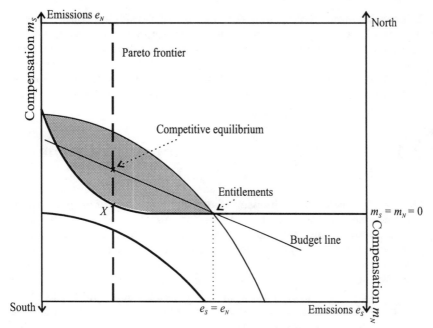

Figure 2.2: An Edgeworth box representation of fair division

the northeast corner as the origin. The two curves in the middle of the figure give the agents' indifference curves at the initial equal allocation of emission entitlements ($e_S = e_N$). At this point, there are no transfers of compensatory payments ($m_S = m_N = 0$), and South's indifference curve is flat because it is satiated given its entitlements.

The Pareto-efficient solutions are given by the points where the indifference curves of the two agents have the same slope, and due to the assumption of quasilinear utility functions this is a straight vertical line. The shaded area characterizes the set of solutions that are individually rational for both agents. Finally, the two bold curves give the stand-alone utilities, which must not be exceeded. Therefore, the only solution satisfying simultaneously the criteria of Pareto efficiency, individual rationality and the stand-alone test is point X. Compared to the competitive equilibrium from equal entitlements, South receives fewer transfer payments.

In applications to environmental problems, the set D may comprise a substantial number of agents. For example, if developing countries were included in a future protocol on the reduction of greenhouse gases, for many of them equal per capita entitlements would be higher than their emissions in the reference path without abatement, unless very strict overall reduction targets were chosen. This is the situation depicted in Figure 2.2. Nevertheless, for $n \geq 2$ it remains to define a general allocation rule for agents that do not belong to set D.

2.5 The Walrasian Mechanism with the Stand-Alone Upper Bound

Often, the Walrasian mechanism, that is an assignment of property rights in proportion to each agent's entitlements and a subsequent allocation via competitive markets, has been advocated for fair division problems (see Young 1994a). Indeed, many writers on climate change have restricted the discussion of fairness concerns to the initial distribution of emission permits, which are then traded on competitive markets. Even though the fairness properties of the Walrasian mechanism have not been discussed in those contributions, it has a number of attractive features. In particular, with quasilinear preferences the Walrasian mechanism has not only a unique efficient solution, but it is also individually rational and satisfies the criterion of envy-freeness, which will be discussed in Section 2.6.

However, the Walrasian mechanism has been criticized because in the general domain of continuous and monotone utility functions it is neither resource nor population monotonic (see Moulin 1990). This is the case even if one restricts attention to the domain of two-good allocation problems with quasilinear preferences.

Proposition 2 *In economies with quasilinear preferences, the Walrasian mechanism operated from equal division produces a unique and stable Pareto-efficient equilibrium which is individually rational and envy-free. However, it may violate population and resource monotonicity and the stand-alone criterion.*

Proof. For uniqueness, stability and Pareto efficiency see Mas-Colell, Whinston, and Green (1995). Individual rationality and envy-freeness are proven in Foley (1967). Violation of population and resource monotonicity and the stand-alone criterion follows straightforwardly from Proposition 1 because members of set D could trade entitlements above their satiation level for a positive price if the common resource is scarce (see also Figure 2.2). □

Other well-known fair division mechanisms like egalitarian equivalence (Pazner and Schmeidler 1978; Crawford 1979) suffer from similar deficiencies (Moulin 1990). In this chapter, I therefore introduce an alternative fair division mechanism, which takes the Walrasian mechanism as the starting point but supplements it by the stand-alone utility as an upper bound.

Definition 5 *Let the WESA mechanism (WESA = Walrasian Mechanism with the Stand-Alone upper bound) be defined as follows. For all $\omega \in R_+^1$, if compensatory payments m_i are feasible, every $i \in N$ should receive the bundle $(e_i^*, m_i(e_i^*))$ from the fair division of a common property resource ω, where e_i^*, p^* denote quantities and prices in the Walrasian equilibrium and the allocation rule for monetary compensations is given as*

$$m_i(e_i^*) = \min\{u_i(\omega) - u_i(e_i^*), (\omega_i - e_i^*)p^* + \kappa_i\}, \qquad (2.6)$$

where $\kappa_i = \dfrac{\sum_{i \in A}((\omega_i - e_i^*)p^* - (u_i(\omega) - u_i(e_i^*)))}{|N \setminus A|}$,

and $A = \{i \in N : m_i(e_i^*) = u_i(\omega) - u_i(e_i^*)\}$.[11]

Accordingly, the WESA mechanism divides the common resource efficiently, and with respect to compensations it distinguishes between two types of agents:

- members of set A receive compensations such that they are exactly as well off as with their stand-alone utility, and

- members of set $N \setminus A$ receive (or pay) compensations as in the Walrasian equilibrium, $(\omega_i - e_i^*)p^*$, plus κ_i which denotes the equal per capita share of the difference between the compensations that members of set A would receive in the Walrasian equilibrium and the compensation they actually receive to reach their stand-alone utility level.

The choice of an equal per capita reallocation of compensations above the stand-alone utility can be justified by arguing that the funds to be reallocated arise from a free service of members of A, from which equal

---

[11] $|N \setminus A|$ denotes the cardinality of the set $N \setminus A$.

agents should benefit equally. In the next section, I will show that this equal per capita reallocation of excess compensations can also be derived from the criterion of envy-freeness.

It is straightforward to show that the WESA mechanism satisfies individual rationality and the stand-alone test for all agents: the stand-alone criterion has been integrated as an upper bound in the formulation of the WESA mechanism. Similarly, individual rationality follows immediately from the fact that all $i \in N$ get either their stand-alone utility or are weakly better off than in the Walrasian equilibrium. In the following section, I shall introduce the last fair division criterion of envy-freeness and explore its relation to the WESA mechanism.

2.6   The No-Envy Criterion

2.6.1   Envy-Freeness from Equal and Proportional Entitlements

An allocation from equal entitlements to a common resource is called envy-free if no agent prefers another's allocation to his own.[12] This describes the ideal that equally entitled agents should have equal liberty to choose from the same budget set. An early version of envy-freeness has been introduced by Tinbergen (1946), but its development is usually credited to Foley (1967) (see also Varian 1974 and Baumol 1986). The popularity of this criterion among economists has often been regarded as very high and Arnsperger (1994, 155) even states that 'envy-freeness has become the first and foremost "distributive companion" to the aggregative requirement of Pareto efficiency in the literature on normative economics'.

Definition 6 *In an exchange economy with k goods, an allocation criterion F is envy-free from equal entitlements if*

$$\text{for all } \omega \in \mathbb{R}_+^k, \text{ all pairs of } i, j \in N : u_i(\mathbf{e}_i) \geq u_i(\mathbf{e}_j). \quad (2.7)$$

In contrast to the previous sections, ω and $\mathbf{e}_i$ are now vectors of k goods. Obviously, this definition depends on the assumption of equal

---

[12]The appropriateness of the term 'envy-freeness' is disputed and some authors prefer to call it the principle of equity. However, the term 'equity' is more commonly used in a broader sense, especially in the non-economics literature. See Kolm (1996) for a recent discussion of the terminology and the philosophical justification of this principle.

entitlements, because otherwise it is likely that the agent with the smallest entitlement would prefer another's share to his own – but such an allocation is not necessarily inequitable. This led some authors to conclude that the no-envy principle 'only applies when parties have equal claims on the good' (Young 1994a, 12). However, there is a relatively straightforward extension to the case where each agent's entitlement can be expressed as a proportional share s_i of the common resource, that is if $\omega_i = s_i\omega$, where $s_i \in [0, 1]$ for all $i \in N$ and $\sum_{i \in N} s_i \leq 1$.

By defining the claimants in an appropriate way, such a problem can always be formulated as one of equal entitlements. To see this, take the simple example of a will, in which it is stated that daughter Anna should receive twice as much of the inheritance as daughter Berta. To apply the no-envy criterion, this problem could easily be revised as one with two clones with preferences identical to Anna's, each of which has the same entitlements as Berta. The no-envy criterion would then require that no clone (or single agent) prefers the allocation of another clone to its own. It is straightforward to extend this procedure to an arbitrary number of agents with proportional entitlements (see Brams and Taylor 1996, 152).

Following the same reasoning, one can also revise the no-envy criterion itself so as to allow for cases with different entitlements. The idea is to compare allocations per entitlements rather than allocations per capita.[13]

Definition 7 *An allocation criterion F is envy-free from proportional entitlements if every agent prefers his allocation to any other agent's allocation adjusted by differences in entitlements, that is if*

$$for\ all\ \omega \in \mathbb{R}_+^k,\ all\ pairs\ of\ i, j \in N : u_i(\mathbf{e}_i) \geq u_i\left(\frac{\omega_i}{\omega_j}\mathbf{e}_j\right). \qquad (2.8)$$

2.6.2   Envy-Freeness with Monetary Compensations

The no-envy criterion has rarely been formulated for the specific case of exchange economies in which agents are characterized by quasilinear utility functions. This is not surprising because the general formulation for envy-freeness from equal entitlements is independent of whether

---

[13]I assume that entitlements ω_i are strictly positive for all $i \in N$ to ensure that envy-freeness from proportional entitlements is defined. Note that in contrast to envy-freeness from equal entitlements, a reallocation such that agent i would in fact receive a share $(\omega_i/\omega_j)\mathbf{e}_j$ will not always be feasible in the revised formulation with proportional entitlements because there may be cases where $(\omega_i/\omega_j)\mathbf{e}_j \geq \omega$.

utility is linear in one good. Nevertheless, if one wants to make the linearity of utility in money explicit, this could be easily done as follows. Let there be a bundle (ω, m) consisting of one good and money to be divided fairly. Envy-freeness from equal entitlements (to ω and m) requires that no agent prefers another's share of the common resource and money to his own, that is $u_i(e_i) + m_i \geq u_i(e_j) + m_j$ for all pairs of $i, j \in N$ (see Moulin 1995).

However, it would be wrong to simply apply this formulation to fair division problems for which monetary compensations are feasible. To see why, take the set D of agents whose entitlements are higher than their emissions without abatement measures. If D contains at least two different agents who receive exactly their stand-alone utility – as has been shown to be the only solution satisfying individual rationality and the stand-alone criterion – then they would envy each other according to the formulation of envy-freeness in the previous paragraph.

This can be seen from Figure 2.3, which depicts abatement costs $c_i(e_i)$ for two agents $i \in D$ as a function of emissions. By definition, abatement costs are zero for members of set D at the point where emissions equal their entitlement ω_i. Efficiency requires that marginal abatement costs are equalized, giving the agents e_1^* and e_2^* respectively. Furthermore, following the solution in Proposition 1, all $i \in D$ are fully compensated for their abatement costs, hence $m_i = c_i(e_i^*)$. Therefore, in the situation depicted agent 1 receives less of every good and would envy agent 2 according to the above formulation of the no-envy criterion.[14]

However, intuitively this result is not very appealing. If, as suggested above, members of set D are exactly compensated for their abatement costs, Figure 2.3 can be interpreted such that the ordinate gives the units of the numeraire good and the cost curves are the indifference curves that secure both agents the utility level of consuming their entitlements. Viewed from this perspective, the fact that some agents receive more of every good is a necessary requirement for equal treatment, in the sense that all $i \in D$ can secure their stand-alone utility levels of the reference situation.

More precisely, in the present fair division problem m_i is not simply a second good in which utility is linear and that otherwise has to be divided fairly together with the common resource ω. It rather serves as compensation to ensure that the efficient allocation of the other goods can be

---

[14] An allocation where one agent receives less of everything than another agent is sometimes called *transparently unequal* (Young 1994a). Obviously, any transparently unequal allocation from equal entitlements produces envy.

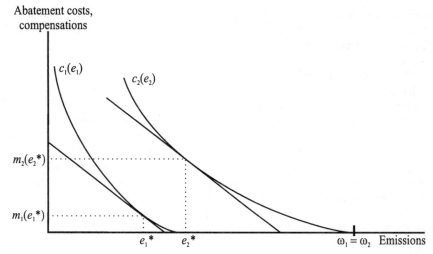

Figure 2.3: *Envy-freeness for low-emission countries*

separated from fairness issues. Accordingly, the purpose of transfers m_i is to compensate agents for utility changes relative to some reference point such that the allocation of $(e_i^*, m_i(e_i^*))$ is not only efficient but also fair for all agents. Therefore, in general agents do *not* have equal entitlements to monetary compensations, and the no-envy criterion has to be adjusted in a similar way as in Definition 7 for the case of proportional entitlements.

Definition 8 *Let agents $i \in N$ have equal entitlements to a common resource and let monetary compensations m_i be feasible. An allocation criterion F is envy-free with respect to a compensation rule if no agent would like to exchange his own bundle against the bundle consisting of another agent's share of the common resource and the compensation he would receive or pay if he had the share of this other agent, that is if*

for all $\omega \in \mathbb{R}_+^1$, all pairs of $i, j \in N$: $u_i(e_i) + m_i(e_i) \geq u_i(e_j) + m_i(e_j)$,
(2.9)

where $m_i(e_i)$ is an allocation rule which determines the monetary compensations an agent i would receive with a share e_i of the common resource.

Thus, the criterion of envy-freeness with monetary compensations has

two components: the allocation of the common resource – to which
agents are assumed to have equal entitlements – and the allocation of
monetary compensations, which is prescribed by a particular allocation
rule $m_i(e_i)$.

Accordingly, compliance with the no-envy criterion depends on the
allocation rule $m_i(e_i)$ for monetary compensations. For example, let
there be two fair division problems (one good and money) and a pair
of agents $i, j \in N$. Agent i receives the same final allocation (e_i, m_i)
for both problems and so does agent j. If this final allocation is based
on different rules for the allocation of monetary compensations, then it
is possible that i envies j in one of the problems but not in the other.
Thereby, the no-envy criterion narrows the set of just allocation rules
for monetary compensations, as will be shown below.

Based on this formulation of envy-freeness with monetary compensations, we come to the central result of this chapter:

Proposition 3 *The WESA mechanism for the fair division of one good
(with equal entitlements) and monetary compensations (in which utility
is linear) produces a unique and stable Pareto-efficient equilibrium which
is individually rational, envy-free with compensations, and satisfies the
stand-alone criterion.*

Proof. Pareto efficiency, stability, uniqueness, individual rationality,
and the stand-alone criterion have already been proved above so that it
remains to analyze envy-freeness. As this entails pairwise comparisons
and the WESA mechanism distinguishes between two types of agents,
this has to be done for pairs of $i, j \in A$, pairs of $i, j \in N \setminus A$, and pairs
of $i \in A, j \in N \setminus A$.

Envy-freeness for pairs of $i, j \in A$

According to Definition 8, the WESA mechanism is envy-free for pairs
of $i, j \in A$, that is agents for which $m_i(e_i^*) = u_i(\omega) - u_i(e_i^*)$, if for all
$\omega \in R_+^1$:

$$u_i(e_i^*) + u_i(\omega) - u_i(e_i^*) \geq u_i(e_j^*) + u_i(\omega) - u_i(e_j^*). \qquad (2.10)$$

This can be simplified to $u_i(\omega) \geq u_i(\omega)$, which is obviously true. In
contrast to the case analyzed above with equal entitlements to money
(Figure 2.3), what matters for i's evaluation is not the compensation j
receives but rather the compensation i would receive if it had j's share
e_j^* of the common resource ω.

Envy-freeness for pairs of $i, j \in N \setminus A$

For pairs of $i, j \in N \setminus A$, that is pairs of agents who are worse off than with their stand-alone utility, the no-envy criterion requires that for all $\omega \in \mathbb{R}^1_+$:

$$u_i(e_i^*) + (\omega_i - e_i^*)p^* + \kappa_i \geq u_i(e_j^*) + (\omega_i - e_j^*)p^* + \kappa_j, \text{ where} \quad (2.11)$$

$$\kappa_i = \frac{\sum_{i \in A}((\omega_i - e_i^*)p^* - (u_i(\omega) - u_i(e_i^*)))}{|N \setminus A|}. \quad (2.12)$$

Taking into account that κ_i is the same for all $i \in N \setminus A$, this inequality can be simplified to $u_i(e_i^*) - u_i(e_j^*) \geq (e_i^* - e_j^*)p^*$. If $e_i^* > e_j^*$, efficiency implies that each unit of e which agent i receives more than j has a marginal utility above the market price for i. Similarly, if $e_i^* < e_j^*$, each unit of e which agent i receives less than j has a marginal utility below the market price for i, which proves the inequality.

Note that if κ_i is not constant for all $i \in N \setminus A$, envy-freeness may be violated. In particular, the amount by which $u_i(e_i^*) - u_i(e_j^*)$ exceeds $(e_i^* - e_j^*)p^*$ may be arbitrarily small so that (2.11) would not hold if $\kappa_i < \kappa_j$. Thereby, the envy-freeness criterion restricts the way of reallocating excess compensations, as suggested on page 26.

Envy-freeness for pairs of $i \in A$ and $j \in N \setminus A$

For pairs of $i \in A$, $j \in N \setminus A$, envy-freeness with compensations requires that for all $\omega \in \mathbb{R}^1_+$:

$$u_i(\omega) \geq u_i(e_j^*) + \min\left\{u_i(\omega) - u_i(e_j^*), (\omega_i - e_j^*)p^* + \kappa_j\right\}, \text{ and}$$

$$u_j(e_j^*) + (\omega_j - e_j^*)p^* + \kappa_j \geq u_j(e_i^*) + \min\left\{u_j(\omega) - u_j(e_i^*), (\omega_j - e_i^*)p^* + \kappa_i\right\}.$$

The left-hand side of the first part of the no-envy criterion denotes agent i's stand-alone utility, which is the upper bound of the WESA mechanism and can therefore never be exceeded. Similarly, if

$$\min\left\{u_j(\omega) - u_j(e_i^*), (\omega_j - e_i^*)p^* + \kappa_i\right\} = (\omega_j - e_i^*)p^* + \kappa_i,$$

the second part of the no-envy criterion becomes

$$u_j(e_j^*) + (\omega_j - e_j^*)p^* + \kappa_j \geq u_j(e_i^*) + (\omega_j - e_i^*)p^* + \kappa_i.$$

This is exactly the same formulation of envy-freeness as inequality (2.11) (only the indices i and j have been exchanged), which has already been shown to be true. Finally, because $u_j(e_j^*) + (\omega_j - e_j^*)p^* + \kappa_j < u_j(\omega)$ by definition of set $N \setminus A$, it follows together with the previous statement that the possibility

$$\min\{u_j(\omega) - u_j(e_i^*), (\omega_j - e_i^*)p^* + \kappa_j\} = u_j(\omega) - u_j(e_i^*)$$

can be excluded.   □

2.7   The WESA Mechanism and the Monotonicity Axioms

In Section 2.4, resource and population monotonicity have been used to derive the stand-alone criterion, which in turn was shown to be satisfied by the WESA mechanism. However, population and resource monotonicity are obviously stronger requirements than the stand-alone criterion. It is therefore of interest to investigate the direct relationship between the monotonicity axioms and the WESA mechanism.

2.7.1   Resource Monotonicity

Let us start by analyzing the relation between the Walrasian mechanism and the criterion of resource monotonicity. If goods are continuously divisible and assuming differentiability, resource monotonicity requires that $du_i/d\omega \geq 0$ for all agents $i \in N$. Agents are assumed to choose emissions e_i so as to maximize utility, which consists of the avoided abatement costs by being allowed to emit e_i and international monetary transfers that arise from differences between final emissions and initial entitlements, evaluated at the international permit price:

$$\max_{e_i} u_i(e_i; \omega) = c_i(0) - c_i(e_i) + (\omega_i - e_i)p. \tag{2.13}$$

Accordingly, to check resource monotonicity we want to know how the optimal value of the objective function changes as the parameter ω changes. Suppose that $e_i^*(\omega)$ is a solution of problem (2.13) and $e_i^*(\omega)$ is a continuously differentiable function of ω. Then, by the envelope theorem[15]

---

[15]The envelope theorem uses the fact that by the first-order condition for unconstrained maximization we must have $\partial u_i(e_i; \omega)/\partial e_i = 0$.

$$\frac{d}{d\omega}u_i(e_i^*(\omega);\omega) \quad = \quad \frac{\partial}{\partial\omega}u_i(e_i^*(\omega);\omega) \tag{2.14}$$

$$= \quad p\frac{\partial\omega_i}{\partial\omega} + (\omega_i - e_i)\frac{\partial p}{\partial\omega}. \tag{2.15}$$

Accordingly, an increase in the total number of emission entitlements has two effects: First, for the additional entitlements, agents receive the permit price p. Second, the price for which countries sell or buy their permit changes.

Despite possible disputes about the initial allocation of entitlements, it seems reasonable to require that each individual agent's entitlements should increase as the size of the common resource increases. Indeed, this would follow from an application of the resource monotonicity criterion to the allocation of entitlements – rather than to the utility derived from using the common property resource. Therefore, I assume that $d\omega_i/d\omega \geq 0$ for all $i \in N$, and with equal per capita entitlements $d\omega_i/d\omega = 1/n$. Furthermore, in Appendix 2.10 it is shown that $dp/d\omega \leq 0$. Intuitively, the price of tradable permits decreases as they become less scarce. Finally, denote by $B = \{i \in N : \omega_i - e_i \leq 0\}$ the set of permit buyers and by $S = \{i \in N : \omega_i - e_i > 0\}$ the set of permit sellers. It then follows straightforwardly from equation (2.15) that for permit-buying agents $i \in B$ we have $du_i/d\omega \geq 0$. Accordingly, resource monotonicity is always satisfied for this group.

However, equation (2.15) can be either positive or negative for agents $i \in S$. For them, a critical point is reached if the absolute values of receiving more entitlements at old prices $|p\omega_i'(\omega)|$ and of receiving a lower price for the permits sold $|(\omega_i - e_i)p'(\omega)|$ are equalized.

To determine such a critical point, denoted $\hat{\omega}$, assume that an agent i could choose ω – the size of the common property resource to be allocated. Then, some utility-maximizing agent $i \in S$ might select an $\omega \leq \omega^s$, where $\omega^s = \min\{\omega \in \mathbb{R}_+^1 : \omega_i(\omega) \geq e_i^s \text{ for all } i \in N\}$ denotes the lowest value of the common resource such that it is abundant and every agent is fully satiated given the entitlements allocation rule $\omega_i(\omega)$. An example is agents $i \in D$, which in the Walrasian mechanism receive more than their stand-alone utility for some levels of ω. This case is depicted in Figure 2.4, where the function $u_i(\omega_i(\omega))$ reaches a maximum in the interval $(0,\omega^s) = \{\omega \in \mathbb{R}_1^+ : 0 < \omega < \omega^s\}$.

The upper graph in Figure 2.4 obviously violates resource monotonicity because utility decreases with increasing ω after the maximum. On the other hand, the WESA mechanism would simply cut away the area above the $u_i = u_i(\omega_i(\omega^s))$ line and therefore satisfy resource monotonic-

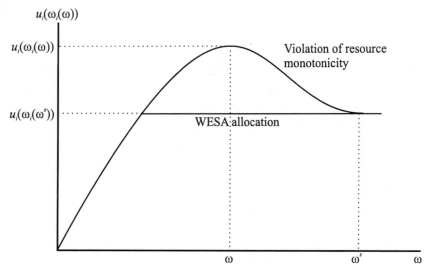

Figure 2.4: Individual utilities in Walrasian and WESA allocation

ity. Leaving aside the reallocated compensatory payments for the moment, this means that one does not have to worry about violations of resource monotonicity in the Walrasian allocation, if those violations occur only above the $u_i = u_i(\omega_i(\omega^s))$ line.

Now, the endpoints are fixed because $u_i(0) = 0$ and $u_i(\omega_i(\omega)) = u_i(\omega_i(\omega^s))$ for all $\omega \geq \omega^s$. Furthermore, $du_i/d\omega$ is positive initially, that is in the right-hand neighborhood of $u_i(0)$. Therefore, a violation of resource monotonicity can only occur if $u_i(\omega_i(\omega))$ reaches a maximum to the left of ω^s. One way to check whether such a maximum lies above the $u_i(\omega_i(\omega^s))$ line and, accordingly, does not occur in the WESA allocation, is to show that for all critical points $\hat{\omega}$

$$u_i(\omega_i(\hat{\omega})) \geq u_i(\omega_i(\omega^s)). \tag{2.16}$$

In the context of climate change and other pollution problems, following equation (2.1) this is equivalent to

$$c_i(0) - c_i(e_i) + (\omega_i(\hat{\omega}) - e_i(\hat{\omega}))p \geq c_i(0) \iff (\omega_i(\hat{\omega}) - e_i(\hat{\omega}))p \geq c_i(e_i). \tag{2.17}$$

It is straightforward to verify that this condition is satisfied for agents

$D = \{i \in N : \omega_i \geq e_i^s\}$. By convexity of abatement cost function

$$c_i'(e_i) \leq \frac{c_i(\omega_i) - c_i(e_i)}{\omega_i - e_i}. \qquad (2.18)$$

For a permit-selling country, indexed S, it follows that

$$(\omega_S - e_S)p \geq c_S(e_S) - c_S(\omega_S), \qquad (2.19)$$

which is equivalent to expression (2.17) if $c_S(\omega_S) = 0$, as is the case for agents $i \in D$. Obviously, the income of those agents exceeds their abatement cost in the Walrasian equilibrium.

Unfortunately, things are more complicated for the larger group of permit-selling countries. From equation (2.15) it follows that for critical points

$$\omega_i(\hat{\omega}) - e_i(\hat{\omega}) = -\frac{p\omega_i'(\omega)}{p'(\omega)}. \qquad (2.20)$$

Substitution into (2.17) gives

$$-\frac{p^2\omega_i'(\omega)}{p'(\omega)} \geq c_i(e_i). \qquad (2.21)$$

Noting that $p = -c_i'(e_i)$ in the Walrasian equilibrium, one gets

$$\frac{d}{d\omega}p = \frac{d}{d\omega}\left(-\frac{dc_i}{de_i}\right) = -\frac{d^2c_i}{de_i^2}\frac{de_i}{d\omega} \qquad (2.22)$$

Using this in equation (2.21) yields

$$\frac{p^2\omega_i'(\omega)}{e_i'(\omega)c_i''(e_i)} \geq c_i(e_i) \text{ so that} \qquad (2.23)$$

$$u_i(\omega_i(\hat{\omega})) \geq u_i(\omega_i(\omega^s)) \text{ if and only if } \frac{c_i'(e_i)}{c_i''(e_i)}\frac{\omega_i'(\omega)}{e_i'(\omega)} \leq \frac{c_i(e_i)}{c_i'(e_i)}. \qquad (2.24)$$

An alternative expression can be derived by explicitly calculating the comparative statics (see Appendix 2.10)

$$p'(\omega) = -\frac{1}{\sum_{i \in N}\frac{1}{c_i''(e_i)}}. \qquad (2.25)$$

Substitution into (2.21) and taking into account that $p = -c_i'(e_i)$ for all $i \in N$ gives

$$p^2 \omega_i'(\omega) \sum_{i \in N} \frac{1}{c_i''(e_i)} \geq c_i(e_i), \text{ so that} \qquad (2.26)$$

$$u_i(\omega_i(\hat{\omega})) \geq u_i(\omega_i(\omega^s)) \text{ if and only if } \sum_{i \in N} \frac{c_i'(e_i)}{c_i''(e_i)} \leq \frac{1}{\omega_i'(\omega)} \frac{c_i(e_i)}{c_i'(e_i)}. \qquad (2.27)$$

I now show that this expression holds at least for the particularly simple case of two countries with equal per capita entitlement and where in the permit-selling country i abatement costs increase quadratically in percentage emission reductions relative to business-as-usual emissions, which are denoted by $\bar{e}_i$. In particular, let

$$c_i(e_i) = \alpha_i \left(1 - \frac{e_i}{\bar{e}_i}\right)^2 \qquad (2.28)$$

so that

$$\frac{c_i'(e_i)}{c_i''(e_i)} = e_i - \bar{e}_i \quad \text{and} \quad \frac{c_i(e_i)}{c_i'(e_i)} = \frac{e_i - \bar{e}_i}{2}. \qquad (2.29)$$

Substitution into (2.27) gives

$$e_i - \bar{e}_i + \frac{c_j'(e_j)}{c_j''(e_j)} \leq 2 \frac{e_i - \bar{e}_i}{2}, \qquad (2.30)$$

which is obviously satisfied for a convex decreasing cost function.

So far, I have abstracted from the excess compensations that are re-allocated by the WESA mechanism and their effect on resource monotonicity. In slight abuse of notation, the upper graph in Figure 2.4 is now interpreted as the aggregate utility of agents which would receive more than their stand-alone utility in the Walrasian mechanism. If the upper graph lies above the $u_i(\omega_i(\omega^s))$ line, excess compensations are given by the distance between the two.

To the west of $\hat{\omega}$ excess compensations increase together with the common property resource ω and, because they are reallocated in equal per capita terms, no conflicts with the criterion of resource monotonicity arise. However, to the east of $\hat{\omega}$ excess compensations decrease as ω increases so that this effect in isolation would violate resource monotonicity. Whether this may indeed happen if the overall effect of an increase in ω is taken into account remains an open question for research.

2.7.2　Population Monotonicity

To simplify the analysis, I assume that there is a continuum of agents, where $I \in \mathbb{R}_+$ signifies the (continuous) number of agents. Then, the criterion of population monotonicity requires that for all $i \in N$, $N \subset N' : du_i/dI \leq 0$, where at the Walrasian equilibrium

$$
\begin{aligned}
\frac{du_i}{dI} &= \frac{\partial u_i}{\partial e_i}\frac{de_i}{dI} + \frac{\partial u_i}{\partial \omega_i}\frac{d\omega_i}{dI} + \frac{\partial u_i}{\partial p}\frac{dp}{dI} \\
&= p\frac{d\omega_i}{dI} + (\omega_i - e_i)\frac{dp}{dI}.
\end{aligned}
\tag{2.31}
$$

Two cases have to be distinguished. In the first, new agents are entitled to a positive share of the fixed common property resource and the entitlements of all original agents decrease, that is $d\omega_i/dI \leq 0$ for all $i \in N$. In the second, new agents receive no entitlements, so that $d\omega_i/dI = 0$. This is related to the discussions on climate change whether countries should receive additional entitlements for population increases (see Grubb, Sebenius, Magalhaes, and Subak 1992).

In both cases, it follows straightforwardly from equation (2.31) that population monotonicity is satisfied for permit-buying agents $i \in B$ because prices always increase if more agents want to consume the common resource ($dp/dI \geq 0$). However, population monotonicity is violated for permit sellers $i \in S$, if new agents get no entitlements, and inconclusive otherwise. Because the issue of population growth has received considerable attention in climate change debates, I summarize this result in the following proposition.

Proposition 4 *Let $N \subset N'$. If new agents $i \in N' \setminus N$ receive zero entitlements, then the Walrasian and the WESA mechanism both violate the criterion of population monotonicity.*

It follows that equity criteria for the fair division of the gains from an exchange of entitlements can have implications for the allocation of the entitlements themselves, namely that new agents should receive a positive entitlement.

In contrast, it has sometimes been argued in the climate change debate that countries might have an incentive to increase population so as to gain from the additional entitlements (Grubb, Sebenius, Magalhaes, and Subak 1992; Grubb 1995). To see whether this remark is justified, I take a closer look at population monotonicity for agents $i \in S$ if $d\omega_i/dI < 0$.

Roughly speaking, S corresponds to the group of developing countries at which the population growth argument is directed.

Let an average agent I_a be defined such that he neither buys nor sells permits, that is $I_a = \{i \in N' : \omega_i = e_i\}$. By definition, if population N increases by such an average agent, he will not engage in trading but simply take away his entitlement from the quantity of the common resource available to the other agents. This means that the effect of a new agent of type I_a on the original population is exactly the same as the effect of a decrease in the common property resource. Therefore, the analysis is the same as in the previous subsection: the Walrasian equilibrium would violate population monotonicity, but if condition (2.24) is satisfied the WESA mechanism does not.

Now, assume that the new agent would be a permit seller, denoted $I_s = \{i \in N' : \omega_i > e_i\}$. Noting that he puts some of his entitlements on the market, the marginal effect on prices of such an agent I_s is smaller than that of the average agent I_a, that is $dp/dI_s \leq dp/dI_a$.[16] Restricting attention to those original agents which are permit sellers, for which population monotonicity may be violated, one gets

$$\frac{dp}{dI_s}(\omega_i - e_i) \leq \frac{dp}{dI_a}(\omega_i - e_i) \quad \text{for all } i \in S. \tag{2.32}$$

Assuming that $(d\omega_i/dI)$ is independent of the type of agent, it follows with equation (2.31) for all $i \in S$ that whenever an allocation rule satisfies population monotonicity for new agents of type I_a, it must also satisfy population monotonicity if new agents of type I_s enter. This has two important implications.

First, current trends show that population increases are highest in developing countries. At the same time, developing countries will usually be permit sellers, at least for climate change. Thus, the empirically much more relevant case is that new agents are of type I_s. It has been shown above that in this case the criterion of population monotonicity is a weaker requirement than resource monotonicity. Nevertheless, from a theoretical point of view the WESA mechanism is defective in that it may not be population monotonic if permit-buying agents $i \in B$ enter.

Second, it has been argued in the literature that a (dynamic) equal per capita allocation would provide an incentive for developing countries to increase their population. However, because developing countries produce agents of type I_s, to the extent that the WESA mechanism satisfies resource monotonicity it also satisfies population monotonicity. This in

---

[16] Assuming, of course, that both receive identical entitlements.

turn implies that utility of all original actors – including those in developing countries – decreases as population increases. Therefore, the claimed incentive to increase population would not exist.

2.8 The WESA Mechanism and Burden Sharing in the Climate Change Regime

In this section, a quantitative application of the WESA mechanism to the climate change regime will be presented. The results have been derived with the RICE model (Regional Integrated model of Climate and the Economy) (Nordhaus and Yang 1996; Nordhaus 1992), which is a regional, dynamic, general-equilibrium model of the economy with particular focus on climate change related activities.

The global level of greenhouse gas emissions and their allocation are based on the assumption of full cooperation, that is emission reduction policies are undertaken efficiently across countries and time so as to maximize global welfare. The WESA mechanism then determines corresponding monetary transfers, depending on the a priori allocation of entitlements to emissions. For the results presented here, equal per capita entitlements have been assumed.[17]

Figure 2.5 depicts control costs – that is abatement costs plus monetary compensations received or paid – in the WESA allocation for six regions: the United States (USA), Japan (JPN), the European Union (EEC), China (CHN), the Former Soviet Union (FSU) and the rest of the world (ROW). For comparison, Figure 2.6 depicts control costs in the Walrasian allocation, using otherwise the same assumptions regarding entitlements and emission allocations.

The main difference between the two allocation mechanisms can be seen immediately. In the Walrasian allocation, the region ROW (essentially the developing countries) and initially also China could yield substantial net gains from emission reductions, because monetary compensations exceed their abatement costs. In contrast, the WESA mechanism cuts off the area of negative control costs and reallocates those 'excess compensations' among the other countries. Accordingly, for regions with positive control costs, these are lower in the WESA allocation

---

[17]In principle, compensatory payments affect countries' growth paths and accordingly their abatement cost functions. These general equilibrium effects have not been taken into account. This can be partly justified by the illustrative character of this empirical section, and by the fact that compensatory payments are usually small relative to GDP levels.

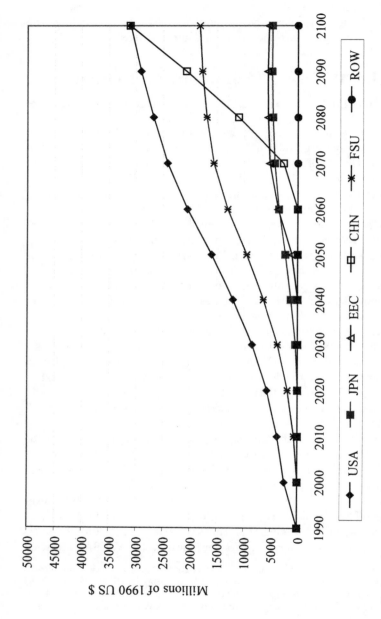

Source: Own calculations based on RICE model (Nordhaus and Yang 1996)

Figure 2.5: Climate change control costs in the WESA allocation

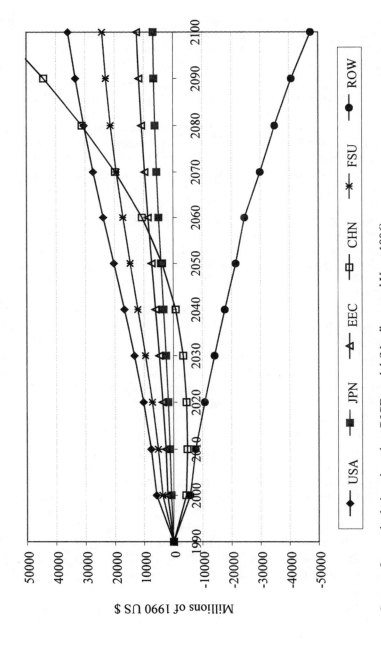

Source: Own calculations based on RICE model (Nordhaus and Yang 1996)

Figure 2.6: Climate change control costs in the Walrasian allocation

than in the Walrasian allocation.

Furthermore, in the RICE model optimal aggregate emissions as well as population size vary over time. Figure 2.5 shows that during the whole time span control costs change for all agents in the same direction. Accordingly, the WESA allocation not only satisfies the stand-alone criterion but also the stronger criteria of resource and population monotonicity.

It should be noted that overall emission reductions in the cooperative RICE path are relatively modest and allow global emissions to increase to roughly four times their current level during the next century. With stricter reductions, it might well be that the Walrasian and the WESA allocation of control costs would be closer to each other, especially for later periods.

Until now, I have not discussed how the WESA allocation might be implemented. Suppose there were a central authority, which cannot control the players' preferences and actions but has the power to design the rules of the (climate change) game. How should this game be set up so that – if played by rational, selfish agents – its outcome would implement the WESA mechanism?[18]

Given perfect information about countries' abatement cost functions, this would not pose a big problem. One possibility would be to allow permit trade on the basis of equal per capita entitlements, and to carry out additional compensatory payments for cases where countries violate the stand-alone criterion ex post. Alternatively, one could use the inverse approach of searching for the initial allocation of tradable entitlements that would lead to the level of control costs in the WESA allocation. This would have the advantage that no intervention into the market would be required after property rights have been defined.

Following the latter procedure, Figure 2.7 depicts the difference between the entitlements to implement the WESA allocation by tradable permits and equal per capita entitlements. As expected, OECD countries and the Former Soviet Union would receive more than their equal per capita entitlements in the WESA allocation. Of particular interest is the fact that the difference between equal per capita and WESA entitlements not only decreases over time, but the values for the individual countries converge towards each other. Thus, the WESA mechanism seems to provide an axiomatic foundation for a characteristic which has

---

[18]For an introduction to implementation theory or mechanism design see Osborne and Rubinstein (1994) as well as Falkinger, Hackl, and Pruckner (1997) for an application to climate change.

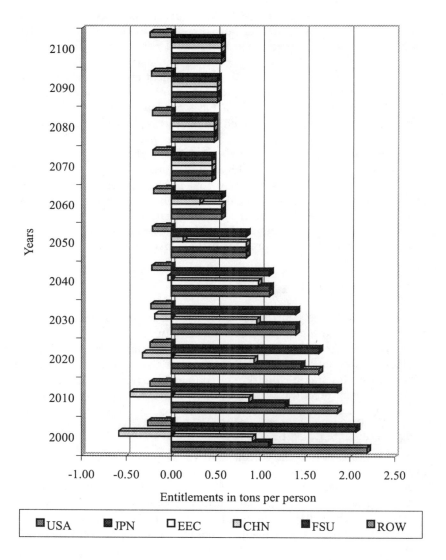

Source: Own calculations based on RICE model (Nordhaus and Yang 1996)

Figure 2.7: Implementation of the WESA allocation

often been advocated as crucial for fair burden sharing – namely that tradable entitlements should initially be related to current emission levels and gradually converge towards an equal per capita allocation (see Cline 1992).

Yet, it seems to be rather a strong simplification to assume that the central authority has complete information over countries' incremental abatement costs, which serve as a basis to determine monetary compensations. The experience gained under the UNFCCC Pilot Program for activities implemented jointly, which was partly undertaken to develop methodologies for certifying such additionality, shows that transaction costs and the length of the approval process may be substantial (UNCTAD 1998, 22). This indicates that implementation of the WESA mechanism would not be as straightforward in practice as the above calculations indicate. For this reason, research into the design of mechanisms for which 'truth telling' about the abatement costs is a solution of the game constitutes an area for further investigations.

2.9   Concluding Remarks

The question of what constitutes a fair burden sharing of climate protection measures is a highly controversial one. In this chapter, the criteria of individual rationality, envy-freeness with monetary compensations, resource monotonicity and population monotonicity were applied to derive a mechanism for the fair division of common property resources.

The justification of the WESA mechanism rests on normative grounds. Obviously, this contrasts with the lack of a central authority to implement the WESA mechanism. Therefore, its attractiveness would gain if it had also some descriptive power.

In this respect, it is interesting that the requirement of imposing 'no harm' on developing countries, which corresponds to the full compensation for abatement costs in the WESA allocation, has been repeatedly mentioned as a central ingredient of any 'acceptable' treaty (Edmonds, Wise, and Barns 1995; Bohm 1997). This principle can in fact be found in some international agreements which have been praised for their fairness. Most prominently, this is so for the international agreement to combat stratospheric ozone depletion (Montreal Protocol), where low-emission countries have been fully compensated for their incremental abatement costs by high-emission countries (see Biermann 1997). The WESA mechanism has also close correspondence to the concept of joint implementation (JI) and the so-called clean development mechanism

(CDM) established with the 1997 Kyoto Protocol.

Let me conclude this chapter with some remarks on the issue of historical emission rights.[19] For pollution stock problems like climate change, optimal emission levels in the current and future periods are partly determined by past emissions. If these have been higher than the natural decay rate in the past, more abatement is required now. One position is to argue that bygones are bygones and, accordingly, the distribution of past emissions should not influence the distribution of current and future emissions.

On the other hand, the principle of *ethical presentism* states that 'past practices are irrelevant to distribution in the present, except to the extent that they left morally relevant and causally efficacious traces in the present' (Elster 1991, 14). For climate change this would imply that there should be no punishment for high past emissions. However, the extent to which different countries have contributed to the current CO_2 concentration level, thereby leaving 'causally efficacious traces in the present' – namely higher mitigation burdens –, should be reflected in the allocation of entitlements.

As entitlements enter the WESA mechanism only as an exogenous argument, its normative appeal is unaffected by this dispute, even though the resulting WESA allocation may change, of course. However, because countries are never more than fully compensated for their abatement costs, granting developing countries additional entitlements for historical reasons would have no effect for the ROW group in Figure 2.5. Also the allocation for China would only be affected after 2060. In particular, the time after which China would have to pay a share of the control costs would be shifted to the future.[20] Hence, if the negotiating partners would accept the fair division principles behind the WESA mechanism, agreement on the allocation of emissions and control costs in the near to medium-term future might be possible even if the dispute about the role of historical emissions remains unresolved.

In summary, the WESA mechanism satisfies a number of intuitively appealing fair division criteria which have received wide support in the literature. Furthermore, the allocation of control costs it induces has some characteristics which make it attractive from a political point of

---

[19] For a discussion of this topic see Smith (1991); Ghosh (1993) as well as Beckerman and Pasek (1995).

[20] The use of historical emission rights would, of course, affect control costs in Annex I countries during the whole period. However, given the similarity of their historical emissions this issue is of considerably less empirical and in particular political relevance.

view as well. On the other hand, a critical issue is whether fair division theory is informationally too impoverished for global environmental problems because it neglects differences in income levels. In the next chapter, I shall respond to this critique by discussing the informationally richer welfarist approach, but also indicate some of the fundamental problems which arise in that framework.

2.10   Appendix: Comparative Statics

In this appendix, the partial derivative $\partial p^*/\partial \omega_i$ will be determined (see equation 2.25). This will also be needed in Chapter 5.

For exogenously given emission allowances ω_i, states choose their mix of own abatement measures and allowances bought or sold so as to minimize the costs of emission reductions:

$$\min_{e_i} c_i(e_i) + (e_i - \omega_i)p, \tag{2.33}$$

with first-order conditions

$$c_i'(e_i^*) + p^* = 0 \qquad \text{for all } i \in N, \tag{2.34}$$

where the asterisks denote equilibrium values. Together with the exogenous constraint on the overall emissions level

$$\sum_{i \in N} e_i^* - \sum_{i \in N} \omega_i = 0, \tag{2.35}$$

this determines the competitive equilibrium of tradable emission allowances.

Linearization of the equation system (2.34) and (2.35) about the equilibrium values $((e_i^*)_{i \in N}, p^*)$ yields

$$\begin{pmatrix} -c_1''(e_1^*) & 0 & \cdots & 0 & -1 \\ 0 & -c_2''(e_2^*) & \cdots & 0 & -1 \\ \vdots & \vdots & \ddots & \vdots & \vdots \\ 0 & 0 & \cdots & -c_n''(e_n^*) & -1 \\ 1 & 1 & \cdots & 1 & 0 \end{pmatrix} \begin{pmatrix} de_1^* \\ de_2^* \\ \vdots \\ de_n^* \\ dp^* \end{pmatrix} = \begin{pmatrix} 0 \\ 0 \\ \vdots \\ 0 \\ \sum d\omega_i \end{pmatrix}.$$

Let J denote the coefficient matrix, or endogenous variable Jacobian. After some messy algebra its determinant can be calculated as

$$\det J = \sum_{j \in N} \left(\frac{\prod_{i \in N} -c_i''(e_i^*)}{-c_j''(e_j^*)} \right) \tag{2.36}$$

which is different from zero if abatement cost functions are non-linear. Accordingly, the above system (2.34) and (2.35) defines the endogenous variables $(e_i^*)_{i \in N}$ and p^* as implicit functions of the exogenously given $\omega = \sum_{i \in N} \omega_i$, at least in the neighborhood of the point $((e_i^*)_{i \in N}, p^*)$.

By Cramer's rule, the partial derivative $\partial p^*/\partial \omega$ can now be calculated as

$$
\begin{aligned}
\frac{\partial p^*}{\partial \omega} &= -\frac{\det \begin{pmatrix} -c_1''(e_1^*) & 0 & \cdots & 0 & 0 \\ 0 & -c_2''(e_2^*) & \cdots & 0 & \vdots \\ \vdots & \vdots & \ddots & \vdots & \vdots \\ 0 & 0 & \cdots & -c_1''(e_n^*) & 0 \\ 1 & 1 & \cdots & 1 & -1 \end{pmatrix}}{\det J} \\
&= \frac{\prod_{i \in N} -c_i''(e_i^*)}{\sum_{j \in N} \left(\frac{\prod_{i \in N} -c_i''(e_i^*)}{-c_j''(e_j^*)} \right)} = -\frac{1}{\sum_{i \in N} \frac{1}{c_i''(e_i^*)}} \leq 0 \qquad (2.37)
\end{aligned}
$$

by convexity of abatement cost functions.

3. A Welfarist Approach to Fair Burden Sharing

> It is not permitted to the most equitable of men to be a judge in his own cause.
>
> Blaise Pascal (1623–1662)

3.1 Introduction

In the previous chapter, burden sharing in international environmental politics has been analyzed as a local justice problem, where – apart from the axiomatic fairness criteria – only actors' entitlements to the common property resources and their abatement cost functions are relevant information for the solution. In particular, if countries differ solely in their income level, they are treated equally by the WESA mechanism.

Obviously, this is not without drawbacks. Imagine an international environmental problem where developing countries are the main source of polluting emissions. Given equal per capita entitlements, the WESA mechanism – but also other solutions in the spirit of local fair division theory – would allocate the greater part of emission reduction burdens to those developing countries. However, many observers would regard this as inequitable and argue that a country's share of the mitigation burdens should not only be determined according to its responsibility for the problem, but also by its capability to shoulder those burdens.[1]

This principle, that burden sharing should take into account countries' 'differentiated responsibilities and their respective capabilities' has indeed been agreed in Article 3 of the Climate Convention and in many other treaties (see Biermann 1998). It is also in accordance with the principle of progressive taxation at the level of nation states, which shifts higher proportional tax burdens to people with higher incomes.

---

[1]One may view this as a problem of second best (Lipsey and Lancaster 1956), meaning that a fair allocation of emission entitlements does not necessarily improve the fairness of the overall situation as long as other resources are allocated in an unfair way.

These are strong arguments to surpass the local perspective of fair division theory and to take welfare differences into account. Section 3.2 introduces social welfare functions and discusses how their specification reflects value judgments. Section 3.3 then analyzes the implications of a welfarist approach for burden sharing in the climate change regime and, in particular, how countries' different responsibilities and capabilities should be taken into account. In the concluding remarks (Section 3.4), the findings are compared to the fair division approach of the previous chapter.

3.2 Social Welfare Functions and Value Judgments

The Arrow impossibility theorem (Arrow 1951) tells us that the prospects of making social choices on the basis of ordinal rational preferences are rather bad. Arrow shows that there is no Pareto-efficient social choice mechanism satisfying the following two desirable conditions: (*i*) independence of irrelevant alternatives, that is social preferences between any two alternatives should depend only on the individual preferences between the same two alternatives, and (*ii*) non-dictatorship, meaning that there should be no agent who determines the social preference independent of the individual preference profiles of the other agents.

A number of approaches to circumvent the Arrow impossibility theorem have been suggested in the literature, for example to relax the assumption of full (economic) rationality or to restrict the analysis to single-peaked preferences (for a discussion see Sen 1970). Welfare theory and cost benefit analysis are based on another approach, namely of reverting to a cardinal preference ordering, which attaches a meaning to utility levels and thereby allows interpersonal comparisons (and hence aggregation) of utility.

A natural objective is to choose emission and consumption levels so as to maximize social welfare:

$$\max_{\{(e_i, x_i)_{i \in N}\}} w(u_1(x_1, e), u_2(x_2, e), \dots, u_n(x_n, e)) \quad \text{s.t.} \quad (u_i)_{i \in N} \in U,$$

(3.1)

where $N = \{1, 2, \dots, n\}$ is the set of agents, indexed i, and $(u_i(x_i, e))_{i \in N}$ is a vector of the individual agents' utility values as a function of private consumption x_i and pollution e. To simplify notation, I assume that the disutility of pollution depends only on aggregate emissions, which is largely appropriate for climate change and ozone depletion, but not for transboundary acidification (see Chapter 6). Finally, U is the utility possibility set and $w(\cdot)$ is a social welfare function that describes how the utility of individual agents is aggregated so as to yield a social welfare index (Bergson 1938; Samuelson 1947).

Cost benefit analysis allows us to make decisions on individual projects – like a particular climate protection strategy – even in a rather imperfect world which is miles away from the bliss point of the welfare maximum. Roughly speaking, a project should be undertaken if it increases social welfare w and rejected otherwise.[2] This means, for example, that policy makers can take account of worldwide income differences in their choice of a climate protection strategy, while not tackling them on a more general level.

However, doing so involves two controversial steps. First, one has to determine how a policy affects the utility of each individual and express those changes in a way that allows interpersonal comparisons. Second, one has to deduce the change in social welfare implied by the changes in the utility of the individual agents. It is in those two steps, which will be addressed in turn, that fairness concerns of transboundary environmental problems enter (for a more extensive discussion see Helm, Bruckner, and Tóth 1999).[3]

3.2.1 Value Judgments at the Level of Individual Agents

Utility changes are not directly observable. On the other hand, to compare a project's effects across different individuals, one has to agree on a common standard of comparison. Using money measures for individual utility changes is a convenient way to tackle these problems, though not necessarily the only one. The two money measures most frequently used are compensating variation and equivalent variation. Compensating variation gives the amount of money that can be taken away from a household after the project so that it is exactly as well off as before the project was undertaken. If an agent gains from a project, this is his willingness to pay for the project. If an agent loses from a project, this is his willingness to accept compensation for the deterioration of his

---

[2]On cost benefit analysis and the derivation of money measures see Boadway and Bruce (1984); Johansson (1993).

[3]In a dynamic framework, value judgments at the intergenerational level that arise from the need to aggregate utilities across time add further controversial value judgments. See Lind (1997) and Tóth (1995) for a discussion.

situation. Similarly, equivalent variation gives the amount of monetary transfers needed to make a household before the project was undertaken exactly as well off as after the project.

Turning from the conceptual idea of money measures towards their empirical specification and interpersonal comparison is anything but an easy exercise. This can be seen nowhere better than in climate change. Among its most important impact categories are effects on human health and mortality, ecosystem damages like wetland, forest and species loss, damages from extreme events like storms, floods and droughts, migration and so on (IPCC 1996b). To a large extent, these impacts concern intangibles, that is goods which are not traded in markets, and, furthermore, the extent of those impacts is highly uncertain. Thus, the usual approach of economists to infer values from evidence based on actual market behavior is often not feasible.

One possibility is to monetize those hard-to-value, non-pecuniary costs indirectly via *implicit markets*. For example, the willingness to pay for national parks and the ecosystems they protect is sometimes approximated from people's travel costs of visiting those parks. Similarly, if two property sites differ only in their susceptibility to flooding, the monetary value of this difference in risk of flooding could be inferred from differences in property values (see Hanley and Spash 1993).

An alternative method is *contingent valuation*, where questionnaires are used to directly elicit individuals' values for the respective goods. For example, a representative sample of people might be asked whether they are willing to accept a certain cost for the prevention of a particular impact, and this information can then be used to estimate demand functions (see Portney 1994; Hanemann 1994).

Although both methods can provide valuable information, they have their shortcomings. For instance, people often attach a value to the mere knowledge that rare ecosystems are protected in national parks, without intending ever to visit them. Such 'existence values' (Krutilla 1967) would not be reflected in estimates derived by the travel cost method. Furthermore, the monetization of intangible values via implicit markets depends on the possibility of isolating those parts of the market behavior that reflect the values one is interested in. For example, one will rarely find property sites which differ only in their risk of flooding.

Contingent valuation surveys, on the other hand, depend on individuals' stated responses to hypothetical questions. Therefore, payments are only symbolic and respondents might not reflect them carefully. Furthermore, as people do not carry their utility functions engraved on their brains, respondents' ability to state their willingness to pay for a particular object requires that they are well informed and at least to some extent familiar with the situation described in the hypothetical question. This problem may be particularly severe if one attempts to elicit respondents' willingness to pay for an impact that will not occur with certainty but only with a certain probability. Nevertheless, such information is important because neglecting people's risk attitude might severely bias results.

Beyond those principal difficulties of eliciting individual agents' valuation for intangibles, in the case of climate change the problem is further aggravated as it will affect almost everyone in a multitude of aspects. Inclusion of all relevant impacts, or even just the most important ones, would prove extremely difficult. Therefore, it is not surprising that most cost benefit studies on climate change rely on highly simplified damage cost functions, which are based in a rather loose way on more elaborate impact studies (see the survey in Schellnhuber and Yohe 1997).

3.2.2 Value Judgments at the Intragenerational Level

Having elicited people's valuations of the avoidance of climate change impacts, these have to be aggregated into social preferences. In other words, one has to decide how much to value a project's effects on different persons relative to each other. Although the precise aggregation rule to be used is highly controversial, there are some properties which are generally regarded as minimum requirements for any social welfare function.

The first criterion is *welfarism* or *non-paternalism*, which means that social preferences should depend only on the individual utility levels, whereas the social planner has no direct preferences on the alternatives. Second, the social welfare function should satisfy the *Pareto criterion* so that an increase in the utility level of every individual also improves social welfare. Third, the social welfare function is usually required to be concave, similar to individual utility functions. While for individual agents the concavity of utility functions signifies the degree of risk aversion, in the context of social welfare functions it rather represents the degree of *inequality aversion*. A final common property is *anonymity* or *symmetry*, which asserts that all agents should be treated equally in the sense that for the evaluation of social welfare only the frequencies of different utility levels matter, but not who enjoys a high or low level of utility. Yet, these four properties still leave a wide range of possible specifications of the social welfare function.

If the global income distribution were in a welfare optimum, the problem of valuing a project's effect on different people would be alleviated considerably. In the optimum, marginal social utility of income must be equal across all agents and, therefore, equal effects (measured in income changes like compensating variation) should be valued equally independent of to which agent they accrue.[4] However, given widespread poverty, it seems hard to argue that the international income distribution is optimal.

If a decision is not made from the position of a global welfare optimum, marginal social utility of income will differ among agents and a global planner would have to decide how to value the effects of a project on different agents relative to each other. The range of value judgments can be illustrated with different types of social welfare functions (SWF), whose indifference curves have shapes that are well known from private consumer and producer theory (see Mas-Colell, Whinston, and Green 1995; Fankhauser, Tol, and Pearce 1997).

Bentham's principle of achieving the greatest good for the greatest number (Bentham 1988) is expressed by a *utilitarian* SWF (Figure 3.1(a)), for which the marginal social welfare of utility is equal across all agents:

$$w = \sum_{i \in N} u_i(x_i, e). \tag{3.2}$$

The utilitarian SWF neglects distributionary aspects in so far as extremely unequal utility allocations – like the endpoints of the indifference curves in Figure 3.1(a) – would be represented by the same welfare index w, as long as the sum of the utility levels remains constant. However, this does not imply indifference towards the income distribution because the marginal utility of income will generally be higher in poorer countries. In equation (3.2), we have $\partial w / \partial u_i = 1$ for all $i \in N$, but $\partial u_i / \partial x_i$ depends on income levels. Neglecting the production side of the economy, global welfare maximization would require marginal utility to be equalized in all countries, thereby supporting a rather egalitarian income distribution. This is illustrated by the point of tangency between the indifference curve and the utility possibility set (UPS) in Figure 3.1(a).[5]

---

[4]This is how many cost benefit studies on climate protection strategies proceed: effects are monetized and then a cost benefit decision criterion, which usually ignores to whom the effects accrue, is applied (for a discussion see Fankhauser, Tol, and Pearce 1997).

[5]The utility possibility sets in Figures 3.1(a) to 3.1(c) will change, of course, with the specification of the social welfare function.

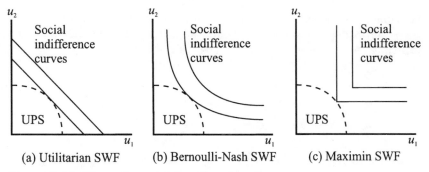

Figure 3.1: Alternative social welfare functions

The second example in Figure 3.1(b) depicts the indifference curves of the Bernoulli-Nash SWF

$$w = \sum_{i \in N} \ln u_i(x_i, e).\tag{3.3}$$

Here, utility improvements for the worse-off agents have a greater effect on social welfare than those for the better-off agents, because $\partial w / \partial u_i = 1/u_i$ depends on individual utility levels. The stronger the curvature of the social indifference curves, the bigger the inequality aversion.

If the curvature tends towards infinity, the indifference curves correspond to those of a maximin SWF depicted in Figure 3.1(c):

$$w = \min\{u_1(x_1, e), u_2(x_2, e), \ldots, u_n(x_n, e)\}.\tag{3.4}$$

In this case, it is only the worst-off group in the society – for which $\partial w / \partial u_i = 1$ – that determines the social welfare level, while $\partial w / \partial u_i = 0$ for all others.

This social welfare function is often termed Rawlsian because of its similarity to Rawls's 'difference principle', according to which inequalities can only be justified if they improve the conditions for the worst-off individual (Rawls 1971). Yet, Rawls was not so much looking for a decision that would somehow maximize the social good; rather he emphasized the process or context in which decisions are made. He was concerned with the establishment of a set of just institutions in which decision making could take place. In particular, Rawls did not focus on the subjective well-being of the individual agents, but on the means and instruments – the so-called primary goods – with which they could foster their well-being. However, Rawls himself has argued that his difference principle cannot be applied to the level of states.[6]

The constant elasticity of substitution function

$$w = \begin{cases} \left(\sum_{i \in N} u_i(x_i, e)^{1-r} \right)^{\frac{1}{1-r}} & \text{if } r \neq 1 \\ \sum_{i \in N} \ln u_i(x_i, e) & \text{if } r = 1 \end{cases} \tag{3.5}$$

allows us to represent the degree of inequality aversion via a single parameter r, including the three special cases just mentioned. In particular, $r = 0$ represents the utilitarian, $r = 1$ the Bernoulli-Nash, and $r = \infty$ the maximin social welfare function.

3.3   Social Welfare Functions and Fairness Concerns in Climate Change

The general formulation of the social welfare function will now be used to analyze distributionary justice concerns of climate change decision making. In doing so, it is important to distinguish whether lump-sum transfers are feasible or not, as emphasized by Chichilnisky, Heal, and Starrett (1993) (see also Chichilnisky and Heal 1994).

Let $f_i(e_i)$ be an increasing and concave production function with emissions as the only input. If transfer payments are feasible and abstracting from any income effects, the decision problem for $r \neq 1$ can be stated as[7]

$$\max_{\{(e_i, x_i)_{i \in N}\}} \left(\sum_{i \in N} u_i(x_i, e)^{1-r} \right)^{\frac{1}{1-r}} \quad \text{s.t.} \quad \sum_{i \in N} x_i = \sum_{i \in N} f_i(e_i)$$

$$\text{and} \quad \sum_{i \in N} e_i = e. \tag{3.6}$$

---

[6]Rawls (1971) states that '[t]he original position is fair between nations; it nullifies the contingencies and biases of historical fate' (see also Rawls 1993 and 1999). Yet, one need not share this view and some authors have indeed argued for an extension of the difference principle to the international level (see Barry 1973 and Beitz 1999).

[7]Extension to the case $r = 1$ is straightforward and will be left out for space considerations.

The Lagrangian is

$$\mathcal{L} = \left(\sum_{i \in N} u_i(x_i, e)^{1-r} \right)^{\frac{1}{1-r}} + \lambda \left(\sum_{i \in N} f_i(e_i) - \sum_{i \in N} x_i \right), \qquad (3.7)$$

with the first-order conditions for all $i \in N$ (assuming an interior solution)

$$\frac{\partial \mathcal{L}}{\partial e_i} = \frac{1}{1-r} \left(\sum_{i \in N} u_i(x_i, e)^{1-r} \right)^{\frac{r}{1-r}} \sum_{i \in N} \left(\frac{(1-r)(\partial u_i / \partial e)}{u_i(x_i, e)^r} \right) + \lambda \frac{\partial f_i}{\partial e_i}$$

$$= \left(\sum_{i \in N} u_i(x_i, e)^{1-r} \right)^{\frac{r}{1-r}} \sum_{i \in N} \left(\frac{\partial u_i / \partial e}{u_i(x_i, e)^r} \right) + \lambda \frac{\partial f_i}{\partial e_i} = 0 \qquad (3.8)$$

$$\frac{\partial \mathcal{L}}{\partial x_i} = \left(\sum_{i \in N} u_i(x_i, e)^{1-r} \right)^{\frac{r}{1-r}} \left(\frac{\partial u_i / \partial x_i}{u_i(x_i, e)^r} \right) - \lambda = 0 \qquad (3.9)$$

$$\frac{\partial \mathcal{L}}{\partial \lambda} = \sum_{i \in N} f_i(e_i) - \sum_{i \in N} x_i = 0. \qquad (3.10)$$

Apart from the marginal abatement cost term $f_i'(e_i)$, equation (3.8) is identical for all actors $i \in N$. Unless $\lambda = 0$, this implies the familiar optimality condition that marginal abatement costs must be equalized across all countries – independently of the specification of the social welfare function. After all, this is hardly surprising because with lump-sum transfers it is always optimal to reduce emissions in the least costly way, and this is achieved by equalizing marginal abatement costs.

Furthermore, solving (3.9) for λ and substituting this into (3.8) gives (subject to the feasibility constraint 3.10)

$$\frac{\sum_{i \in N} (u_i(x_i, e)^{-r} \partial u_i / \partial e)}{\partial f_i / \partial e_i} = -\frac{\partial u_i / \partial x_i}{u_i(x_i, e)^r} \qquad \text{for all } i \in N. \qquad (3.11)$$

Following the previous argument, the left-hand side in (3.11) is the same for all countries. Hence, a utilitarian social welfare function (with $r = 0$ the denominator on the right-hand side is equal to 1) requires an allocation of the consumption good x such that marginal utilities of consumption are equalized across countries. These are usually regarded as higher in poorer countries so that even a utilitarian social welfare function would allocate to them a higher share of the consumption good

x_i. Accordingly, developing countries receive transfer payments which might substantially exceed their abatement costs. This contrasts with the WESA mechanism of the previous chapter, where full compensation for abatement costs constitutes an upper bound on transfers.

For $r > 0$, countries with lower utility levels $u_i(x_i, e)$ should face lower marginal utilities of consumption so as to keep the quotient on the right-hand side of (3.11) the same for all agents, as required by the optimality conditions. This effect is more pronounced the higher the r, because it accentuates the differences in utility levels. Accordingly, as we move away from the utilitarian social welfare function and increase r, transfer payments (in terms of the consumption good x_i) to poorer countries increase. Furthermore, because the values for $u_i(x_i, e)$ depend also on a country's disutility from pollution, with a higher r the compensation for countries which suffer high damages from pollution increases.

Turning to the case without lump-sum transfers, domestic consumption x_i must equal domestic production $f_i(e_i)$ (assuming non-satiation) so that the optimization problem for the case $r \neq 1$ becomes

$$\max_{\{(e_i, x_i)_{i \in N}\}} \left(\sum_{i \in N} u_i(x_i, e)^{1-r} \right)^{\frac{1}{1-r}} \quad \text{s.t.} \quad x_i = f_i(e_i) \ \forall \, i \in N, \quad (3.12)$$

$$\text{and} \quad \sum_{i \in N} e_i = e. \quad (3.13)$$

The Lagrangian is

$$\mathcal{L} = \left(\sum_{i \in N} u_i(x_i, e)^{1-r} \right)^{\frac{1}{1-r}} + \sum_{i \in N} \lambda_i (f_i(e_i) - x_i) \quad (3.14)$$

with the first-order conditions for all $i \in N$ (assuming an interior solution)

$$\frac{\partial \mathcal{L}}{\partial e_i} = \left(\sum_{i \in N} u_i(x_i, e)^{1-r} \right)^{\frac{r}{1-r}} \sum_{i \in N} \left(\frac{\partial u_i / \partial e}{u_i(x_i, e)^r} \right) + \lambda_i \frac{\partial f_i}{\partial e_i} = 0 \quad (3.15)$$

$$\frac{\partial \mathcal{L}}{\partial x_i} = \left(\sum_{i \in N} u_i(x_i, e)^{1-r} \right)^{\frac{r}{1-r}} u_i(x_i, e)^{-r} \frac{\partial u_i}{\partial x_i} - \lambda_i = 0 \quad (3.16)$$

$$\frac{\partial \mathcal{L}}{\partial \lambda_i} = f_i(e_i) - x_i = 0. \quad (3.17)$$

In contrast to the case with lump-sum transfers, the Lagrangian multiplier λ_i is now country-specific. Therefore, marginal abatement costs

$f_i'(e_i)$ in optimality condition (3.15) may differ among countries. In particular, solving (3.16) for λ_i and substituting this into (3.15) gives (subject to the feasibility constraint 3.17)

$$\frac{\partial f_i}{\partial e_i} = -\frac{u_i(x_i, e)^r \sum_{i \in N} (u_i(x_i, e)^{-r} \partial u_i / \partial e)}{\partial u_i / \partial x_i} \quad \text{for all } i \in N. \quad (3.18)$$

This is exactly the same formulation as the optimality condition (3.11) with lump-sum transfers, but its interpretation differs because marginal abatement costs are no longer the same across countries. Considering first the case of a utilitarian social welfare function ($r = 0$) and noting that the summation term is the same for all countries, equation (3.18) requires that marginal abatement costs must be inversely proportional to marginal utilities of consumption in the optimum (see Proposition 1 in Chichilnisky and Heal 1994). Because the latter are higher in poorer countries, they should face lower marginal abatement costs in the optimum than richer countries. As r increases, the term $u_i(x_i, e)^r$ further accentuates this effect.

In summary, if lump-sum transfers are feasible, these can be used to implement the value judgments expressed by the social welfare function, while abatement measures are undertaken in the least costly manner. Without lump-sum transfers, value judgments are expressed by the allocation of abatement burdens so that richer countries face higher abatement cost at the margin.

The question then arises which of the two cases is more realistic. Chichilnisky and Heal (1994) criticize the assumption of lump-sum transfers because no international institution executing such transfers exists.[8] However, by the same reasoning the whole approach of framing the problem as one of social welfare maximization would then be flawed because there exists no world government to implement those recommendations. So, regarding the analysis mainly as a normative thought experiment, I find it more consistent to give the 'global welfare maximizer' the tool of lump-sum transfers as well.

---

[8]The World Bank, the International Monetary Fund and other national and international development agencies are only a poor substitute for such an institution. On the other hand, political scientists in particular have emphasized the increasing role of international institutions for decision making, for which they introduced the term 'global governance' (Young 1997). The most prominent example of this is the World Trade Organization (WTO) founded in 1994, which has the power to pass binding judgment in the case of disputes (Helm 1995). Recently, a number of observers have argued for a World Environment Organization with similar powers (see Biermann and Simonis 1998).

3.4   Concluding Remarks

In a critical review of various theories of distributive justice to climate change, Beckerman and Pasek (1995, 405) come to the rather skeptical conclusion that

> it is highly unlikely anyway that any widely accepted ethical principles could be found that have any bearing on the equitable international allocation of tradable emission permits, in spite of the impression to the contrary given by discussion of various 'equitable' allocations of emission permits. The main reason for this is that the discussion implicitly assumes that there are some clear principles of distributive justice between nations that are simple extensions of those relating to distributive justice between individuals within any nation. But ... this assumption is quite unwarranted.

Rawls's explicit statement that his difference principle is not applicable to the international level might be referred to in support of such a claim (Rawls 1999). However, in the light of the preceding discussion I wouldn't go as far as supporting the position of Beckerman and Pasek (1995), while still admitting that substantial problems exist.

In particular, the WESA mechanism is based on fairness principles for which widespread support can be found in the literature. Resourcist theories of justice also offer some guidance for the allocation of entitlements. And it has been shown that a fairly precise burden-sharing rule follows from fair division theory. A shortcoming of this approach, however, is its neglect of differences in income levels across countries.

By contrast, these are given a very central position in the welfarist approach to burden sharing in international environmental politics. Yet, here the criticism of Beckerman and Pasek (1995) seems more applicable. Beyond the problem of relying on interpersonal, cardinal comparisons of utility[9] and the difficulties of valuing effects on individual agents, there exists no agreement on the social welfare function, that is how to evaluate individual effects at the global level. In spite of those uncertainties there exists, however, common ground in that any specification of the distributionary parameter r in the generalized social welfare function (3.5) would shift higher mitigation burdens to the richer regions in the world.

---

[9]Note that none of the fair division criteria in Chapter 2 involves such interpersonal, cardinal comparisons of utility. For a recent defense of cardinalism see Ng (1997); see also Harsanyi (1955) and his derivation of an additive social welfare function based on von Neumann-Morgenstern utility functions.

Judging from the statement in the Climate Change Convention that burden sharing should take account of countries' 'differentiated responsibilities and their respective capabilities', the fair division approach is heavily biased towards the responsibilities component and the welfare approach towards the capabilities component. Fortunately, at least for the case of climate change the general results of the two approaches are largely in harmony with each other: the WESA mechanism shifts most of the abatement burdens to richer countries, and is therefore in accordance with countries' different capabilities. Similarly, a welfarist approach would shift most of the abatement burdens to high-emission countries, and is therefore in accordance with countries' different responsibilities.

However, there are two reasons which might make the fair division approach considerably more relevant for international environmental negotiations. First, in my opinion the fair division criteria are less controversial than the specification of the social welfare function. And second, from a political point of view I regard any solution as unrealistic which entails transfers to developing countries that substantially exceed their abatement costs.

This sets the stage for the remaining two parts of the book. The analysis has until now been purely normative, and issues of political acceptability have only been alluded to loosely. In the following chapter, international environmental cooperation is framed as a coalitional game. Thereby, acceptability of burden-sharing rules will move to the forefront, but issues of fairness will retain a considerable role as a selection criterion if there is more than one 'acceptable' solution.

PART II

International Policy in the Cooperative Mode

4. Environmental Cooperation as a Coalitional Game

Thinking:
The talking of the soul with itself.

Plato (428/427–348/347 BC)

4.1 Introduction

In the first part of the book, international environmental policy was analyzed from a normative point of view. The search was for 'fair' agreements, not for those that would be 'acceptable' to sovereign states. However, there exists no superior institution like a world government which disposes of the power and information to implement a fair outcome.

This, of course, need not mean that fair agreements must necessarily prove unacceptable. Indeed, I have argued that at least some characteristics of the WESA mechanism resemble provisions in international environmental treaties – in particular the principle that low-emission developing countries should be compensated for their incremental abatement costs. However, that interpretation was based on *ad hoc* arguments, not on a systematic analysis of the strategic interaction of sovereign decision makers. This will be the topic of the remaining two parts of the book, first using concepts from cooperative game theory and then turning to non-cooperative game theory.

Of the two, cooperative game theory is based on the more optimistic view of the world because it is assumed that agents can negotiate effectively: if it is feasible for a coalition of agents to improve the payoff of all its members, then they will be able to reach agreement on this, unless some agents would do even better by joining another coalition.[1] Put differently, cooperative game theory starts from an imaginary position of cooperation, and then analyzes whether it is self-enforcing. This is, of course, a simplifying perspective because the process of coalition

---

[1] For an introduction to cooperative game theory see Osborne and Rubinstein (1994), Myerson (1991) and Shubik (1984).

formation – which may involve threats, promises, or certain negotiation rules – is left out of the analysis. However, an explicit modeling of the negotiation process would substantially increase the complexity of any analysis and often render it intractable.

Any observer or participant of international environmental negotiations will agree that coalition formation plays a central role.[2] For example, in climate change negotiations there are not only well-known groups like the EU, the OPEC or the G-77/China (group of developing countries). Further alliances have been formed by states with common interests in this particular issue area so as better to coordinate their policies – like the Alliance of Small Island States (AOSIS) or the JUSS-CANNZ group (Japan, USA, Switzerland, Canada, Australia, Norway and New Zealand).

Nevertheless, with some exceptions (Chander and Tulkens 1995, 1997; Egteren and Tang 1997; Eyckmans 1997; Funaki and Yamato 1999; Uzawa 1999), concepts from cooperative game theory have received relatively little attention in the literature on international environmental politics. A central question regards the conditions under which a transboundary pollution game – or more generally, an economy with multilateral environmental externalities – has a non-empty core, meaning that cooperation by the grand coalition comprising all players is stable with respect to defection by subcoalitions. As will be shown in the first part of this chapter, a non-empty core exists even without restrictive assumptions regarding payoff functions (as in Chander and Tulkens 1997) or retaliation strategies (as in Egteren and Tang 1997).

This immediately raises another question, namely whether some allocations from the core are more appealing than others, be it for positive or normative reasons. Fairness principles are one, if not the, central criterion to pick a solution from the core. This establishes a bridge towards the preceding part, but now the search for a fair outcome is restricted to the set of core-stable solutions. Accordingly, none of the solution candidates that will be discussed in the following are fully convincing from a normative point of view. Besides fairness issues, another common theme carried over from the previous part is the assumption that players can make transfer payments, in which utility is linear (for a discussion of this issue see Barrett 1994; Carraro and Siniscalco 1993).

The structure of this chapter is as follows. After introducing some

---

[2]For an informative and indeed quite exciting description of such negotiations see the account by Benedick (1997, 1998), who headed the US delegation in the early stages of the international ozone negotiations.

basic concepts of cooperative game theory (Section 4.2), a transboundary pollution game will be shown to be balanced so that it has a non-empty core (Section 4.3). In the rest of the chapter, the Shapley value (Section 4.4.1), the ratio equilibrium (Section 4.4.2) and the egalitarian equivalent allocation (Section 4.4.3) will be discussed as selection candidates from the core.

4.2   Coalition Formation and the Role of Blocking Rules

A *coalitional game* (N, v) consists of a finite set N of players, indexed by $i = \{1, 2, \ldots, n\}$ and a characteristic function v that specifies the worth $v(S)$ of every non-empty coalition $S \subset N$. For a coalitional game with transferable utility, $v(S)$ is a real number, namely the total payoff that members of coalition S can allocate among themselves. The central stability concept in cooperative game theory is the core.

Definition 9 *Given a coalitional game with transferable utility* (N, v), *a payoff vector* $(\pi_i)_{i \in N}$ *is in the core if*

$$\sum_{i \in N} \pi_i = v(N), \qquad \text{and for all } S \subset N : \ v(S) \leq \sum_{i \in S} \pi_i. \qquad (4.1)$$

The first part of this definition ensures that the payoff vector $(\pi_i)_{i \in N}$ is feasible for the *grand coalition* N. The second part introduces a stability requirement such that no subcoalition S by acting on its own can achieve an aggregate payoff which is higher than the share that it receives under global cooperation. Thereby, the concept of 'individual rationality' as discussed in Chapter 2 is extended to one which also requires 'group rationality'.

In their seminal paper on the core of an economic system with externalities, Shapley and Shubik (1969) presented different examples involving external *diseconomies*, some of which have a non-empty core and some of which do not. They also raised the question whether there are restricted classes of models for which general existence or non-existence theorems can be established. In analyzing this issue, they found the treatment of blocking rules to be crucial (Foley 1970; Rosenthal 1971; Scarf 1971; Starrett 1973).

In particular, Rosenthal (1971, 182) argued that 'for economies in which externalities have beneficial effects, the core does not necessarily describe intuitively stable outcomes'. The reason is that it may involve non-credible threats. A simple example – similar to the one provided by Rosenthal (1971, 187) – shall illustrate that the same critique applies to economies with *negative* externalities.

Let there be three individuals, each endowed with one unit of an all-purpose input good. An individual i can transform input goods on a one-to-one basis into an output good x_i, which generates a negative externality e_i. The payoff functions are given by

$$\pi_1 = x_1 - 3e_2, \tag{4.2}$$

$$\pi_2 = x_2 - 3e_3, \tag{4.3}$$

$$\pi_3 = x_3 - 3e_1 - 2e_3. \tag{4.4}$$

Accordingly, the externality generated from production by agents 1 and 2 affects only a neighbor, but agent 3 is affected by his own production externality as well. Because the benefits of producing an output good are exceeded by the damages of the associated externality, the Pareto-optimal solution involves zero production; hence the worth of the grand coalition is $v(N) = 0$. No coalition of two individuals can guarantee itself a positive payoff – and thereby block the grand coalition – regardless of the action of the third individual.

However, for agent 3 it is never 'reasonable' to produce his own output good because this would decrease his payoff by $x_3 - 2e_3$. Thus, if agent 3 behaves individually rationally, 1 and 2 could agree to use their input goods jointly to produce two units of the output good x_1. This would yield a coalition value $v(\{1,2\}) = 2$, because the externality e_1 that is associated with the production of x_1 affects only agent 3. The grand coalition would be dominated via the coalition $\{1,2\}$.

Accordingly, existence of a non-empty core depends on whether we consider agent 3's threat to produce an output good as credible, even though this behavior would be self-damaging. For the special case of transboundary pollution problems, the following behavioral assumptions for agents that act in response to a blocking coalition S can be made: They might

- act to minimize the coalition payoff $v(S)$ (called α-characteristic function),

- follow their emissions in the business-as-usual path without any abatement measures (called δ-characteristic function), or

- choose their emissions individually as a best reply to the action of coalition S (called γ-characteristic function).

The first alternative (α-characteristic function) corresponds to allowing agent 3 to threaten with the production of an output good. It would pose the strongest threat to a blocking coalition S and is, therefore, most effective in sustaining global cooperation. The α-characteristic function has been used by Egteren and Tang (1997) to show that a solution called 'maximum victim benefits', which maximizes the benefits to the victims of pollution while ensuring that polluters are willing to join the scheme, is core-stable.

However, in transboundary pollution games agents that respond to a blocking coalition S can lower the worth $v(S)$ of this coalition only by increasing their own emissions. This does not appear to be a credible threat, because these emissions would cause – possibly substantial – environmental damages to the agents that execute the punishment themselves (Mäler 1989). Furthermore, the production of emissions above the business-as-usual level will usually be costly. Being aware of those problems, Egteren and Tang (1997) justify their assumption that agents outside a blocking coalition act to minimize the coalition payoff by citing Polinsky (1980, 1092) that 'Unions strike, nations go to war, and parties go to court rather than settle outside of court more cheaply'. While I agree that retaliation constitutes a common fact in politics – and not only there – there are, however, few examples of retaliation regardless of costs.[3]

According to the second alternative (δ-characteristic function), agents that do not belong to a blocking coalition would threaten to stop their emission abatement efforts. Thus, the basic idea of retaliation is kept, but not regardless of costs, which makes this strategy more plausible.

However, Chander and Tulkens (1997) have objected that, due to the self-damaging effect of emissions, this strategy also would not constitute an optimal response for coalition external agents. Instead, they argue that those agents would adopt individually best-reply strategies (γ-characteristic function), and they call the outcome a 'partial agreement equilibrium with respect to S'. Thereby, Chander and Tulkens (1997) combine solution concepts from cooperative and non-cooperative game theory.

In the following sections, I will restrict attention to the last two alternatives, namely that agents outside a blocking coalition S will stop their

---

[3]The issue of reciprocity, which includes retaliation, is receiving increased attention in the literature on theoretical game theory and experimental economics (see Rabin 1993; Dufwenberg and Kirchsteiger 1998). However, Rabin (1993), whom Egteren and Tang (1997) quote in support of their position, also argues that there is a trade-off between the incentives for reciprocal behavior and the costs it leads to.

emission abatement efforts or follow individual best-reply strategies.

4.3 The Core of a Transboundary Pollution Game

I consider a simple economy with multilateral environmental externalities. A unique private consumption good is produced at the non-negative level $x_i \geq 0$ from the quantity of input $e_i \geq 0$. The technology is described by a production function $x_i = f_i(e_i)$, which is assumed to be increasing, differentiable and strictly concave in e_i. Each agent's preferences are represented by a quasilinear utility function $u_i(x_i, e) = x_i - d_i(e)$. Here, $d_i(e)$ is i's disutility as a positive, increasing, differentiable and strictly convex function of the level of the externality $e = \sum_{i \in N} e_i$. This setting is general enough to comprise a large class of environmental pollution problems and for concreteness I will refer to $d_i(e)$ as agent i's damages caused by overall emissions e.

The characteristic function of this economic-ecological model is defined by

$$v(S) = \max_{\{(x_i, e_i)_{i \in S}\}} \sum_{i \in S} u_i(x_i, e) \qquad (4.5)$$

subject to $\quad \sum_{i \in S} x_i \leq \sum_{i \in S} f_i(e_i) \quad$ and $\quad e = \sum_{i \in S} e_i + \sum_{i \in N \setminus S} \tilde{e}_i, \quad (4.6)$

where $\tilde{e}_i$ denotes emission levels of agents outside a coalition S.

In the case of the δ-characteristic function, $\tilde{e}_i$ represents emissions in the business-as-usual path without abatement efforts. In the case of the γ-characteristic function, for all $i \in N \setminus S : (x_i, \tilde{e}_i)$ maximizes $u_i(x_i, e)$ subject to $x_i \leq f_i(\tilde{e}_i)$ and $e = \tilde{e}_i + \sum_{\substack{j \in N \\ j \neq i}} e_j$. A proof that such a γ-characteristic function exists is provided in Chander and Tulkens (1997).

A standard procedure to check whether a game has a non-empty core arises from the Bondareva-Shapley theorem (Bondareva 1963; Shapley 1967), which establishes a necessary and sufficient condition for a non-empty core. This core existence theorem elaborates on the following concept of balanced weights:

Given the set N of agents, denote by $\mathcal{C}$ the set of all coalitions that can be formed and by $\mathcal{C}_i = \{S \in \mathcal{C} : i \in S\}$ the subset of those coalitions of which i is a member. Furthermore, for any coalition S denote by

$(1_S) \in R^N$ its characteristic vector with entries given by

$$(1_S)_i = \left\{ \begin{array}{ll} 1 & \text{if } i \in S \\ 0 & \text{otherwise.} \end{array} \right.$$

Accordingly, $(1_N) \in R^N$ denotes the vector with all entries equal to one.

Definition 10 *A vector $(\delta_S)_{S \in C} : \delta_S \in [0,1]$ for all $S \in C$ is a balanced collection of weights if*

$$\sum_{S \in C} \delta_S(1_S) = (1_N), \text{ or equivalently if for all } i \in N : \sum_{S \in C_i} \delta_S = 1.$$

A good way to think about this is that the weights δ_S represent the fraction of the available time budget that an actor i spends in coalition S. Adding this over all coalitions of which i is a member yields $\sum_{S \in C_i} \delta_S = 1$, meaning that i has used up his complete time budget. This establishes a feasibility constraint for actor i's time allocation. However, for a coalition to be active for the fraction of time δ_S, *all* its members have to devote δ_S of their time to it and, therefore, the feasibility constraint needs to be extended to the whole set N of agents. If there exists a pattern such that each coalition S is active for the fraction of time δ_S and each member consumes up exactly his available time, then such a time allocation over all coalitions $(\delta_S)_{S \in C}$ is called a balanced collection of weights.

As an example, let $n = 4$ players form the coalitions $\{1, 2\}$, $\{1, 3\}$, $\{1, 4\}$ and $\{2, 3, 4\}$. These are balanced with the weights given by $1/3$, $1/3$, $1/3$, and $2/3$, respectively.

The Bondareva-Shapley theorem builds upon this concept of balanced weights as follows:

Proposition 5 *(Bondareva 1963; Shapley 1967) A coalitional game with transferable payoff (N, v) has a non-empty core if and only if*

$$\sum_{S \in C} \delta_S v(S) \leq v(N) \tag{4.7}$$

for every balanced collection of weights.

Accordingly, for the core to be non-empty there must be no feasible pattern of coalition formation that yields a higher aggregate payoff than the grand coalition can achieve. To show that this condition is satisfied for the above economic-ecological model, the following lemma will prove useful.

Lemma 2 *Let $(e_i^S)_{i \in S}$ be an optimal input vector for coalition S, given that agents $i \in N \backslash S$ choose inputs $\tilde{e}_i$. For the coalitional game with multilateral externalities as defined by the characteristic function specified in equations (4.5) and (4.6):*

$$\sum_{S \in C \backslash C_i} \delta_S \sum_{i \in S} e_i^S \leq \sum_{S \in C_i} \delta_S \sum_{i \in N \backslash S} \tilde{e}_i. \qquad (4.8)$$

Proof. Elaborating on the γ-characteristic function, Chander and Tulkens (1997, 389) have shown that 'for any coalition $S \subset N$, [...] the individual emission levels of players outside of S are not lower than those at the disagreement equilibrium, although the total emissions are not higher', where the disagreement equilibrium describes the Nash equilibrium of the game. Their argument proceeds roughly along the following lines. Assume that aggregate emissions in the partial agreement equilibrium, denoted $e^P = \sum_{i \in S} e_i^S + \sum_{i \in N \backslash S} \tilde{e}_i$, exceed those in the disagreement (Nash) equilibrium $e^N = \sum_{i \in N} e_i^N$. By convexity of the damage cost functions, this implies that $d_i'(e^P) \geq d_i'(e^N)$ for all $i \in N$. The well-known equilibrium conditions for the Nash equilibrium are $f_i'(e_i^N) = d_i'(e^N)$ for all $i \in N$, and those for the partial agreement equilibrium follow straightforwardly from the γ-characteristic function as

$$f_i'(e_i^S) = \sum_{j \in S} d_j'(e^P) \ \forall \, i \in S \quad \text{and} \quad f_i'(\tilde{e}_i) = d_i'(e^P) \ \forall \, i \in N \backslash S. \quad (4.9)$$

Taken together this yields

$$f_i'(e_i^S) = \sum_{j \in S} d_j'(e^P) \geq d_i'(e^P) \ \geq \ d_i'(e^N) = f_i'(e_i^N) \ \forall \, i \in S, \text{ and} \quad (4.10)$$

$$f_i'(\tilde{e}_i) = d_i'(e^P) \ \geq \ d_i'(e^N) = f_i'(e_i^N) \ \forall \, i \in N \backslash S. \quad (4.11)$$

However, by concavity of the production function this would imply that emissions in the partial agreement equilibrium are lower than those in the Nash equilibrium for *all* agents – a contradiction to the initial assumption that $e^P > e^N$. Hence, we must have $e^P \leq e^N$, and therefore $d_i'(e^P) \leq d_i'(e^N)$. Reversing the sign in (4.11) accordingly gives the desired result that $\tilde{e}_i \geq e_i^N$ for all $i \in N \backslash S$. Intuitively, external agents free-ride on the emission reductions achieved by cooperation within the coalition as compared to the Nash equilibrium.

We can now show that

$$\sum_{S \in \mathcal{C} \setminus \mathcal{C}_i} \delta_S \sum_{i \in S} e_i^S \leq \sum_{S \in \mathcal{C} \setminus \mathcal{C}_i} \delta_S \sum_{i \in S} e_i^N = \sum_{S \in \mathcal{C}_i} \delta_S \sum_{i \in N \setminus S} e_i^N \leq \sum_{S \in \mathcal{C}_i} \delta_S \sum_{i \in N \setminus S} \tilde{e}_i$$

$$(4.12)$$

what includes the lemma. From the information on aggregate emissions and on emissions of agents $i \in N \setminus S$, it follows immediately that $\sum_{i \in S} e_i^S \leq \sum_{i \in S} e_i^N$, as it is used in the first step of expression (4.12).

To see that the '=' sign in (4.12) is true, note that the expressions on the left- and right-hand side of it both completely describe for the same collection of balanced weights the emissions of agents outside of the coalitions containing i. In particular, on the left-hand side we look at those coalitions that do not contain i, and then consider the action of agents that belong to those coalitions. On the right-hand side, we look at the coalitions that do contain i, and then consider the action of agents that do not belong to those coalitions.

For illustration, take the previous example of coalitions $\{1,2\}$, $\{1,3\}$, $\{1,4\}$, and $\{2,3,4\}$ with balanced weights 1/3, 1/3, 1/3, and 2/3. For $i = 1$, the part of (4.12) that involves the '=' sign becomes

$$\frac{2}{3} \left(e_2^N + e_3^N + e_4^N \right) = \frac{1}{3} \left(e_3^N + e_4^N \right) + \frac{1}{3} \left(e_2^N + e_4^N \right) + \frac{1}{3} \left(e_2^N + e_3^N \right)$$

$$e_2^N + e_3^N + e_4^N = e_2^N + e_3^N + e_4^N.$$

Similarly, for $i = 4$ the expression becomes

$$\frac{1}{3} \left(e_1^N + e_2^N \right) + \frac{1}{3} \left(e_1^N + e_3^N \right) = \frac{2}{3} e_1^N + \frac{1}{3} \left(e_2^N + e_3^N \right)$$

$$2 e_1^N + e_2^N + e_3^N = 2 e_1^N + e_2^N + e_3^N.$$

Finally, the last step in (4.12) follows from $e_i^N \leq \tilde{e}_i$ for all $i \in N \setminus S$ as was shown above. Obviously, these three steps also hold if agents outside a blocking coalition choose their business-as-usual emission so that the lemma holds equally for the γ- and the δ-characteristic function. $\quad\square$

Equipped with Lemma 2, we can now prove non-emptiness of the γ-core, which arises from the γ-characteristic function, by showing that the underlying game is balanced. While Chander and Tulkens (1997) established existence of the γ-core only for a relatively small range of functions,[4] the following proof relies on the much weaker assumption of

---

[4]Chander and Tulkens (1997, 395) assume that for all $S \subset N, |S| \geq 2 : d_i'(e^N) \leq \sum_{j \in S} d_j'(e^*), i \in S$, where the superscript * indicates Pareto-efficient emission levels. Roughly speaking, this means that marginal damage costs of pollution do not fall 'too much' between the Nash equilibrium and the Pareto optimum.

convex damage functions and concave production functions.

Proposition 6 *The coalitional game with multilateral externalities as defined by the characteristic function specified in equations (4.5) and (4.6) is balanced and therefore has a non-empty core.*

Proof. For each $i \in N$ let $e_i^C = \sum_{S \in C_i} \delta_S e_i^S$ denote i's total emissions from emitting in each coalition of which it is a member the optimal level e_i^S, weighted by the associated δ_S. By concavity[5] of the production function,

$$f_i(e_i^C) = f_i\left(\sum_{S \in C_i} \delta_S e_i^S\right) \geq \sum_{S \in C_i} \delta_S f_i(e_i^S). \qquad (4.13)$$

Turning to the damage function one gets

$$d_i\left(\sum_{i \in N} e_i^C\right) = d_i\left(\sum_{i \in N} \sum_{S \in C_i} \delta_S e_i^S\right) = d_i\left(\sum_{S \in C} \delta_S \sum_{i \in S} e_i^S\right) \quad (4.14)$$

$$= d_i\left(\sum_{S \in C_i} \delta_S \sum_{i \in S} e_i^S + \sum_{S \in C \setminus C_i} \delta_S \sum_{i \in S} e_i^S\right) \qquad (4.15)$$

$$\leq d_i\left(\sum_{S \in C_i} \delta_S \sum_{i \in S} e_i^S + \sum_{S \in C_i} \delta_S \sum_{i \in N \setminus S} \tilde{e}_i\right) \qquad (4.16)$$

$$= d_i\left(\sum_{S \in C_i} \delta_S \left(\sum_{i \in S} e_i^S + \sum_{i \in N \setminus S} \tilde{e}_i\right)\right) \qquad (4.17)$$

$$\leq \sum_{S \in C_i} \delta_S d_i\left(\sum_{i \in S} e_i^S + \sum_{i \in N \setminus S} \tilde{e}_i\right). \qquad (4.18)$$

Here, (4.14) follows from the fact that i's total emissions from passing through all coalitions of which it is a member summed over all agents are equivalent to the emissions of each individual coalition S summed

---

[5]A function f is called concave on an interval I if and only if

$$f((1 - \delta)a + \delta b) \geq (1 - \delta)f(a) + \delta f(b)$$

for all $a, b \in I$ and all $\delta \in [0, 1]$. The condition for convexity is obtained by using the $\leq$ instead of the $\geq$ sign. Expression (4.13) follows straightforwardly by replacing the values a, b by $\{(e_i^{\bar{S}})_{S \in C_i}\}$ and noting that $\sum_{S \in C_i} \delta_S = 1$.

over all coalitions. Lemma 2 is used in the step leading to (4.16), and (4.18) follows from convexity of the damage function.

Finally, by cohesiveness[6]

$$v(N) \geq \sum_{i \in N} f_i(e_i^{\mathcal{C}}) - \sum_{i \in N} d_i \left(\sum_{i \in N} e_i^{\mathcal{C}} \right) \tag{4.19}$$

$$\geq \sum_{i \in N} \sum_{S \in \mathcal{C}_i} \delta_S f_i(e_i^S) - \sum_{i \in N} \sum_{S \in \mathcal{C}_i} \delta_S d_i \left(\sum_{i \in S} e_i^S + \sum_{i \in N \setminus S} \tilde{e}_i \right) \tag{4.20}$$

$$= \sum_{S \in \mathcal{C}} \delta_S \sum_{i \in S} f_i(e_i^S) - \sum_{S \in \mathcal{C}} \delta_S \sum_{i \in S} d_i \left(\sum_{i \in S} e_i^S + \sum_{i \in N \setminus S} \tilde{e}_i \right) \tag{4.21}$$

$$= \sum_{S \in \mathcal{C}} \delta_S \left(\sum_{i \in S} f_i(e_i^S) - \sum_{i \in S} d_i \left(\sum_{i \in S} e_i^S + \sum_{i \in N \setminus S} \tilde{e}_i \right) \right) \tag{4.22}$$

$$= \sum_{S \in \mathcal{C}} \delta_S v(S), \tag{4.23}$$

where the last step follows from the definition of the characteristic function. □

4.4 Choosing an Allocation from the Core of a Transboundary Pollution Game

In the previous section it has been shown that the core of the game with multilateral environmental externalities is non-empty. Accordingly, once an allocation from the core has been selected, no coalition on its own can improve the payoff of all its members. This indicates that states might be able to agree on efficient solutions to transboundary pollution problems – assuming that the model setup and the core solution concept appropriately represent the agents' interactions.

---

[6] A coalitional game (N, v) with transferable payoff is *cohesive* if

$$v(N) \geq \sum_{k=1}^{K} v(S_k) \quad \text{for every partition } \{S_1, \ldots, S_k\} \text{ of } N.$$

Accordingly, no partition can achieve a greater aggregate utility than the grand coalition. This is a special case of the condition of *superadditivity*, which requires that for every pair of coalitions $S, T \in N : \ S \cap T = \emptyset \implies v(S \cup T) \geq v(S) + v(T)$.

In general, however, the core contains more than one allocation, which limits its usefulness as a descriptive solution concept.[7] Indeed, as will be argued in the following subsection, there are reasons to suspect that the core of a transboundary pollution game may be fairly large. The question then becomes whether there are criteria according to which certain allocations from the core are 'better' than others. From a normative perspective, such criteria may relate to desirable equity principles. From a positive perspective, such criteria may serve as focal points to coordinate the individual agents' actions.

In the following, I will discuss three different concepts to pick a unique solution for a coalitional game: the Shapley value, a ratio equilibrium and an egalitarian equivalent solution.

4.4.1 The Shapley Value and Convexity of the Transboundary Pollution Game

Probably the best-known *normative* solution concept for coalitional games is the Shapley value (Shapley 1953).

Definition 11 *The Shapley value S_i of a coalitional game (N,v) is defined by the condition*

$$S_i(N,v) = \sum_{S \subseteq N \setminus i} \frac{|S|!\,(|N| - |S| - 1)!}{|N|!}(v(S \cup i) - v(S)) \ \text{for each} \ i \in N.$$

$$(4.24)$$

There are $|N|!$ different orderings of the agents in $|N|$. Given that each ordering is equally likely, $(|S|!\,(|N| - |S| - 1)!)/(|N|!)$ denotes the probability that the coalition S comes before agent i. The second term in (4.24) denotes i's marginal contribution to this coalition S. Taken together, for each agent i the Shapley value is his average marginal contribution to the set of his predecessors.

Roughly speaking, this means that each agent should be paid according to how valuable his cooperation is for the other agents. However, the normative appeal of the Shapley value stems not only from the equitableness of this principle as such, but also from the fact that it is the only solution satisfying the following four axioms (Shapley 1953):

- *Efficiency:* $\sum_{i \in N} S_i(N,v) = v(N)$

---

[7]An important exception is the equivalence of the core with the set of competitive allocations for large economies (Debreu and Scarf 1963).

- *Symmetry*: For any permutation $\pi : N \to N$ and any agent $i \in N$: $\mathcal{S}_{\pi(i)}(N, \pi v) = \mathcal{S}_i(N, v)$. This requires that only an agent's role in the coalitional game, but not his name or labeling, should matter.

- *Dummy player*: If $v(S \cup \{i\}) - v(S) = 0$ for all $S \subset N$, then $\mathcal{S}_i(N, v) = 0$. Accordingly, the joint worth of a coalitional game should be divided only among those agents who contribute to the worth of the game.

- *Additivity*: For any two coalitional games v and w: $\mathcal{S}_i(v + w) = \mathcal{S}_i(v) + \mathcal{S}_i(w)$ for all $i \in N$, where $v + w$ is the game defined by $(v + w)(S) = v(S) + w(S)$ for every coalition S.

While the first three properties are intuitively appealing, the additivity axiom has sometimes been criticized as being hard to motivate from a normative point of view (Luce and Raiffa 1957, 248).[8]

For the special class of convex coalitional games, the normative appeal of the Shapley value and the positive appeal of the core supplement each other in an ideal way. Every convex game has a non-empty – usually very large – core, and this core always contains the Shapley value (Shapley 1971). In particular, the Shapley value obtains a central position in the core of a convex game and therefore constitutes a natural selection point (see Moulin 1995).

Definition 12 *A coalitional game with transferable utility (N, v) is convex if for all coalitions $S \subseteq T$ and $k \notin T$:*

$$v(S \cup k) - v(S) \leq v(T \cup k) - v(T). \tag{4.25}$$

In words, a coalitional game with transferable utility is convex if the marginal contribution of a new adherent k is larger for larger coalitions so that cooperation becomes increasingly profitable with coalition size.[9]

There is indeed some reason to conjecture that this might be the case for transboundary pollution games: the larger a coalition, the more pollution sources it can control and the more beneficiaries from such control it includes. Furthermore, climate change has some similarity to a game, which is sometimes used as an illustrative example of a convex game – namely the pollution of a lake by a number of surrounding factories,

---

[8]For a defense see Myerson (1991, 437). From a mathematical point of view, the additivity axiom is convenient because together with the dummy axiom it restricts the solution set to convex combinations of marginal contribution vectors (Weber 1988).

[9]For statements which are equivalent to convexity see Shapley (1971) and Ichiichi (1981).

which have to clean the water prior to usage (Shubik 1984, 542). Unfortunately, the convexity conjecture turns out to be wrong.

Proposition 7 *The coalitional game with multilateral externalities as defined by the characteristic function specified in equations (4.5) and (4.6) is not convex.*

Proof. Because the proof is somewhat tedious, I relegate it to the Appendix.

Without convexity of the transboundary pollution game, the Shapley value loses much of its appeal as a solution candidate, raising the question of alternative proposals.

4.4.2 A Ratio Equilibrium

Another well-known solution concept, which has received attention especially in the context of public good problems, is the ratio equilibrium (Kaneko 1977; Mas-Colell and Silvestre 1989; Chander 1993). It expresses the principle that agents should pay in proportion to the marginal benefit they derive from a public good. On the basis of this personalized price system, the level of public good provision is chosen such that all agents demand the same amount of it.[10]

For public good problems, the natural reference point for cost allocation is an economy in which the public good is not provided. When the problem is one of multilateral environmental externalities, another reference point representing the case of cooperation failure is needed. Accordingly, Chander and Tulkens (1997) define a 'ratio equilibrium with respect to the disagreement equilibrium', where the disagreement equilibrium is the state induced by the Nash equilibrium of the game. More specifically, they propose to share the costs of environmental protection such that

$$x_i^* = f_i(e_i^N) - \frac{d_i'(e^*)}{\sum_{i \in N} d_i'(e^*)} \sum_{i \in N} \left(f_i(e_i^N) - f_i(e_i^*) \right) \quad \text{for all } i \in N, \quad (4.26)$$

where $\sum_{i \in N} x_i^* = \sum_{i \in N} f_i(e_i^*)$ and superscripts * denote Pareto-efficient levels. Accordingly, each agent gets the goods he produces in the Nash equilibrium minus a weighted share of the difference between the Nash production level and the (lower) Pareto-efficient production level.

---

[10]Note the similarity to the Lindahl equilibrium (Lindahl 1919).

Chander and Tulkens (1997) show that for certain specifications of the damage cost functions (see footnote 4) the ratio equilibrium as defined above lies in the γ-core of a transboundary pollution game. However, the ratio equilibrium has some unattractive normative features, especially if applied to transboundary pollution problems.

Due to the weighting factor, the ratio equilibrium allocates the highest share of the environmental protection costs to those countries that face the highest environmental damage costs. The source of damaging emissions plays only a very minor role (through the selection of the Nash equilibrium as the reference point). Accordingly, the ratio equilibrium implements the victim pays principle rather than the polluter pays principle. As marginal rather than absolute damages matter, the ratio equilibrium may even give a complete free ride to some countries if their marginal damage costs evaluated at the efficient emissions level e^* is zero.

With respect to the empirical importance of this deficiency, many studies indicate that climate change would be particularly detrimental to developing countries (IPCC 1996a).[11] If this is true, the ratio equilibrium would allocate to them the main part of the protection costs, while most of the damaging emissions actually originate from activities in the industrialized countries. This outcome stands in sharp contrast to a cost allocation which is based on axiomatic fairness principles (Chapter 2) or on a welfarist approach (Chapter 3), and therefore must be criticized on normative grounds. Furthermore, in the ratio equilibrium the costs for developing countries might amount to a substantial part of their GDP so that the assumption of quasilinear utility functions – which is a weak point of the analysis anyway – becomes fairly inadequate.

The choice of the Nash equilibrium as the reference point representing cooperation failure slightly alleviates this criticism of the ratio equilibrium. According to the allocation mechanism (4.26), no actor receives more of the private consumption good x than in the Nash equilibrium. Therefore, he cannot exploit increased emission reductions of other actors by reducing his own reduction efforts, as would be in his interest if adopting a best-reply strategy to a cooperating coalition.[12] However, the ratio equilibrium selects a solution from the core only if this effect

---

[11] In a thorough analysis one would have to distinguish more carefully between primary damages and how seriously those damages are taken by the individual countries. If damages occur mainly in the long run, their discounted perceived costs may not actually be so high in developing countries compared to industrialized countries.

[12] Remember that $\tilde{e}_i \geq e_i^N$ for all $i \in N \setminus S$, as has been shown in the proof of Lemma 2 on page 72.

plays a minor role, in particular if the damage cost function is linear or at least not too curved (see footnote 4). Therefore, in cases where the ratio equilibrium with respect to the disagreement equilibrium has a feature that is attractive from a normative perspective, it may no longer be in the core of the coalitional game.

Violation of the principle of cost monotonicity, which requires that the welfare of no agent should go up as cost functions increase, is a further unattractive feature of the ratio equilibrium (see Moulin 1995). Finally, it is difficult to implement because the Lindahlian auctioneer whom it requires faces a much tougher task than his Walrasian counterpart: he has to know countries' damage cost functions, which are usually even more difficult to estimate than abatement cost functions.

However, to a considerable extent the criticized bias towards the victim pays principle is unavoidable because the core is in the first place a positive solution concept and one needs quite heroic assumptions about actors' preferences so that a country with high emissions but low damage costs would accept its responsibility for shouldering a major share of the emission reduction burdens. On the other hand, there may well be a solution in the core which is more attractive from a normative point of view. One such alternative is proposed in the following section.

4.4.3   Egalitarian Equivalent Solutions

The egalitarian equivalent allocation is a well-known solution concept that is ordinal in nature and treats agents symmetrically. It was first proposed by Pazner and Schmeidler (1978, 672) for the allocation of private goods:

> Specifically, an allocation is said to be egalitarian equivalent if there exists a fixed commodity bundle (the same for each agent) that is considered by each agent to be indifferent to the bundle that he actually gets in the allocation under consideration. In other words, an egalitarian equivalent allocation has the special property that its underlying welfare distribution could have been generated by an egalitarian economy.

A version of this concept has been applied to cost sharing of public goods (Mas-Colell 1980; Moulin 1987). In this context, an allocation is called egalitarian equivalent if it equalizes individual benefits measured as units of free public goods. It is relatively straightforward to extend this to an economy with multilateral externalities.

In public good problems, cooperation failure implies non-provision of the public good and, accordingly, zero costs for all agents. For economies with multilateral environmental externalities, an equivalent reference point has to be found. Candidates are to measure egalitarian equivalence as free environmental protection either relative to business-as-usual emissions or relative to emissions in the Nash equilibrium (Eyckmans 1997). As it turns out, the first candidate lies in the δ-core, and – under the same conditions that Chander and Tulkens (1997) use for the ratio equilibrium – the second candidate lies in the γ-core.

Definition 13 *Let $\bar{e}_i$ denote emissions in the business-as-usual path. An outcome $(e_i^*, x_i)_{i \in N}$, where $\sum_{i \in N} x_i = \sum_{i \in N} f_i(e_i^*)$, is called δ-egalitarian equivalent if $\check{e}$ is the lowest feasible level of the multilateral externality such that*

$$u_i(e^*, x_i) = u_i(\check{e}, f_i(\bar{e}_i)) \text{ for all } i \in N. \tag{4.27}$$

Definition 14 *Let e_i^N denote emissions in the Nash equilibrium of a game. An outcome $(e_i^*, x_i)_{i \in N}$ is called γ-egalitarian equivalent if $\check{e}$ is the lowest feasible level of the multilateral externality such that*

$$u_i(e^*, x_i) = u_i(\check{e}, f_i(e_i^N)) \text{ for all } i \in N. \tag{4.28}$$

In words, the δ-egalitarian equivalent solution equalizes individual benefits measured as free environmental protection relative to the case without any emission abatement measures. The γ-egalitarian equivalent solution uses the Nash equilibrium emission levels as the reference point.

Proposition 8 *The coalitional game with multilateral externalities as defined by the characteristic function specified in equations (4.5) and (4.6) has a unique δ-egalitarian equivalent allocation which lies in the δ-core of the game. Furthermore, if for all $S \subset N, |S| \geq 2 : \sum_{j \in S} d_j'(e^*) \geq d_i'(e^N)$ for all $i \in S$, then the coalitional game has a unique γ-egalitarian equivalent allocation which lies in the γ-core of the game.*

Note that this assumption is the same that Chander and Tulkens (1997) used to show that the ratio equilibrium lies in the γ-core. This arises from the fact that both – the γ-egalitarian equivalent solution as well as Chander and Tulken's ratio equilibrium – use emissions in the Nash equilibrium as the reference point from which to start cost sharing.

Proof. I will concentrate on the γ-egalitarian equivalent solution, because the proof is more involved. Occasionally, I will mention how the proof for the δ-egalitarian equivalent solution differs. Loosely following the procedure as used in Moulin (1987) for public goods, I first show that a unique γ-egalitarian equivalent allocation exists.

Every $i \in N$ is a member of some coalition $S \subset N$. Therefore, the assumption $d_i'(e^N) \leq \sum_{j \in S} d_j'(e^*)$ for all $i \in S$ implies that $d_i'(e^N) \leq \sum_{j \in N} d_j'(e^*)$ for all $i \in N$. It then follows that

$$f_i'(e_i^N) = d_i'(e^N) \leq \sum_{j \in N} d_j'(e^*) = f_i'(e_i^*) \text{ for all } i \in N \qquad (4.29)$$

so that $e_i^N \geq e_i^*$ for all $i \in N$ by concavity of the production function. Using this in the first step of the following expression and the fact that $(e_i^N)_{i \in N}$ is not a Pareto-optimal emission vector for the grand coalition in the second step yields

$$\sum_{i \in N} u_i(e^*, f_i(e_i^N)) \geq \sum_{i \in N} u_i(e^*, x_i) \geq \sum_{i \in N} u_i(e^N, f_i(e_i^N)). \qquad (4.30)$$

By assumption, $u_i(e)$ is continuous and monotonically decreasing in the interval $[e^*, e^N]$. Thus, by (4.30) there must be a unique level $\check{e} \in [e^*, e^N]$ such that $\sum_{i \in N}(\check{e}, f_i(e_i^N)) = \sum_{i \in N} u_i(e^*, x_i)$, which establishes existence and uniqueness of a γ-egalitarian equivalent allocation.

Existence of a δ-egalitarian equivalent solution follows straightforwardly by replacing Nash equilibrium emissions e_i^N with emissions in the business-as-usual path $\bar{e}_i$. In this case, the first inequality in (4.30) is trivial because $\bar{e}_i \geq e_i^*$ for all $i \in N$ holds obviously.

Turning to the core property of the γ-egalitarian equivalent allocation, assume by contradiction that there is a coalition $S \subset N$ which has an objection, say $((e_i^S)_{i \in S}, (\bar{e}_i)_{i \in N \setminus S}, (x_i^S)_{i \in S})$, where $(e_i^S)_{i \in S}$ is as usual an optimal emission vector for coalition S, $(\bar{e}_i)_{i \in N \setminus S}$ is an emissions vector for the coalition external agents, and $\sum_{i \in S} x_i^S \leq \sum_{i \in S} f_i(e_i^S)$. Denoting aggregate emissions of this partial agreement equilibrium by $e^P = \sum_{i \in S} e_i^S + \sum_{i \in N \setminus S} \bar{e}_i$, this would imply that

$$u_i(e^*, x_i) = u_i(\check{e}, f_i(e_i^N)) \leq u_i(e^P, x_i^S) \text{ for all } i \in S, \qquad (4.31)$$

where at least one inequality is strict.

Suppose that $e^P \leq \check{e}$. Together with $\bar{e}_i \geq e_i^N$ for all $i \in N \setminus S$ – as was shown in the proof of Lemma 2 – it then follows that

$$u_i(e^*, x_i) = u_i(\check{e}, f_i(e_i^N)) \leq u_i(e^P, f_i(\bar{e}_i)) \text{ for all } i \in N \setminus S. \qquad (4.32)$$

Accordingly, agents $i \in N \setminus S$ would also benefit from the objection of coalition S and we would have a Pareto improvement, violating efficiency of the egalitarian equivalent allocation.

Hence we must have $e^P > \breve{e}$. Together with (4.31) this implies that $u_i(\breve{e}, f_i(e_i^N)) \leq u_i(\breve{e}, x_i^S)$ for all $i \in S$, and accordingly $f_i(e_i^N) \leq x_i^S$ for all $i \in S$.

Next, assume that $e^P < e^*$ so that by convexity of damage cost functions $d_i'(e^P) \leq d_i'(e^*)$ for all $i \in N$. Together with the first-order conditions of the partial agreement equilibrium it follows that

$$f_i'(e_i^S) = \sum_{j \in S} d_j'(e^P) \leq \sum_{j \in S} d_j'(e^*) \;\leq\; \sum_{j \in N} d_j'(e^*) = f_i'(e_i^*) \; \forall \, i \in S, \text{ and}$$

$$f_i'(\tilde{e}_i) = d_i'(e^P) \leq d_i'(e^*) \;\leq\; \sum_{j \in N} d_j'(e^*) = f_i'(e_i^*) \; \forall \, i \in N \setminus S.$$

By concavity of production functions this would imply that emissions in the partial agreement equilibrium exceed those in the efficient solution for all agents, a contradiction. Hence we must have $e^P \geq e^*$ and $\sum_{i \in S} d_i'(e^P) \geq \sum_{i \in S} d_i'(e^*)$. Finally, using the restriction $\sum_{j \in S} d_j'(e^*) \geq d_i'(e^N)$ for all $i \in S$ we get

$$f_i'(e_i^S) = \sum_{j \in S} d_j'(e^P) \geq \sum_{j \in S} d_j'(e^*) \geq d_i'(e^N) = f_i'(e_i^N) \; \forall \, i \in S. \quad (4.33)$$

Therefore, $e_i^S \leq e_i^N$ for all $i \in S$ and $\sum_{i \in S} f_i(e_i^N) \geq \sum_{i \in S} x_i^S = \sum_{i \in S} f_i(e_i^S)$.[13]

Together with the previous result that $f_i(e_i^N) \leq x_i^S$ for all $i \in S$ it follows that $f_i(e_i^N) = x_i^S$ for all $i \in S$ and (4.31) becomes

$$u_i(\breve{e}, f_i(e_i^N)) \leq u_i(e^P, f_i(e_i^N)) \text{ for all } i \in S \quad (4.34)$$

with at least one strict inequality. However, this cannot be true because $\breve{e} < e^P$ and utility decreases in aggregate emissions e, providing the desired contradiction to the claim that there is a coalition $S \subset N$ which has an objection to the γ-egalitarian equivalent allocation.

Replacing e_i^N by $\bar{e}_i$, the proof for the δ-egalitarian equivalent solution follows straightforwardly. Indeed, it is less involved because $\sum_{i \in S} f_i(\bar{e}_i) \geq \sum_{i \in S} x_i^S$ holds by the simple argument that it can never be an optimal decision to emit more than the business-as-usual emissions. $\quad\square$

---

[13] This result follows immediately from Proposition 5 in Chander and Tulkens (1997, 395) and the preceding has adopted their elaborations.

Having shown that the egalitarian equivalent mechanism picks an allocation from the δ-core of a transboundary pollution game, and under certain conditions also from the γ-core, let me turn to some of its normative features. Judged from a fair division or welfarist perspective as in Part I of this book, this principle is again defective because the symmetric way in which the egalitarian equivalent allocation treats different agents neglects states' different responsibility for environmental pollution. However, it has been argued above that implementation of the polluter pays principle would not constitute a core-stable solution because it provides insufficient incentives for cooperation to agents with high emissions but low damages.

For public good problems, it is a well-known result that the egalitarian equivalent mechanism meets the desirable normative criteria of population and cost monotonicity (Moulin 1987; Moulin 1995). For the δ-core much of this normative appeal of the egalitarian equivalent mechanism carries through if applied to economies with multilateral environmental externalities, although it satisfies only the somewhat weaker condition of population solidarity.[14] Unfortunately, this cannot be said of the γ-core.

Definition 15 *An allocation mechanism for the surplus of a coalitional game satisfies population solidarity if for all agents $i \in N : N \subset N'$, utility changes in the same direction as the population increases from N to N'.*

The normative appeal of this criterion is straightforwardly seen. If none of the original agents can be made responsible for the new adherent who enters the scene, then everyone should be affected in the same direction. Indeed, the principle is very similar to that of population monotonicity in Chapter 2 on fair division theory, although monotonicity is a somewhat stronger criterion in that it also prescribes the direction in which utility has to change for all agents.

Definition 16 *Let $(f_i(e_i))_{i \in N}$ and $(g_i(e_i))_{i \in N}$ be two production function profiles such that $g_i(e_i) \geq f_i(e_i)$ for all $i \in N$, and $g_i(\bar{e}_i) = f_i(\bar{e}_i)$. An allocation mechanism for the surplus of a coalitional game is said to satisfy cost monotonicity if a move of the economy from profile $(f_i(e_i))_{i \in N}$ to the more productive profile $(g_i(e_i))_{i \in N}$ leads to an increase in the utility of every agent.*

---

[14]For an extensive analysis of the population solidarity axiom see Chun (1986) as well as Thomson (1983a, 1983b).

Note that this definition is restricted to cases where the change in production functions does not affect the level of business-as-usual emissions. Put differently, I assume that the improved technology facilitates emission abatement but does not affect emissions in the scenario without abatement measures.

As the previous criterion of population solidarity, cost monotonicity also expresses a solidarity ideal: if the emission abatement technologies of one or several agents improve, this should be to no one's disadvantage. Accordingly, cost monotonicity emphasizes the shared responsibility for environmental protection.

Proposition 9 *Consider the coalitional game with multilateral externalities as defined by the characteristic function specified in equations (4.5) and (4.6). If agents outside a blocking coalition choose their business-as-usual emissions, then the δ-egalitarian equivalent mechanism satisfies the criteria of population solidarity and cost monotonicity.*

Proof. By assumption, an agent's emissions in the business-as-usual path $\bar{e}_i$ are not affected by population size N. Hence, the individual agents' utility in the egalitarian equivalent allocation $u_i(\check{e}, f_i(\bar{e}_i))$ depends only on how the change in population affects the level $\check{e}$, which is the same for all agents. This proves population solidarity.

However, while the egalitarian equivalent allocation with private or public goods can be shown to be population *monotonic* (Moulin 1995), this is not the case for multilateral externalities. To see this, imagine the extreme example of a new adherent with positive damage costs but zero own emissions. In the egalitarian equivalent solution, this agent would bear a positive cost share without causing any damage to the previous agents, whose aggregate utility would increase accordingly. On the other hand, if the new adherent has positive emissions but suffers no damages, the egalitarian equivalent solution would allocate to him a zero cost share (otherwise he would object cooperation) and therefore aggregate utility of the previous agents would decrease.

To see why the γ-egalitarian equivalent mechanism need not satisfy population solidarity, remember that utility is given by $u_i(\check{e}, f_i(e_i^N))$. It can be shown that the isolated changes in $\check{e}$ respectively $f_i(e_i^N)$, which are induced by a population increase, are in the same direction for all agents. However, the effect of changes in $\check{e}$ respectively $f_i(e_i^N)$ on utility may have an opposite direction, and the net effect of the two may have a different sign for different agents.

Turning to *cost monotonicity*, use superscripts $'$ to indicate variable levels that arise with the more productive technology. Obviously, aggregate Pareto-efficient utility increases with the improved technology so that $\sum_{i\in N} u_i(\check{e}', g_i(\overline{e}_i)) \geq \sum_{i\in N} u_i(\check{e}, f_i(\overline{e}_i))$. As $g_i(\overline{e}_i) = f_i(\overline{e}_i)$ for all $i \in N$ by assumption, this implies that $\check{e}' \leq \check{e}$. Using this in the second step of the following expression,

$$u_i(e'^*, x_i') = u_i(\check{e}', g_i(\overline{e}_i)) \geq u_i(\check{e}, f_i(\overline{e}_i)) = u_i(e^*, x_i), \qquad (4.35)$$

as was to be shown.   □

4.5   Concluding Remarks

If transboundary environmental policy is modeled as a coalitional game, the prospects of attaining a Pareto-efficient level of cooperation appear to be considerably better than suggested by the simple Prisoner's Dilemma story, which is often used as an analogy for the free-rider problems behind the 'tragedy of the commons' (Hardin 1968; Ostrom 1990). In particular, the grand coalition has been shown to be core-stable for a reasonably wide range of production and damage functions and for different behavioral assumptions about agents outside a blocking coalition.

However, the discussion of different candidates from the core has made clear that there exists a trade-off between the (political) stability of a solution and its fairness. In particular, a substantial bias towards the victim pays principle seems unavoidable because otherwise polluters would have no incentive to join a cooperative agreement. These fairness aspects have not been analyzed in full detail and further solution candidates can be found in the literature (see Moulin 1992a), even though their applicability to international environmental problems would have to be tested.

Despite those limitations, and beside the fact that the highly stylized model can hardly serve as an appropriate description of the real world, the perspective of cooperative game theory may still be too optimistic. For one thing, the empirical picture of existing international environmental agreements seems to be mixed: there are successes as well as failures, rather than a persistent pattern of full cooperation (Helm and Sprinz 1999; Simonis 1996b; Victor, Raustiala, and Skolnikoff 1998). Furthermore, studies using stability concepts from non-cooperative game theory to analyze coalitions in international environmental politics mostly come to the conclusion that cooperating coalitions will be rather small, at least if free-rider incentives – and hence the potential gains from cooperation

– are substantial.[15]

One aspect that substantially improved the prospects of international cooperation was the unlimited feasibility of transfer payments. In Chapter 5, which opens the third part of this book, I shall still allow transfer payments, but the only mechanism to do so is via the initial allocation and subsequent international trade of emission permits. However, the more fundamental breach with the preceding two parts is that for the rest of the book I will rely on concepts from non-cooperative game theory and in particular on solution concepts based on the Nash equilibrium. It will no longer be assumed that countries can 'negotiate effectively', and this makes global environmental cooperation considerably more difficult to achieve.

4.6 Appendix: Convexity of the Transboundary Pollution Game

To prove violation of convexity as stipulated in Proposition 7, note that (assuming that the new adherent $k \notin N$)[16]

$$v(S \cup \{k\}) = \sum_{S \cup \{k\}} \left[f_i(e_i^{S'}) - d_i \left(\sum_{S \cup \{k\}} e_i^{S'} + \sum_{N \setminus S} \tilde{e}_i \right) \right], \text{ and } \quad (4.36)$$

$$v(T) = \sum_{T} \left[f_i(e_i^T) - d_i \left(\sum_{T} e_i^T + \sum_{N \setminus T} \tilde{e}_i \right) \right], \quad (4.37)$$

where $(e_i^{S'})_{i \in S \cup \{k\}}$ and $(e_i^T)_{i \in T}$ are payoff-maximizing emission profiles for coalitions $S \cup \{k\}$ and T respectively.

Assume that $e_k^{S'} \leq e_k^{T'}$, that is optimal emissions of the new adherent k are lower if he joins the smaller coalition $S \subseteq T$. This may be the case,

---

[15]This is true for coalition-proof Nash equilibria (Bernheim, Peleg, and Whinston 1987) as well as for the stability concept introduced by D'Aspremont and Gabszewicz (1986), which checks the incentives of *individual* countries to join or defect from a coalition. Even though these results will not be discussed in more detail here, this is certainly an important strand of the literature and the reader is referred to Carraro and Siniscalco (1993), Barrett (1994), Hoel (1994) as well as Finus and Rundshagen (1998), among others.

[16]In what follows, the summation index is always i; hence I skip it for ease of notation so that, for example, $\sum_{S \cup \{k\}}$ stands for $\sum_{i \in S \cup \{k\}}$.

for example, if the set $T \setminus S$ contains primarily agents whose abatement cost functions lie below those of agent k. Then,

$$v(S \cup \{k\}) + v(T) \le \sum_S f_i(e_i^{S'}) - \sum_{S \cup \{k\}} d_i \left(\sum_{S \cup \{k\}} e_i^{S'} + \sum_{N \setminus S} \tilde{e}_i \right)$$

$$+ f_k(e_k^{T'}) + \sum_T f_i(e_i^T) - \sum_T \left[d_i \left(\sum_T e_i^T + \sum_{N \setminus T} \tilde{e}_i \right) \right]. \qquad (4.38)$$

To prove violation of convexity, it suffices to consider the case of linear damage cost functions. Thus, assuming that $d_i(e) = \beta_i e$, one gets

$$\sum_{S \cup \{k\}} d_i \left(\sum_{S \cup \{k\}} e_i^{S'} + \sum_{N \setminus S} \tilde{e}_i \right) \qquad (4.39)$$

$$= \sum_S d_i \left(\sum_{S \cup \{k\}} e_i^{S'} + \sum_{N \setminus S} \tilde{e}_i \right) + d_k \left(\sum_{S \cup \{k\}} e_i^{S'} + \sum_{N \setminus S} \tilde{e}_i \right)$$

$$= e_k^{S'} \sum_S \beta_i + \sum_S d_i \left(\sum_S e_i^{S'} + \sum_{N \setminus S} \tilde{e}_i \right) + e_k^{S'} \beta_k + d_k \left(\sum_S e_i^{S'} + \sum_{N \setminus S} \tilde{e}_i \right).$$

Equivalently,

$$\sum_{T \cup \{k\}} d_i \left(\sum_T e_i^T + e_k^{T'} + \sum_{N \setminus T} \tilde{e}_i \right) \qquad (4.40)$$

$$= \sum_T d_i \left(\sum_T e_i^T + e_k^{T'} + \sum_{N \setminus T} \tilde{e}_i \right) + d_k \left(\sum_T e_i^T + e_k^{T'} + \sum_{N \setminus T} \tilde{e}_i \right)$$

$$= e_k^{T'} \sum_T \beta_i + \sum_T d_i \left(\sum_T e_i^T + \sum_{N \setminus T} \tilde{e}_i \right) + e_k^{T'} \beta_k + d_k \left(\sum_T e_i^T + \sum_{N \setminus T} \tilde{e}_i \right).$$

Inserting (4.39) into (4.6), note that

$$\sum_S f_i(e_i^{S'}) - \sum_S d_i \left(\sum_S e_i^{S'} + \sum_{N \setminus S} \tilde{e}_i \right) \le v(S), \qquad (4.41)$$

because $(e_i^{S'})_{i \in S \cup \{k\}}$ is an optimal emission profile for coalition $S \cup \{k\}$ but not for S. Similarly, solving (4.40) for $\sum_T d_i \left(\sum_T e_i^T + \sum_{N \setminus T} \tilde{e}_i \right)$ and inserting this into (4.6), note that

$$
f_k(e_k^{T'}) + \sum_T f_i(e_i^T) - \sum_{T \cup \{k\}} d_i \left(\sum_T e_i^T + e_k^{T'} + \sum_{N \setminus T} \tilde{e}_i \right) \leq v(T \cup \{k\}),
$$
(4.42)

because $(e_i^T)_{i \in T}$ is an optimal emission profile for coalition T but not for $T \cup \{k\}$.

Given that the emission profiles $(e_i^{S'})_{i \in S}$ and $(e_i^{S})_{i \in S}$ as well as $(e_i^{T'})_{i \in T}$ and $(e_i^T)_{i \in T}$ may be arbitrary close to each other, the convexity requirement

$$
v(S \cup \{k\}) + v(T) \leq v(T \cup \{k\}) + v(S)
$$

may be violated unless – collecting the remaining terms in (4.39) and (4.40) –

$$
d_k \left(\sum_S e_i^{S'} + \sum_{N \setminus S} \tilde{e}_i \right) + e_k^{S'} \sum_{S \cup \{k\}} \beta_i
$$
(4.43)

$$
\geq d_k \left(\sum_T e_i^T + \sum_{N \setminus T} \tilde{e}_i \right) + e_k^{T'} \sum_{T \cup \{k\}} \beta_i.
$$

As $S \subset T$ and $e_k^{S'} \leq e_k^{T'}$ by the initial assumption, condition (4.43) may easily be violated.[17] $\qquad \square$

Note that this proof did not depend on the specification of the strategy $\tilde{e}_i$ of coalition external agents. An example of a non-convex transboundary pollution game is given in Eyckmans (1997, 182).

---

[17]In the preceding analysis it has been assumed that the new adherent k has not been a member of the original population N. On the other hand, if $k \in N$, when joining coalition S or T his original emissions $\tilde{e}_k$ as an agent outside of those coalitions have to be subtracted from emissions of the set $N \setminus S$ respectively $N \setminus T$. In doing this analysis, the term $\tilde{e}_k \sum_S \beta_i$ has to be added to the left-hand side of condition (4.43) for convexity. To see that this revised condition may still be violated, take the extreme example $\beta_i = 0$ for all $i \in S$ but $\beta_i > 0$ for all $i \in T \setminus S$.

PART III

International Policy in the Non-Cooperative Mode

5. International Emissions Trading and the Choice of Allowances

> The difficulty lies, not in the new ideas,
> but in escaping the old ones, which ramify,
> for those brought up as most of us have been,
> into every corner of our minds.
>
> John Maynard Keynes (1883–1946)

5.1 Introduction

The potential importance of transfer payments to deal effectively with transboundary pollution problems has been recognized widely (Barrett 1994; Buchholz and Konrad 1995; Chander and Tulkens 1997). This was also demonstrated in the previous chapters, where transfers contributed to the fairness and stability of cooperation.

Transfer payments have indeed become an element of many international environmental agreements. Primarily, they are intended to partly or fully compensate poorer countries for the costs that arise from their participation in pollution abatement efforts (Biermann 1997; Keohane and Levy 1996). On the other hand, transfer payments are rather uncommon among the OECD countries; not even the European regime on transboundary acidification, which includes East European countries, involves compensations to any substantial extent. Thus, the scale of monetary transfers in international environmental politics has hitherto been limited.

With the establishment of an emissions trading system in Article 17 of the Kyoto Protocol, the role of compensatory payments in international politics has entered new dimensions in a number of respects: the expected size of transfers is unprecedented; in principle, the trading system is open to all countries that accept binding emission caps; and by using markets to execute transfers, the aim to achieve protection targets in the most efficient way moves to the forefront. This interpretation is somewhat qualified by the fact that the Kyoto Protocol left open the task of defining the relevant principles, modalities, rules and guidelines for emissions trading. It is planned that these will be agreed at the sixth Conference of the Parties (COP6) at the end of the year 2000.[1] The success or failure of emissions trading can have far-reaching implications beyond climate change politics in that it may become a model for other areas of international cooperation as well.

The principal idea of emissions trading is simple and intuitively appealing. In a first step, the number of pollution allowances is fixed, which determines the emission target. These allowances are then traded on competitive markets until marginal abatement costs are equalized across all actors so that the target is met at least cost.[2] Furthermore, this cost-minimization property of tradable permits is compatible with different initial allocations of allowances so that a central authority can use them to pursue its distributional goals.

After those ideas had been introduced by Dales (1968), they were formalized by Montgomery (1972) and dealt with in detail by Tietenberg (1985) and others. With the maturing of international environmental problems, and especially in the context of climate change, the question arose as to their applicability to the international level (see OECD 1992; Chichilnisky and Heal 1994; Simonis 1996a; Koutstaal 1997). An important difference from a domestic permit system is the absence of a central authority at the international level, which disposes of the power to determine the initial allocation of tradable allowances. To the contrary, this allocation will be the outcome of negotiations among sovereign states. In this chapter, I shall therefore analyze how a trading regime affects states' incentives when they choose their level of allowances in the non-cooperative mode of international environmental politics.

It is widely accepted that the cost savings argument for emissions trading can be straightforwardly extended to the international level. The hope is that due to those lower abatement costs, countries will choose higher reduction targets. For example, the UNCTAD report on greenhouse gas emissions trading, which was prepared for COP4 in Buenos Aires, states: 'Allowance trading systems have been designed to achieve

---

[1]In particular, there exists a dispute, with the USA and the EU as the main antagonists, whether the extent to which national emission targets can be achieved by permit purchases should be limited.

[2]Obviously, this does not apply to environmental problems for which the location of pollution sources matters – like transboundary acidification (see Klaassen 1996). The efficiency property of a tradable permit system may also be violated if there are transaction costs (see Stavins 1995) or if there is imperfect competition on the permit market (see Section 5.6.

stringent environmental standards while reducing costs of compliance, allowing acceptance of more stringent standards' (UNCTAD 1998, 1).

The climate negotiation process in Kyoto offered indeed some support for this view. Many observers argued that the USA accepted their reduction obligations only because they hoped to reduce abatement costs by buying permits from other countries – in particular from Russia and Ukraine. On the other hand, these two countries received emission allowances which even exceed their projected business-as-usual emissions. In the literature on climate change, the difference between the two is often referred to as 'hot air'. It may be a substantial amount. For example, Victor, Nakiçenovic, and Victor (1998) estimate that during the Protocol's 2008–2012 budget period this bubble will range from 9 MtC (million tons of carbon) to 900 MtC for Russia and 3 MtC to 200 MtC for Ukraine, depending on various modeling assumptions. The potential importance of hot air can also be inferred from Figure 2.1 on page 12 by comparing the projected business-as-usual emissions for the Former Soviet Union with the Kyoto target (this is the line labeled 'Kyoto Russia + Ukraine').

The prospect of selling surplus emission allowances seems to have induced those countries to strive for *higher* entitlements than they would have done without a tradable permit system. This suggests that if countries decide on the allocation of tradable emission allowances rather than the level of emission reductions which they actually have to undertake domestically, some countries might choose less, but others more, emission allowances. Such an effect has already been pointed out by Bohm (1992), but his analysis is restricted to a diagrammatic approach, which differs from the one in Section 5.3. Furthermore, the analytic approach pursued in most of this chapter makes it possible to analyze the incentive effects of emissions trading more systematically and will lead to a number of new insights.

The outline of this chapter is as follows. In the next section, I introduce some elementary concepts of non-cooperative game theory and set up the basic model. In Sections 5.3 and 5.4, I analyze the choice of emission allowances using a diagrammatic and analytic approach, respectively. In the remaining, the welfare implications of emissions trading are explored (Section 5.5) and some of the previous results are reconsidered for the case of imperfect competition on the permit market (Section 5.6).

5.2   Transboundary Pollution as a Non-Cooperative Game

In Part II of this book, coalitions of players were the primitives in the analysis of a transboundary pollution game. From now onwards, individual players will take their place as the primitives of the game and it is no longer assumed that players can negotiate effectively to form coalitions.[3] Each player $i \in N = \{1, 2, \ldots, n\}$ is characterized by a set of available actions A_i and a preference relation on the set of feasible outcomes of the game. An outcome depends not only upon a player's own action $a_i \in A_i$, but also on the action taken by the other players, thereby introducing the sort of strategic considerations which distinguish game theory from decision theory.

The choice of emission allowances is modeled in strategic (or normal) form, meaning that players choose their strategy – that is their plan of action for the complete game – simultaneously. Put differently, a game in strategic form is completely described by the set of players, strategies and preference relations, while complexities arising from the sequence of moves as in extensive form games are neglected.

The Nash equilibrium describes the steady state in which the strategies of all players are best replies to each other so that none of them has an incentive to change his strategy.

Definition 17 *A Nash equilibrium of a game in strategic form is a profile of actions* $(a_i^N)_{i \in N} \in \times_{i \in N} A_i$ *such that for every player* $i \in N$ *we have*

$$(a_i^N, a_{-i}^N) \succeq (a_i, a_{-i}^N) \qquad for\ all\ a_i \in A_i, \qquad (5.1)$$

where the index $-i$ *refers to all players other than* i.

The subsequent analysis is based on comparing the Nash equilibria of the two games in which states choose their tradable respectively nontradable emission allowances. Admittedly, this gives a rather stylized picture of the international negotiation process. It may also be too pessimistic, because there is no give and take here, and countries' potential for cooperation is restricted to the introduction of internationally tradable emission allowances.

On the other hand, a substantial part of the empirical literature suggests that emission targets as codified in international environmental

---

[3]For an introduction to non-cooperative game theory see Fudenberg and Tirole (1991); Myerson (1991); Osborne and Rubinstein (1994) as well as Gibbons (1992).

agreements often differ only slightly from the single-shot Nash equilibrium (Murdoch and Sandler 1997; Murdoch, Sandler, and Sargent 1997), even if the underlying game is more complicated.[4]

A possible explanation for this is provided by the literature on coalition formation, which has emphasized the difficulties to make binding commitments at the international level so that agreements have to be self-enforcing (Carraro and Siniscalco 1993; Barrett 1994; Finus and Rundshagen 1998). In particular, it has been shown that cooperating coalitions which comprise more than two or three countries will usually not be stable, meaning that there are countries which want to either accede or leave the coalition. In these situations, internationally tradable emission allowances appear to be a promising policy tool, because the associated cost savings may lead countries to choose stricter emission reduction targets – even if they interact non-cooperatively.

Anyhow, the intention with this chapter is not to give a 'realistic' description of the negotiation process on transboundary pollution problems, or even of a specific example like the Kyoto Protocol, although the latter is sometimes used to motivate the analysis. Rather, the aim is to identify strategic incentives that arise from the possibility to trade emission allowances with other nations; and for this purpose a non-cooperative game structure is particularly well suited.

I first consider the non-cooperative game of transboundary emission choices *without* trading. A country's action set consists of the feasible emissions $e_i \in \mathbb{R}_+$. The preference relation is represented by a national welfare or payoff function u_i, which depends on abatement costs $c_i(e_i)$ as a function of domestic emissions and damage costs $d_i(e)$ as a function of global emissions ($e = \sum_{i \in N} e_i$). As in the previous chapters, abatement cost functions are assumed to be non-negative, convex and decreasing in national emissions, while damage cost functions are non-negative, convex and increasing in global emissions.

For a transboundary pollution game, the Nash equilibrium is obtained if each player maximizes his payoff function while taking the other players

---

[4]In a collaborative work with Detlef Sprinz, we introduced a unifying framework and a simple indicator ranging from 0 to 1 to assess a regime's effectiveness (Helm and Sprinz 1999; Sprinz and Helm 1999). Here, a value of 0 corresponds to the non-cooperative Nash equilibrium and a value of 1 to the scenario of full cooperation. Applying this to the European regime on transboundary acidification, the results indicate that the potential for cooperation could only partly be translated into political action – with regime effectiveness scores of 0.39 for the reduction of SO_2 emissions and 0.31 for the reduction of NO_x emissions.

emission choices e^N_{-i} as given:

$$\max_{e_i} u_i(e_i, e^N_{-i}) = -d_i(e) - c_i(e_i) \qquad \text{for all } i \in N \qquad (5.2)$$

so that in the Nash equilibrium

$$\frac{\partial d_i}{\partial e} + \frac{\partial c_i}{\partial e_i} = 0. \qquad (5.3)$$

Accordingly, countries choose emissions such that domestic marginal abatement costs equal domestic marginal damage costs.

In contrast, if emission allowances are *tradable*, entitlements $\omega_i \in \mathbb{R}_+$ and actual emissions e_i usually differ so that the money paid or received for permit transfers at price p has to be added to the countries' payoff functions. Thus, the problem becomes

$$\max_{\omega_i} u_i^{trade}(\omega_i, \omega^N_{-i}) = -d_i(\omega) - c_i(e^*_i) - (e^*_i - \omega_i)p^* \text{ for all } i \in N, \quad (5.4)$$

where u_i^{trade} is the payoff with emissions trading, $\omega = \sum_{i \in N} \omega_i = \sum_{i \in N} e^*_i$, and superscripts * denote equilibrium values in a competitive permit market. The first-order condition for optimality is

$$\frac{\partial d_i}{\partial \omega} + \frac{\partial c_i}{\partial e^*_i}\frac{\partial e^*_i}{\partial \omega_i} + \left(\frac{\partial e^*_i}{\partial \omega_i} - 1\right)p^* + (e^*_i - \omega_i)\frac{\partial p^*}{\partial \omega_i} = 0. \qquad (5.5)$$

Initially, I assume that there is a great number of actors on the permit market so that countries can influence the permit price via the choice of their initial entitlements ω_i but not via the choice of their actual emissions e_i. This seems particularly reasonable if states pass on their allowance budgets and trading takes place on the level of firms. However, if (a relatively small number of) countries trade only directly with each other, it may be more appropriate to model the permit market as one with imperfect competition, as will be done in Section 5.6.

Given the assumption of a competitive permit market, in equilibrium we have $\partial c_i/\partial e^*_i = -p^*$. This can be used to solve equation (5.5) for the best-reply functions

$$\omega_i(\omega^N_{-i}) = \frac{\partial d_i/\partial \omega + \partial c_i/\partial e^*_i}{\partial p^*/\partial \omega_i} + e^*_i. \qquad (5.6)$$

The model of the permit market – with the emission allowance profile $(\omega_i)_{i \in N}$ taken as an exogenous variable – is exactly the same as in

Appendix 2.10 on page 46. Hence, the partial derivative of prices with respect to allowances is again given by[5]

$$\frac{\partial p^*}{\partial \omega_i} = -\frac{1}{\sum_{i \in N} \frac{1}{c_i''(e_i^*)}} \leq 0. \tag{5.7}$$

According to equation (5.6), countries which in the competitive allocation accept higher marginal abatement costs than their marginal damage costs are compensated by receiving allowances that exceed their after-trade emission level ($\omega_i > e_i^*$), and vice versa.

5.3 The Choice of Emission Allowances – Diagrammatic Approach

In the general form of the preceding section, the optimality conditions with and without trading can not be solved explicitly for the allocation of emission allowances, which could then be compared to each other. To do so analytically, abatement and damage cost functions have to be specified further. This will be done in the next section, but first consider the graphical treatment in Figure 5.1.

For two countries, indexed i and j, the solid downward-sloping lines give marginal abatement costs as a function of domestic emissions. Similarly, the solid upward-sloping lines give marginal damage costs as a function of overall emissions. In the Nash equilibrium without trading, denoted by superscripts ^{N}, $-c_i'(e_i) = d_i'(e^N)$, $-c_j'(e_j) = d_j'(e^N)$, and $e_i^N + e_j^N = e^N$, as it is required by the optimality condition in equation (5.3).

Turning to the case with allowance trading, we can sum up the best-reply functions (5.6) over all countries. Taking into account that $\partial p^* / \partial \omega_i$ is the same for all countries (see equation 5.7) and $\sum_{i \in N} \omega_i = \sum_{i \in N} e_i^*$, this yields

$$\sum_{i \in N} \frac{\partial d_i}{\partial e} = -\sum_{i \in N} \frac{\partial c_i}{\partial e_i}, \tag{5.8}$$

---

[5]Note that $\partial \omega / \partial \omega_i = 1$ because $\omega = \omega_i + \sum_{j \in N \setminus \{i\}} \omega_j^N$ and each country i chooses its emission allowances as a best reply to given levels ω_j^N of the other countries. Hence it makes no difference whether one differentiates with respect to ω as in Appendix 2.10 or with respect to ω_i as in equation (5.6).

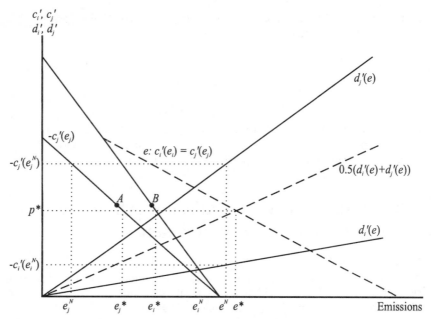

Figure 5.1: Nash emission levels with and without trading

where the derivatives are evaluated at the efficient emission levels e_i^*.[6] Because marginal abatement costs are equalized in the competitive equilibrium, for the case of two countries

$$0.5 \left(\frac{\partial d_i}{\partial e} + \frac{\partial d_j}{\partial e} \right) = -\frac{\partial c_i}{\partial e_i} = -\frac{\partial c_j}{\partial e_j} = p^*. \tag{5.9}$$

This expression makes it possible to draw the solution with allowance trading. The dashed upward-sloping line gives the left-hand side of equation (5.9), and the dashed downward-sloping line gives overall emissions e such that marginal abatement costs are the same in both countries, as required by the right-hand side. The resulting after-trade emission levels have been marked with superscripts *.

---

[6]In principle, equation (5.8) also holds for the case with non-tradable emission allowances (equation 5.3), but marginal damage and abatement costs are not evaluated at the efficient emission level e_i^*; hence individual and overall emissions will usually differ with and without trading.

Even though non-tradable emission allowances e_i^N can not be compared directly to those with trading, we can do so for after-trade emissions e_i^* instead, because in the aggregate these are equal to the initial allocation of tradable allowances. This exercise reveals that overall emissions increase if initial entitlements are tradable ($e^* > e^N$). Equalization of marginal abatement costs on the permit market causes that emissions in country i fall relative to the non-trade case ($e_i^* < e_i^N$), but this reduction is more than compensated by the emission increase in the other country ($e_j^* > e_j^N$).

The mechanism that leads to this result may be explained as follows. Fix overall emission allowances as in the Nash equilibrium without trading, but allocate these allowances such that marginal abatement costs are equalized – as in points A and B. Now, let the countries reconsider their choice of allowances.

In point B, the low-damage country i faces marginal abatement costs above its marginal damage costs. Accordingly, i has an incentive to increase its number of allowances relative to point B. When doing so in a regime with trading, it will base its optimality calculus not on the original marginal abatement cost function, but on the 'flatter' function which is the aggregate of the two countries' individual marginal abatement cost functions. Therefore, it will choose tradable emission emission allowances ω_i (which are not drawn in the figure) that lie to the right of those without trading (e_i^N).

Similarly, in point A the high-damage country j has an incentive to reduce its allowances, and with trading it will base this decision on the aggregate marginal abatement cost function. Therefore, it will choose tradable emission emission allowances that lie to the left of those without trading. Finally, because i's marginal abatement cost curve is steeper than j's, the effect of using the aggregate marginal abatement cost function – rather than the domestic one – is more pronounced for the low-damage country i so that overall emissions increase with trading.

Put differently, if the low-damage country increases its emission allowances – taking allowances of the other country as given – its marginal abatement costs decrease less in the case with trading because the permit market would allocate some of the additional allowances to the other country. Thus, the wedge that an increase of emission allowances would drive between marginal damage and abatement costs in the low-damage country is smaller if these allowances are traded afterwards; hence also the incentive to abstain from such an increase is smaller.

Conversely, if the high-damage country considers a reduction of its emission allowances, marginal abatement costs increase less with trading, thereby offering stronger incentives to strive for such a reduction. Accordingly, the possibility of trading introduces an additional strategic advantage for the low-damage country, which it can exploit in terms of transfer payments that exceed its additional abatement cost with trading.

However, before coming to a negative conclusion on emissions trading, I wish to emphasize that it is easy to construct graphs which yield an opposite result with $e^N > e^*$. In the following, I will pursue an analytic approach to analyze in more detail under which conditions a perverse permit effect as just described occurs.

5.4   The Choice of Emission Allowances – Analytic Approach

In order to solve analytically for the allocation of tradable and non-tradable emission allowances, I will restrict the analysis to the relatively simple case of two countries with quadratic abatement and damage cost functions. While this admittedly limits the generalization of the results, an extension to more than two countries or more general functional forms would seriously hamper the tractability of the analysis. For this reason, several authors have relied on similar or even more restrictive assumptions in their studies of international environmental cooperation (e.g., Hoel 1992; Barrett 1994; Finus and Rundshagen 1998). Furthermore, to show that a negative effect of emissions trading on the choice of environmental targets is possible, it suffices to do so for the specific example of quadratic damage and abatement cost functions.

Let abatement costs increase quadratically in percentage emission reductions relative to business-as-usual emissions without any abatement efforts, which are denoted by $\bar{e}_i$:

$$c_i(e_i) = \alpha_i \left(1 - \frac{e_i}{\bar{e}_i} \right)^2, \qquad (5.10)$$

with first and second derivatives

$$\frac{\partial c_i}{\partial e_i} = -\frac{2\alpha_i}{\bar{e}_i} \left(1 - \frac{e_i}{\bar{e}_i} \right), \qquad (5.11)$$

and

$$\frac{\partial^2 c_i}{\partial e_i^2} = \frac{2\alpha_i}{\bar{e}_i^2}. \tag{5.12}$$

Similarly, let damage costs increase quadratically in the level of overall emissions:

$$d_i(e) = \beta_i(e_i + e_j)^2, \tag{5.13}$$

with first and second derivatives

$$\frac{\partial d_i}{\partial e} = 2\beta_i(e_i + e_j), \tag{5.14}$$

and

$$\frac{\partial^2 d_i}{\partial e^2} = 2\beta_i. \tag{5.15}$$

Because countries' damage cost functions differ only in the coefficient β, I will sometimes refer to the country with the lower β as the low-damage country and to the country with the higher β as the high-damage country.

To determine Nash emission levels e_i^N in the non-trade case, I substitute equations (5.11) and (5.14) into the optimality condition (5.3) to get

$$2\beta_i(e_i + e_j) - \frac{2\alpha_i}{\bar{e}_i}\left(1 - \frac{e_i}{\bar{e}_i}\right) = 0. \tag{5.16}$$

Solving for e_i yields country i's reaction function

$$e_i(e_j) = \frac{\alpha_i/\bar{e}_i - \beta_i e_j}{\beta_i + \alpha_i/\bar{e}_i^2}. \tag{5.17}$$

Country j's reaction function follows straightforwardly by exchanging the indices. Solving both simultaneously gives the Nash equilibrium of emission levels without trading[7]

$$e_i^N = \frac{\bar{e}_i(\alpha_i\alpha_j - \alpha_j\beta_i\bar{e}_i\bar{e}_j + \alpha_i\beta_j\bar{e}_j^2)}{\alpha_i\alpha_j + \alpha_j\beta_i\bar{e}_i^2 + \alpha_i\beta_j\bar{e}_j^2}, \tag{5.18}$$

---

[7]Throughout this and the following chapter I assume that interior solutions with non-negative emission levels exist. As the conditions for this follow straightforwardly from the equations for equilibrium emission levels, I abstain from writing them down explicitly.

and equivalently for country j.

Turning to the case with trading, I start with the second stage game, where efficient emission levels e_i^* are determined as a function of overall emission allowances. On a competitive permit market, marginal abatement costs are equalized across countries and the sum of efficient emissions equals the sum of emission allowances, yielding the conditions

$$-\frac{2\alpha_i}{\bar{e}_i}\left(1 - \frac{e_i^*}{\bar{e}_i}\right) = -\frac{2\alpha_j}{\bar{e}_j}\left(1 - \frac{e_j^*}{\bar{e}_j}\right) \text{ and } \omega_i + \omega_j = e_i^* + e_j^*. \quad (5.19)$$

These two equations with two unknowns can be solved for the efficient emission levels

$$e_i^* = \frac{\alpha_i \bar{e}_i \bar{e}_j^2 - \alpha_j \bar{e}_j \bar{e}_i^2 + \alpha_j \bar{e}_i^2 (\omega_i + \omega_j)}{\alpha_i \bar{e}_j^2 + \alpha_j \bar{e}_i^2}. \quad (5.20)$$

Inserting this together with the respective derivatives of the abatement and damage cost functions (equations 5.11, 5.12, and 5.14) into optimality condition (5.6) yields country i's reaction function $\omega_i(\omega_j^N)$ and equivalently for j. If these are solved simultaneously, one gets the desired Nash equilibrium of emission allowances with trading

$$\omega_i^N = \frac{\alpha_i(2\alpha_j \bar{e}_i + 2\beta_j \bar{e}_i \bar{e}_j^2 + \beta_j \bar{e}_j^3 - \beta_i \bar{e}_j^3) + \alpha_j(\beta_j \bar{e}_i^3 - \beta_i \bar{e}_i^3 - 2\beta_i \bar{e}_i^2 \bar{e}_j)}{2\alpha_i \alpha_j + \alpha_j \beta_i \bar{e}_i^2 + \alpha_j \beta_j \bar{e}_i^2 + \alpha_i \beta_i \bar{e}_j^2 + \alpha_i \beta_j \bar{e}_j^2}. \quad (5.21)$$

The first interesting exercise is to compare countries' choices of emission allowances in the trading case (ω_i^N) against emission allowances without trading (e_i^N). The difference between the two is given by

$$\omega_i^N - e_i^N = \frac{(\beta_j - \beta_i)(\bar{e}_i + \bar{e}_j)(\alpha_i^2 \alpha_j \bar{e}_j^2 + \alpha_j^2 \beta_i \bar{e}_i^4 + \alpha_i^2 \beta_j \bar{e}_j^4)}{(\alpha_i \alpha_j + \bar{e}_i^2(\alpha_j \beta_i + \alpha_i \beta_j))(2\alpha_i \alpha_j + \bar{e}_i^2(\alpha_i + \alpha_j)(\beta_i + \beta_j))}. \quad (5.22)$$

Although this equation looks a bit messy at first sight, it is easy to interpret, because its sign depends solely on the term $\beta_j - \beta_i$, that is on the ratio of the two countries' marginal damage costs.[8] The first result follows straightforwardly:

---

[8]Note that $d_i'(e)/d_j'(e) = 2\beta_i e / 2\beta_j e = \beta_i/\beta_j$.

Proposition 10 *Given are two countries with quadratic damage and abatement cost functions as specified above. Comparing emission entitlements in the Nash equilibria of the games with and without emissions trading,*

$$\omega_i^N \gtreqless e_i^N \quad if \quad d_i'(e) \lesseqgtr d_j'(e).$$

Accordingly, the low-damage country chooses more emission allowances in the equilibrium with trading. As has already been indicated, in Figure 5.1 ω_i would lie to the right of e_i so that country i's income from permit transfers, $(\omega_i - e_i^*)p^*$, exceeds its additional abatement costs, which are represented by the area under its marginal abatement cost curve for the interval $[e_i^*, e_i^N]$. The intuition for this result has already been explained in the previous section.

Proposition 10 proves the conjecture made in the introduction, that some countries might choose more – rather than fewer – emission allowances if these are tradable. Given the restriction to two countries and the assumed functional specifications, the result is even stronger because there will *always* be a country which chooses higher emission allowances in the case with trading.

How does this result relate to the climate negotiations process? It has often been argued that climate change damages would be relatively modest in Russia compared to the USA and other OECD countries (IPCC 1996a), or at least they do not receive as much political attention (Biermann 1998). Thus, the pattern which could be observed in Kyoto – with the high-damage country USA consenting to receive less emission allowances after agreement on a tradable permit system and the low-damage country Russia successfully negotiating for more emission allowances – is nicely reflected in Proposition 10.

It has already been mentioned that in the Kyoto Protocol some Eastern European countries, in particular Russia and Ukraine, received even higher emission allowances than their projected business-as-usual emissions – the difference being called 'hot air'. It is feared that the inclusion of developing countries into a regime of tradable allowances could have a similar effect – termed 'tropical air'.

The conditions under which this occurs in the context of the present model follow straightforwardly by taking the difference of tradable entitlements ω_i^N as specified in equation (5.21) and business-as-usual emission $\bar{e}_i$:

$$\omega_i^N - \bar{e}_i = \frac{(\bar{e}_i + \bar{e}_j)(\alpha_i\beta_j\bar{e}_j^2 - 2\alpha_j\beta_i\bar{e}_i^2 - \alpha_i\beta_i\bar{e}_j^2)}{2\alpha_i\alpha_j + \alpha_j\beta_i\bar{e}_i^2 + \alpha_i\beta_i\bar{e}_j^2 + \alpha_j\beta_j\bar{e}_i^2 + \alpha_i\beta_j\bar{e}_j^2}. \qquad (5.23)$$

Some re-arrangements in the numerator yield that $\omega_i^N > \bar{e}_i$ if $\frac{\beta_j}{\beta_i} > 2\frac{\alpha_j/\bar{e}_j^2}{\alpha_i/\bar{e}_i^2} + 1$. Here, the left-hand side is simply the quotient of the two countries' marginal damage cost functions and the right-hand side equals twice the quotient of the second derivative of the abatement cost functions plus 1 (see equations 5.12 and 5.15).

Proposition 11 *Given are two countries with quadratic damage and abatement cost functions as specified above. Comparing emission entitlements in the Nash equilibrium of the game with trading and business-as-usual emissions,*

$$\omega_i^N \gtreqless \bar{e}_i \qquad if \qquad \frac{d_j'(e)}{d_i'(e)} \gtreqless 2\frac{c_j''(e_j)}{c_i''(e_i)} + 1.$$

In Proposition 10 it was stated that a country i chooses more emission allowances in the case with trading if $d_j'(e)/d_i'(e) > 1$. According to Proposition 11, the conditions for choosing allowances which even exceed business-as-usual emissions are stricter and depend also on abatement cost functions. Underlying this result is the same intuition as above: the wedge that an increase of emission allowances would drive between marginal damage and abatement costs in the low-damage country, say i, is smaller with trading. In particular, this effect is more pronounced the steeper country i's marginal abatement cost function in relation to that of country j so that the incentive to choose higher emission allowances – and thereby the possibility to demand compensation – increases with trading.

It remains to determine the effect of a tradable permit system on overall emissions. This can be calculated straightforwardly by summing equation (5.22) over both countries, yielding

$$\omega^N - e^N = \frac{(\beta_i - \beta_j)(\alpha_j\bar{e}_i^2 - \alpha_i\bar{e}_j^2)(\alpha_i\alpha_j(\bar{e}_i + \bar{e}_j))}{(\alpha_i\alpha_j + \bar{e}_i^2(\alpha_j\beta_i + \alpha_i\beta_j))(2\alpha_i\alpha_j + \bar{e}_i^2(\alpha_i + \alpha_j)(\beta_i + \beta_j))}. \qquad (5.24)$$

Proposition 12 *Given are two countries with quadratic damage and abatement cost functions as specified above. Furthermore, let i denote the* *country with lower marginal damage costs $(d_i'(e) < d_j'(e))$. Comparing total emissions in the Nash equilibria with and without trading,*

$$\omega^N \gtreqless e^N \quad if \quad c_i''(e_i) \gtreqless c_j''(e_j).$$

Thus, a system of international allowance trading increases aggregate emissions if the country with the lower marginal damage costs has the steeper marginal abatement cost curve. This is exactly the case depicted in Figure 5.1.

5.5 Welfare Effects of Emissions Trading

In the previous section I focused on the environmental effect of emissions trading. However, from a welfare-theoretic perspective it is more interesting to analyze the conditions under which the introduction of a tradable permit system would increase countries' payoffs, rather than their emissions. Given the previous analysis, one might conjecture that the environmentally more concerned country would be worse off with emissions trading: even though it accepts fewer emission allowances for itself, emissions in the low-damage country increase. However, the high-damage country also gains from undertaking emission reductions in the most efficient way, as it is achieved by a competitive permit market. A priori, it is not clear whether those gains can outweigh the losses due to the other country's choice of more emission allowances.

Unfortunately, even with the relatively simple payoff functions as used in the preceding sections, the results turned out to be too complex to interpret. One possibility to proceed would be to use numerical examples (as, for example, in Barrett 1992). Here, I pursue the alternative of further simplifying the payoff functions.

A particularly simple case arises if both countries have identical abatement cost functions.

Proposition 13 *Given are two countries with quadratic damage cost functions and identical quadratic abatement cost functions (that is, $\alpha_i = \alpha_j$ and $\bar{e}_i = \bar{e}_j$). In this case, aggregate welfare increases with emissions trading.*

Proof. With $\alpha_i = \alpha_j$ and $\bar{e}_i = \bar{e}_j$ it follows straightforwardly from equation (5.24) that overall emissions with and without trading are identical $(e^N = \omega^N)$ – and because I have assumed that the location of pollution sources does not matter, the state of the environment will be

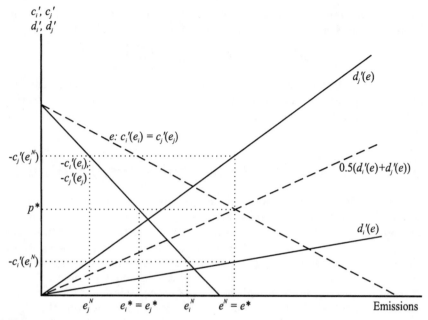

Figure 5.2: Emissions trading with identical abatement cost curves

identical as well. As trading enables countries achieve their targets in the most efficient way, aggregate welfare unambiguously improves. □

The equivalence of total emission levels with and without trading can also be seen from Figure 5.2. It differs from Figure 5.1 on page 100 only in that marginal abatement cost functions are identical for both countries.

In principle, the same intuition as in the preceding section explains this result. If the low-damage country considers increasing its allowances, with trading its marginal abatement costs fall only half as much as without trading because – given identical abatement cost functions – the competitive permit market allocates exactly half of the additional emissions to the other country. Conversely, if the high-damage country considers lowering its allowance level, with trading its marginal abatement costs rise only half as much as without trading. Accordingly, one country's incentives to increase its allowances are of the same magnitude as the other country's incentives to decrease its allowances so that the overall level of allowances remains the same with and without trading.

Proposition 13 depends crucially on the assumption of identical abatement cost functions. If damage cost functions are simplified to be linear instead – an assumption that is not uncommon in the literature (e.g., Mäler 1989) – the following result arises:

Proposition 14 *Given are two countries with linear damage cost functions, $d_i(e) = \beta_i e$, and quadratic abatement cost functions. In this case, the welfare effect of allowing emissions trading is always positive for the low-damage country, but it may be positive or negative for the high-damage country as well as for the group of both countries, compared to a system without trading.*

Proof. Substitute the Nash equilibrium levels for tradable and non-tradable allowances as well as after-trade emission levels into the respective payoff functions with and without trading (equations 5.4 and 5.2). With linear damage cost functions this yields the welfare effects of trading for an individual country

$$
u_i^{trade} - u_i = \frac{(\beta_j - \beta_i)(3\alpha_j\beta_i\bar{e}_i^2 + 2\alpha_i\beta_j\bar{e}_j^2 + \alpha_j\beta_j\bar{e}_i^2 - 2\alpha_i\beta_i\bar{e}_j^2)}{16\alpha_i\alpha_j}, \quad (5.25)
$$

and for the aggregate of both countries

$$
u^{trade} - u = \frac{(\beta_j - \beta_i)(3\alpha_j\beta_j\bar{e}_i^2 - 3\alpha_i\beta_i\bar{e}_j^2 + \alpha_j\beta_i\bar{e}_i^2 - \alpha_i\beta_j\bar{e}_j^2)}{16\alpha_i\alpha_j}. \quad (5.26)
$$

First, let i denote the low-damage country ($\beta_i < \beta_j$). Then the first bracket in (5.25) is positive, and because $2\alpha_i\beta_j\bar{e}_j^2 - 2\alpha_i\beta_i\bar{e}_j^2 > 0$ the second bracket as well. Next, let i denote the high-damage country ($\beta_i > \beta_j$). A sufficient – though not necessary – condition for its welfare to decrease with trading is that it has the flatter marginal abatement cost curve.[9] Together with Proposition 12 this implies that an increase of overall emissions is always associated with a welfare loss for the high-damage country. Conversely, its welfare increases if the slope of the other country's marginal abatement costs $\alpha_j/\bar{e}_j^2$ is sufficiently small relative to his own one.

---

[9] With $c_i''(e_i) < c_j''(e_j)$ we have $\alpha_i\bar{e}_j^2 < \alpha_j\bar{e}_i^2$ so that the term $3\alpha_j\beta_i\bar{e}_i^2 - 2\alpha_i\beta_i\bar{e}_j^2$ is always positive.

Finally, to see that the overall welfare effect of trading may be negative, denote the high-damage country again by i. Then, for equation (5.26) to be negative, its second bracket must be positive. This is the case if

$$(3\beta_j + \beta_i)\frac{\alpha_j}{\bar{e}_j^2} > (3\beta_i + \beta_j)\frac{\alpha_i}{\bar{e}_i^2}. \tag{5.27}$$

Roughly speaking, this means that the low-damage country j must have a *substantially* steeper marginal abatement cost curve. Accordingly, the condition for a negative welfare effect is stricter than the one for an increase in overall emissions, where it suffices that the low-damage country has a steeper marginal abatement cost curve (Proposition 12). The reason is, of course, that even with higher overall emissions, countries still benefit from the cost savings of allowance trading. □

Alternatively, this result can be obtained graphically. Figure 5.3 differs from the previous two in that both countries have constant marginal damage costs of $d_i'(e) = \beta_i$ and $d_j'(e) = \beta_j$, with $\beta_i > \beta_j$. Because the high-damage country i faces a flatter marginal abatement cost curve, after a trading system is introduced its emissions increase by more than country j's emissions decrease.[10] Thus, we have a particularly simple example where allowance trading leads to an increase in overall emissions.

The associated welfare effects are given by the areas under the marginal abatement and damage cost curves. Assuming that marginal damage costs in the two countries differ only slightly, we can restrict attention to the area below the $d_j'(e) = \beta_j$ line. The hatched area below i's marginal abatement cost curve measures i's welfare gain that arises from its increased emissions with trading. Because $e^* - e = (e_i^* - e_i) + (e_j^* - e_j)$, this area is of the same size as the sum of the shaded areas, that represent country j's welfare loss due to it's reduced emissions and its welfare loss due to the additional damage costs. However, the additional damage costs have to be counted twice – as the area under i's *and* under j's marginal damage cost curve – so that the overall welfare effect of emissions trading is negative.

Propositions 13 and 14 are restricted to rather stylized cases. Nevertheless, they suffice to illustrate some important points. The most interesting finding is that aggregate welfare may decrease with trading. However, this has been shown only for the case of linear damage cost functions, for which the free-rider incentives are relatively low (see Helm

---

[10]Remember that the horizontal dashed line, described by $0.5(d_i'(e) + d_j'(e)) = 0.5(\beta_i + \beta_j)$, lies exactly half-way in between i's and j's marginal damage cost curves.

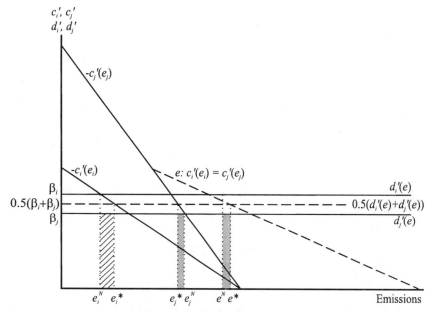

Figure 5.3: Emissions trading with constant marginal damage costs

and Sprinz 1999). Even then, a necessary condition for this to occur is that the country with higher damage costs has lower abatement costs, as follows immediately from equation (5.26). Thus, a negative effect of emissions trading on aggregate welfare seems to be the exception rather than the rule, which is also supported by Proposition 13.

Nevertheless, the question arises why countries should introduce a permit system in those cases where it has a negative welfare effect. Such a decision has been left out of the analysis until now, as I have simply compared the choice of emission allowances with and without trading. However, a system of international allowance trading will usually be declined by countries which would loose from it. On the other hand, those countries that would benefit from it have an incentive to propose an allocation of allowances such that a trading system becomes profitable for all participants.

If decisions on a trading system and on the allocation of initial allowances were taken successively, such a promise to compensate potential losers would not be credible because after agreement on trading there would be no incentive to stick to this promise. In consequence, a trading system would be introduced only if it were beneficial for all countries without compensations.

However, it seems more reasonable to assume that decisions on the level of allowances and their tradability are taken simultaneously. During the negotiations of the Kyoto Protocol, these two issues were indeed linked to each other. Thus, countries' strategies are pairs specifying their vote on a trading system, which can only be introduced with unanimity, and their allowance choices in the systems with respectively without trading. As the following proposition summarizes, this may have substantial effects on the distribution of the gains that arise with emissions trading.

Proposition 15 *Let two countries decide simultaneously on the allocation of emission allowances and their tradability.*

- *There always exists a Nash equilibrium without trading, in which countries choose emission allowances such that domestic marginal abatement and damage costs are equalized.*

- *There also exists an equilibrium with trading and this equilibrium is Pareto-preferred to the one without trading. In the trading equilibrium, countries choose their allowances as specified in equation (5.21) if this leads to a solution $u_i^{trade} \geq u_i$ for both countries. Alternatively, let there be a (high-damage) country, say j, for which $u_j^{trade} < u_j$. The allocation of allowances will be adjusted such that this country is equally well off in the systems with and without trading, while the other country gets all the gains that arise from the improved efficiency in a trading regime.*

Proof. A system without trading and emission levels as in equation (5.18) constitutes a Nash equilibrium because no country can unilaterally introduce a trading system. Similarly, it is straightforward to see that trading constitutes a stable equilibrium if the Nash levels of allowances as specified in equation (5.21) lead to a solution $u_i^{trade} \geq u_i$ for both countries.

Next, consider the case $u_j^{trade} < u_j$ so that j would decline a trading system. Suppose that the allocation of allowances were adjusted such that country j receives a payoff $u_j^{trade^*} > u_j$, where the superscript $^{trade^*}$ indicates that payoffs in the trading regime follow from allowance choices which are no longer best replies as specified in equation (5.21). But if they are no best replies and their adjustment would not immediately affect the approval of a trading system, then they cannot constitute an equilibrium.

Hence the only remaining candidate for a trading equilibrium is one with $u_j^{trade^*} = u_j$. This can be established as an equilibrium if i chooses its allowances such that j's best response leads to $u_j^{trade^*} = u_j$. This yields two equations in two unknowns with a unique solution, assuming that the equations are linearly independent and an interior solution exists. Country j clearly has no incentive to change its action because it is a best response within the trading system and j wouldn't improve its payoff by blocking such a trading system. By contrast, if country i followed its best response strategy within a trading system, it would want to increase its allowances. However, this would induce country j to veto trading, leaving i with its no-trade payoff. Clearly, this is lower than the payoff with trading, because j is exactly as well off as without trading so that i can appropriate all the gains that arise from a more efficient use of resources in a trading regime.

Finally, note that such an equilibrium exists even if the best-reply strategies within a trading regime would lead to a decrease of overall welfare (Proposition 14). The reason is simply that an allocation where one country receives its no-trade payoff and the other country is better off than without trading is always feasible due to the efficiency gains that arise from trading. □

Accordingly, if we endogenize the decision about international emissions trading, we can be assured that such a system will (weakly) improve the welfare of each individual country. However, the allocation of the gains that are arise from a trading system may be distributed quite unevenly in favor of the environmentally less concerned country.

5.6 Imperfect Competition on the Permit Market

The elaborations in the previous sections were based on the assumption of perfect competition on the permit market. This seems to be reasonable if international trading takes place on the level of firms or branches because there will then be a great number of sellers and buyers. For such a scenario, the experience with national tradable permit systems indicates that market power issues are not a major problem, and they may be effectively dealt with by mechanisms like the annual auctioning of 3 per cent of allowances under the US Acid Rain Program (UNCTAD

1998, 25; Schwarze and Zapfel 1998).

However, on the international level it is also possible that states retain the exclusive right to implement permit transfers. In this case the number of market participants would be considerably smaller and there might be countries with market power. To see how this affects the results of the previous analysis, I will model stage 2 of the game with imperfect competition on the permit market along the lines of the seminal work of Hahn (1984), and then analyze its implications for states' choices of allowances in stage 1 of the game.[11]

In particular, let country 1 be the actor with market power, while the other $i = 2, ..., n$ market participants (e.g., the firms in country 2) are price takers. Country 1 can be either a seller or a buyer of permits. Thus, there is a monopoly or monopsony player with a competitive fringe. As usual, price takers buy or sell permits until their marginal cost of abatement equals the permit price. In contrast, country 1 can influence the permit price and as a seller of permits it therefore faces a trade-off between either selling more permits at a lower price or fewer permits at a higher price. If country 1 is a buyer of permits, this trade-off is reversed.[12] More precisely, for a given profile of allowances $(\omega_i)_{i \in N}$, the problem for the country with market power is to

$$\min_p c_1(e_1) + (e_1 - \omega_1)p \qquad \text{s.t.} \quad e_1 = \omega - \sum_{i=2}^n e_i(p), \qquad (5.28)$$

with the first-order condition for an interior minimum

$$\frac{\partial c_1}{\partial e_1} \frac{\partial e_1}{\partial p} + \left(\omega - \sum_{i=2}^n e_i(p) - \omega_1 \right) - p \sum_{i=2}^n \frac{\partial e_i}{\partial p} = 0. \qquad (5.29)$$

As ω is exogenous, it follows from differentiating both sides of the constraint with respect to p that $-\partial e_1/\partial p = \sum_{i=2}^n \partial e_i/\partial p$ so that (5.29) can be written as

$$\left(-\frac{\partial c_1}{\partial e_1} - p \right) \sum_{i=2}^n \frac{\partial e_i}{\partial p} + \left(\omega - \sum_{i=2}^n e_i(p) - \omega_1 \right) = 0. \qquad (5.30)$$

---

[11] On imperfect competition on the permit market see also Fehr (1993); Egteren and Weber (1996).

[12] I abstract from the possibility of price discrimination, although there might be some scope for it in an international trading regime.

As can be seen from equation (5.30), marginal abatement costs of the country with market power will equal the equilibrium price only if its share of allowances equals the amount it actually chooses to use (Hahn 1984, 756). In all other cases, the tradable permit system will not lead to global cost minimization of abatement efforts. This is in sharp contrast to the case of perfect competition, where the initial allocation of allowances does not affect the efficiency property of the final equilibrium (see Montgomery 1972).

Hahn (1984) also showed that inefficiency increases the more the number of permits allocated to the actor with market power differs from its permit use after trading. While this is an important result if a government agency has to decide how best to hand out emission rights to the individual firms, in the present framework this initial allocation of emission rights is determined endogenously through the strategic interaction of sovereign states. Therefore, I am not so much interested in the way that imperfect competition affects the costs to achieve a given abatement target, but rather how it affects countries' equilibrium choices of initial allowances and the welfare implications thereof.

As in the previous section, I confine the analysis to the simple case of two countries (or groups of countries) with quadratic abatement and damage cost functions. The game is solved by backwards induction. In stage 2, the optimality conditions for the country with market power (equation 5.30) and for the competitive fringe, indexed 2, $(p = -c_2'(e_2))$ together with the condition for market clearance $(e_1 + e_2 = \omega_1 + \omega_2)$ yield each country's optimal emission levels as a function of emission allowances ω_1 and ω_2.

Turning to stage 1 of the game at which countries choose their allowances, the objective functions maximizing the payoff in a trading regime (equation 5.4) remain unchanged, and for the competitive fringe also the general solution as specified in equation (5.6) is the same with imperfect competition. However, the country with market power is usually characterized by $-c_1'(e_1) \neq p$ so that its best response function becomes

$$
\omega_1(\omega_{-1}^N) = \left(\frac{\partial d_1}{\partial \omega} + \frac{\partial e_1}{\partial \omega_1} \left(\frac{\partial c_1}{\partial e_1} + p \right) - p \right) \Big/ \frac{\partial p}{\partial \omega_1} + e_1. \tag{5.31}
$$

Solving the response functions for the country with market power and the competitive fringe simultaneously, thereby using the above information on e_1 and e_2, yields the Nash equilibrium of emission allowances in a trading regime with imperfect competition:[13]

$$\omega_1^N = \frac{\overline{e}_i \alpha_1 \alpha_2 (2\alpha_1 + 3\alpha_2 + \overline{e}_i^2 (6\beta_2 - 5\beta_1)) + \overline{e}_i^3 (\alpha_1^2 (3\beta_2 - \beta_1) - 3\alpha_2^2 \beta_1)}{2\alpha_1^2 \alpha_2 + 3\alpha_1 \alpha_2^2 + \overline{e}_i^2 (\alpha_1^2 (\beta_1 + \beta_2) + \alpha_1 \alpha_2 (3\beta_1 + 2\beta_2) + 3\alpha_2 \beta_1)},$$

$$(5.32)$$

and

$$\omega_2^N = \frac{\overline{e}_i \alpha_1 \alpha_2 (2\alpha_1 + 3\alpha_2 - \overline{e}_i^2 (6\beta_2 - 5\beta_1)) - \overline{e}_i^3 (\alpha_1^2 (3\beta_2 - \beta_1) - 3\alpha_2^2 \beta_1)}{2\alpha_1^2 \alpha_2 + 3\alpha_1 \alpha_2^2 + \overline{e}_i^2 (\alpha_1^2 (\beta_1 + \beta_2) + \alpha_1 \alpha_2 (3\beta_1 + 2\beta_2) + 3\alpha_2 \beta_1)}.$$

$$(5.33)$$

Some findings derived for the case of perfect competition on the permit market remain valid or change only marginally if there is a country with market power. In particular, whether a country chooses more or fewer allowances if these are tradable depends again solely on its being a low or high-damage country (Proposition 10). I abstain from writing down those results in detail and concentrate on two particular issues: aggregate emissions and welfare.

In particular, together with the results of the previous section, the above equations can be used to compare total emission levels with imperfect permit markets (ω_{ic}^N) to those without trading (e^N), and to those with competitive permit markets (ω_{pc}^N):

$$\omega_{ic}^N - e^N = \frac{2(\beta_2 - \beta_1)\alpha_1^2 \alpha_2 (\alpha_1 + \alpha_2) \overline{e}_i^3}{(\alpha_1 \alpha_2 + \alpha_2 \beta_1 \overline{e}_i^2 + \alpha_1 \beta_2 \overline{e}_i^2)(x + \alpha_1^2 \beta_2 \overline{e}_i^2 + \beta_1 \overline{e}_i^2 (\alpha_1^2 + 3\alpha_2))},$$

$$(5.34)$$

where $\qquad x = \alpha_1 \alpha_2 (3\alpha_2 + 3\beta_1 \overline{e}_i + 2\beta_2 \overline{e}_i^2 + 2\alpha_1),$ and

$$\omega_{ic}^N - \omega_{pc}^N = \frac{2\alpha_2 \overline{e}_i^3 (\beta_2 - \beta_1)(\alpha_1 + 3\alpha_2)}{2\alpha_1 + 3\alpha_2 + \overline{e}_i^2 (\alpha_1 (\beta_1 + \beta_2)/\alpha_2 + (3\beta_1 + 2\beta_2) + 3\beta_1/\alpha_1)}.$$

$$(5.35)$$

The next proposition follows straightforwardly.

Proposition 16 *Given are a country with market power and a competitive fringe, indexed 1 and 2 respectively, both of which have quadratic abatement and damage cost functions.*

---

[13] As in a previous section, results are written for the special case $\overline{e}_1 = \overline{e}_2 = \overline{e}_i$ so as to reduce the complexity of the solution – without any effects on the main conclusion.

- *Comparing total emissions in the Nash equilibria with imperfect competition on the permit market and without trading,*
$$\omega_{ic}^N \gtreqless e^N \quad \text{if} \quad d_1'(e) \lesseqgtr d_2'(e).$$

- *Comparing total emissions in the Nash equilibria with imperfect and perfect competition on the permit market,*
$$\omega_{ic}^N \gtreqless \omega_{pc}^N \quad \text{if} \quad d_1'(e) \lesseqgtr d_2'(e).$$

Accordingly, if Russia is conceived as a country that has low damages and that is (nearly) a monopoly seller of permits, then the first part of this proposition would support the conjecture that trading may have increased overall emissions. For this scenario it also provides an environmentalist's argument that emission permits should be handed down to the level of firms so as to increase the number of traders and ensure a competitive permit market.

The principal intuition behind Proposition 16 is the same as in the foregoing section: the wedge that an increase of emission allowances would drive between marginal damage and abatement costs is lower if these allowances are traded afterwards, even if competition on the permit market is imperfect. For this reason, it also remains valid that whether a country chooses more or fewer allowances if these are tradable depends solely on its being a low- or high-damage country.

However, there is now a second effect, which arises from the asymmetry of the situation with imperfect competition. A country with market power that faces relatively high marginal damage costs can use its influence on the permit price towards a solution with lower aggregate emissions, and vice versa. As a consequence, the situation that total allowances are higher with trading is more likely if the permit market is non-competitive; in particular, it suffices if the country with market power faces higher marginal damage costs (compare the conditions in Propositions 12 and 16). Similarly, total emissions are lower with imperfect than with perfect competition only if it is the country with market power that suffers most from high emissions.

The same mechanism resurfaces in an analysis of the welfare effects of imperfect competition. As in much of Section 5.5, for reasons of tractability the following is confined to the simple case of linear damage cost functions. Calculating the aggregate payoff with imperfect competition on the permit market u_{ic}^{trade} and comparing this to the case of perfect competition u_{pc}^{trade} yields

$$u_{pc}^{trade} - u_{ic}^{trade} = \frac{(\beta_2 - \beta_1)(\beta_1 y + \beta_2 z)\bar{e}_i^2}{16\alpha_1\alpha_2(2\alpha_1 + 3\alpha_2)^2}, \tag{5.36}$$

where

$$y = -8\alpha_1^3 - 32\alpha_1^2\alpha_2 - 27\alpha_1\alpha_2^2 + 9\alpha_2^3, \text{ and}$$
$$z = 8\alpha_1^3 + 40\alpha_1^2\alpha_2 + 63\alpha_1\alpha_2^2 + 27\alpha_2^3.$$

Proposition 17 *Given are two countries with linear damage cost functions $(d_i(e) = \beta_i e)$, and quadratic abatement cost functions. Imperfect competition on the permit market always implies a lower level of aggregate welfare than with perfect competition if the competitive fringe has higher damages than the country with market power $(\beta_2 > \beta_1)$. In contrast, if the high-damage country has market power $(\beta_1 > \beta_2)$, then in some cases aggregate welfare may be higher than with perfect competition.*

Proof. The first part of Proposition 17 follows straightforwardly from equation (5.36). To see the second part, note that for $\beta_1 > \beta_2$ equation (5.36) yields a negative value if

$$\frac{\beta_1}{\beta_2} < \frac{8\alpha_1^3 + 40\alpha_1^2\alpha_2 + 63\alpha_1\alpha_2^2 + 27\alpha_2^3}{8\alpha_1^3 + 32\alpha_1^2\alpha_2 + 27\alpha_1\alpha_2^2 - 9\alpha_2^3}. \quad \Box \tag{5.37}$$

Such a result is more likely the higher the abatement cost coefficients α_i, especially those of the competitive fringe, and the more similar damage costs are. Intuitively, with steeper abatement cost functions the country with market power can use its influence on the permit price more effectively.

Hahn (1984) and others have pointed out that imperfect competition infringes on the efficiency of the permit market and accordingly lowers aggregate welfare. Proposition 17 shows that this needs to be qualified if the initial allocation of emission entitlements is determined endogenously rather than given exogenously, for example by some government agency. However, the potentially welfare-improving effect of imperfect competition is restricted to the case where the country with market power faces higher damage costs.

This hints at the theory of second-best, according to which a reduction in the number of unsatisfied optimality conditions does not necessarily lead to a welfare improvement if at least one such condition remains violated (Lipsey and Lancaster 1956). In the present analysis, one market failure relates to the fact that countries do not take into account the damages they cause to others, which is particularly detrimental for a high-damage country. If a second market failure is introduced by giving the high-damage country an influence on permit prices, it uses this power to pursue its interest in low emissions, and therefore partly corrects the first market failure. But obviously, if the country with market power faces relatively low damage costs, the negative effects of the two market failures can also add to each other.

5.7 Concluding Remarks

It is generally argued that emissions trading leads to lower abatement cost and as such entails the potential to reach agreement on more ambitious reduction targets. In this chapter it has been shown that this statement needs to be qualified: under unfavorable conditions trading may have the opposite effect of resulting in higher rather than lower overall emissions.

What policy implications follow from this analysis? Certainly, the findings should *not* be interpreted as an argument against an international system of emissions trading. The highly stylized model and the underlying behavioral assumptions are not intended to give a 'realistic' description of the negotiation process, but rather to investigate a particular incentive effect, which has hitherto not received enough attention, in my opinion.

Nevertheless, the point addressed in this chapter is an important one. For one thing, the Kyoto Protocol, which for the first time provides for emissions trading at the international level, showed its empirical relevance quite drastically. Some countries received emission allowances which even exceed their projected business-as-usual emissions – the so-called 'hot air'. This has led to severe criticism especially on the part of environmental groups and partly undermined the credibility of the Kyoto agreement in general and of the emissions trading system in particular.

One could regard this as an unpleasant but in the end only minor flaw of the Protocol because it does not affect the overall reduction target of 5.2 per cent for the period 2008–2012.[14] Indeed, Article 17 on emissions trading entered the Protocol only during the last round of negotiations in Kyoto, which lasted for the whole night until the early hours of the morning. Given these circumstances, it may be that negotiators have overlooked the formation of 'hot air', did not want to jeopardize agreement at the last minute, or simply wanted to go to bed.

On the other hand, developing countries refused to accept any reduction obligations in Kyoto and it is this group of countries for which the

---

[14]This assumes that countries comply with the negotiated targets. Some observers have argued that monitoring of greenhouse gas emissions may pose particularly severe problems with respect to the 'hot air' countries like Russia and Ukraine.

perverse incentive effects introduced by the possibility to sell surplus allowances may be particularly strong. Large amounts of such 'tropical air' would probably pose a much more serious threat to climate protection policies than the limited extent of 'hot air'.

On the occasion of COP4 in Buenos Aires, Argentina as the first developing country pledged to announce voluntary emission targets, hoping that it would then be allowed to participate in the trading system. Although this voluntary acceptance of emission targets in spite of major opposition from other developing countries deserves encouragement, negotiators would be well advised to give the issue of 'tropical air' close attention. In this context it is worth pointing out that the fair division criteria introduced in Chapter 2 are incompatible with any allocation of emission allowances which more than compensates a country for its abatement costs.

In the following chapter, the empirical focus is shifted away from climate change. Instead, I choose the European regime on transboundary acidification as the example which motivates the analysis. On the theoretical side, countries will still be assumed to interact in the non-cooperative mode, but now they interact repeatedly and aspects of uncertainty will be introduced. In particular, I shall explore how countries can use the 'veil of scientific uncertainty' to hide their distributional interests.

6. Cooperation Behind the Veil of Scientific Uncertainty

> The most important fundamental laws and facts of
> physical science have all been discovered, and these
> are now so firmly established that the possibility
> of their ever being supplemented in consequence
> of new discoveries is exceedingly remote.
>
> Albert Abraham Michelson (1852–1931)

6.1 Introduction

In the preceding chapters I have abstracted from any aspects of uncertainty and instead assumed that actors have complete knowledge about their own as well as about other actors' abatement and damage cost functions. This served to keep the analysis focused on other issues, but it goes without saying that uncertainties are paramount in international environmental politics. Hence, decision makers have to negotiate about abatement measures even though they do not know the true model of the ecological system and have only a rough idea about the costs and benefits of their action. In the following, I shall analyze how this kind of 'model uncertainty' – where players not only have incomplete information about the payoff functions of the other players, but also about their own payoff function – may affect the prospects of international cooperation (see Helm 1998).

The basic proposition is that countries can use model uncertainty as a fig-leaf to hide the true reasons for their opposition to substantive international regulation, which are often founded on purely national interests (see Boehmer-Christiansen 1988). Therefore, science not only assists decision makers in defining the right policy choice, but itself becomes an object of negotiations. In particular, I shall argue that the common prior assumption, according to which differences in subjective probability estimates of distinct individuals have to be explained by differences in information, is not convincing in the context of international environmental negotiations. In contrast, there exists a plurality of legitimate perspectives, and that gives countries a certain leeway in the interpretation of uncertain scientific knowledge.

I approach these issues again within the framework of non-cooperative game theory. However, in addition to the introduction of uncertainty into the analysis, there is a second extension compared to the previous chapter. I will take account of the fact that countries interact repeatedly with each other. Accordingly, they have the opportunity to respond to other actors' behavior in previous rounds, including the use of punishment strategies.

A well-known result for such repeated games is that Pareto-efficient cooperation can always be sustained as a (subgame perfect) Nash equilibrium if future payoffs are not discounted too much (see Fudenberg and Tirole 1991). Yet, from an empirical point of view this seems somewhat unrealistic, at least in the area of international environmental policy.

In the present chapter, I will retain the basic idea that punishment strategies can be used to induce cooperation. However, it will be argued that scientific uncertainty renders their use more difficult, leading to solutions of partial cooperation, which seem to be in better conformity with observed behavior.

The outline of this chapter, which puts more emphasis on the empirical side than the previous ones, is as follows. After a short overview of the role of uncertainty in international environmental politics (Section 6.2), a basic model for the analysis of uncertainty and distributional interests will be set up (Section 6.3). In the following two Sections, 6.4 and 6.5, it will be extended to repeated interaction and repeated interaction under scientific uncertainty. Finally, the model will be illustrated quantitatively (Section 6.6) and qualitatively (Section 6.7) for the example of the negotiations of the first Sulphur Protocol to combat transboundary acidification in Europe.

6.2   Scientific Uncertainty and International Environmental Negotiations

A number of recent studies has emphasized the detrimental effects of the strategic use of private information for cooperation (for an overview see Fudenberg and Tirole 1991). For example, Morrow (1994) argues that actors have an incentive to misrepresent their available information in order to pursue their distributional interests and thereby forgo the benefits of honestly sharing their knowledge. Similarly, the literature on two-level games has shown how asymmetric information about domestic constraints can lead to cooperation failures (see Dupont 1994).

However, the ability to hide or misrepresent private information is limited in the domain of international environmental problems. Empirical data and the results of new studies are spread rapidly within an increasingly international research community. Furthermore, monitoring systems and standardized guidelines for national communication serve as barriers to secretly cheat on the implementation of obligations under international environmental agreements.

In contrast, there have been fierce discussions in recent negotiations about the true model of the ecological system on which countries should base their cooperative actions. This can be seen from the disputes about the assessment reports of the International Panel on Climate Change (IPCC) in the emerging climate change regime (Shackley 1997; Helm and Schellnhuber 1998), but also from the negotiations on transboundary acidification (see Section 6.7). This type of uncertainty, where players have incomplete information not only about the payoff function of other players but also about their own payoff functions, has been termed *model uncertainty* (sometimes also analytic or scientific uncertainty, Iida 1993). A primary area of application has been studies on the benefits of macroeconomic policy coordination where, for example, uncertainty consists of governments' ignorance of whether the Keynesian or the monetarist model is the more appropriate description of the economy (see Frankel and Rockett 1988).

In the issue area of environmental protection, model uncertainty means that actors do not properly understand an environmental problem in its full complexity. This may include uncertainty about

- the cause effect relationship between pollutants and environmental damages,

- the costs of environmental damages or, conversely, the potential benefits of mitigation and adaptation measures,

- the effectiveness and costs of different mitigation and adaptation measures, and

- international ecological interdependence, that is the extent of transboundary emission transfers.

Knowledge of these issues is incomplete, but the pool of conflicting models is assumed to be common knowledge so that uncertainty pertains equally to all countries. The central question is whether such model uncertainty affects the prospects of international environmental cooperation and, if so, whether there are reasons to expect that the effects of model uncertainty are biased towards favoring or impeding effective international cooperation.

In decision theory it is usually assumed that decision makers act as expected utility maximizers who update their beliefs with the improvement of scientific knowledge, for example regarding the damage caused by a specific pollutant. Whether there will be a general bias towards too strict or too lax environmental policies depends mainly on actors' risk attitude. On average, actors will choose stricter environmental measures if they are risk-averse and laxer measures if they are risk-taking, compared to the policy chosen by risk-neutral actors. Mostly, risk neutrality is considered as the adequate approach for political decision makers, although risk aversion might be more appropriate in the presence of environmental irreversibilities (Arrow and Lind 1970; Arrow and Fisher 1974).

Thus, if governments act as expected utility maximizers, one would expect that model uncertainty should, on average, be either neutral (case of risk neutrality) or favorable (case of risk aversion) towards the choice of strict environmental policy measures. Only if the value of future information is very high, and the costs of waiting comparatively low, might rational actors choose a protection strategy which is less strict than would be optimal according to the present stage of knowledge (Yohe and Wallace 1996).

However, these results have to be reconsidered if one takes into account the process of international negotiations. Young (1994b, 42–46) has emphasized the positive role 'good uncertainty' can play. He argued that a high degree of uncertainty can soften the problems associated with distributive bargaining, because no country knows how much it will win or lose relative to others. Similarly, in institutional bargaining uncertainty about how a country's position will be affected by a particular agreement tends to favor provisions that are regarded as fair because they minimize the prospects for potentially disastrous results (Brennan and Buchanan 1985).

Yet, even a high degree of model uncertainty usually not does preclude countries from having at least a rough idea about the distributional consequences of environmental regulations. For example, despite the uncertainty of the knowledge about transboundary acidification, net emission exporters and countries with low exceedance of critical loads are likely to benefit less from uniform emission reductions than net emission importers. In this case, the veil of uncertainty offers countries an opportunity to hide their distributional interests. They can deny the existence of serious environmental dangers or at least argue that more research is needed to substantiate them, thereby delaying effective international cooperation and making it more difficult to achieve.

This raises the question why countries should try to hide their distributional interests in the first place. A legalistic answer would be to point to the norms of international law to act cooperatively and not to cause damage to other states. Alternatively, it can be argued that countries fear some kind of punishment if they openly disregard the interests of other states. This might simply stem from the fear that in other cases the upstream/downstream constellation of pollution transfers will be in the opposite direction and they will be dependent on the cooperative behavior of others, as will be assumed in the following sections. However, punishment could also take place in completely different issue areas, or simply consist in a loss of reputation (on issue linkages see Folmer, v. Mouche, and Ragland 1993; McGinnis 1986).

6.3   Model Uncertainty and Distributional Interests – Game-Theoretic Approach

As usual, $N = \{1, 2, \ldots, n\}$ denotes the set of players or countries, indexed alternatively i or j, and each country minimizes its disutility of polluting emissions. In contrast to previous chapters, no side-payments are allowed and there are now transport coefficients a_{ij} which describe the share of j's emissions that is deposited in country i. This source receptor relationship for emissions characterizes problems like acid rain, for which environmental damages are caused by national depositions rather than the global emission level (Mäler 1991; Klaassen 1996). Country i's optimization problem can then be stated as

$$\min_{e_i} c_i(e_i) + d_i(q_i), \qquad \text{s.t. } q_i = \sum_{j \in N}(a_{ij}e_j), \qquad (6.1)$$

where $c_i(e_i)$ are the abatement costs of achieving the emission level e_i, with $c_i'(e_i) \leq 0$ and $c_i''(e_i) \geq 0$, and $d_i(q_i)$ are the damages from depositions q_i, with $d'(q_i) \geq 0$ and $d''(q_i) \geq 0$. Solving this optimization problem yields the Nash equilibrium of the international pollution game, in which each country chooses emissions such that

$$\frac{\partial c_i}{\partial e_i} = a_{ii} \frac{\partial d_i}{\partial q_i}, \tag{6.2}$$

that is marginal abatement costs are equated with marginal damage costs weighted by the share of emissions deposited domestically.

Now, assume that countries are contemplating a treaty on international emission reductions. Let e_i^t and e_i^{nt} be country i's emissions with and without a treaty, respectively, and denote by q_i^t and q_i^{nt} the associated deposition levels. The benefits v of emission reductions induced by the treaty can be calculated for each country as

$$v_i = d_i(q_i^{nt}) - d_i(q_i^t) + c_i(e_i^{nt}) - c_i(e_i^t), \tag{6.3}$$

that is as the difference between the damages that the abated emissions had caused in country i and the costs of its own emission reductions $r_i = e_i^{nt} - e_i^t$.

Of the different sources of uncertainty listed above, uncertainty about the damage function is probably the most prevalent.[1] A simple way to model this is to assume that damages $d_i(q_i, \theta)$ depend not only on depositions but also on the state of nature θ, where θ is a continuous random variable with probability density function $f(\theta)$, which describes the seriousness of damages. The optimization problem will then be to minimize expected costs of emissions $E(c_i(e_i) + d_i(q_i, \theta))$:

$$\min_{e_i} c_i(e_i) + \int d_i(q_i, \theta) f(\theta)\, d\theta, \qquad \text{s.t. } q_i = \sum_{j \in N}(a_{ij} e_j), \tag{6.4}$$

and if risk is multiplicative this can be specified as

$$\min_{e_i} c_i(e_i) + d_i(q_i) E(\theta), \qquad \text{s.t. } q_i = \sum_{j \in N}(a_{ij} e_j). \tag{6.5}$$

If actors are risk-neutral expected utility maximizers, and the random variable θ has mean 1, the solution to the optimization problem as well as the expected benefits of an international emission reductions treaty are independent of the degree of uncertainty, that is of the variance of the density function. This suggests that in a simple static game played among risk-neutral actors, the degree of uncertainty has no immediate effect on the choice of emission levels.

---

[1] Uncertainty about transport coefficients and abatement costs could easily be modeled in a similar way.

6.4 Repeated Interaction between Emission Exporting and Importing Countries

In the following, I consider the case where the game is not played just once but countries interact repeatedly with each other. To keep things simple and with a view to the empirical analysis in Sections 6.6 and 6.7, the repeated version of a transboundary pollution game will be restricted to the case of two countries, a net emission importer I and a net emission exporter E, which can also be viewed as two groups of countries.[2] Furthermore, I assume that the action space is the same for all countries and consists only of two elements, called r^h for high reductions and r^n for no reductions. Although this setting is rather simple, it corresponds well to the negotiations on transboundary air pollution in Europe, which were dominated by two groups of countries bargaining over uniform emission reduction targets (see Section 6.7).

The normal form representation of the stage game is given in Table 6.1, where the payoffs are the expected net benefits of countries' actions as compared to the status quo (r^n, r^n), which can be calculated following equation (6.3).

The following preference ordering will be assumed. To introduce potential gains from mutual cooperation, (r^h, r^h) is the outcome with the highest total payoff. However, the individual interests of the two countries are quite different. To take into account the net emission importer's interest in high emission reductions, (r^h, r^h) is its best and (r^n, r^n) its worst outcome. Conversely, the best and the worst outcome for the net emission exporter are (r^h, r^n) and (r^n, r^h) respectively, reflecting its interest in not reducing its own emissions.

Accordingly, payoffs are $a > b > 0$ and $a > c > 0$ for country I as well as $y > 0 > z$ and $y > x > z$ for country E. In the Nash equilibrium of the stage game (r^h, r^n), typed in bold letters, the net emission importer chooses high reductions while the emission exporting country will abstain from reduction measures.

Finally, the following trigger strategy often used for supergames is assumed. A country cooperates in the first and all future rounds as long as the other country cooperates as well. Cooperation is defined as the choice of the action that maximizes the expected joint payoff of the stage game. Defection is punished by the choice of the stage game's Nash

---

[2]Alternatively, the countries could differ in their ecological vulnerability rather than their transboundary pollution balances.

Table 6.1: The transboundary pollution stage game

		Country E	
		r^h	r^n
Country I	r^h	a, x	$\mathbf{b, y}$
	r^n	c, z	$0, 0$

strategy for the rest of the game.[3] In a deterministic framework, the so-called 'folk theorem' states that this trigger strategy sustains mutual cooperation as a subgame perfect Nash equilibrium of the game if players are sufficiently patient.[4]

Two different types of model uncertainty will be considered. In the first case, there exists uncertainty about the environmental damages caused by polluting depositions, and hence about the total gains from cooperation. These depend on the state of nature θ, which is unknown to both countries and can be observed only as a random variable as defined above. In the second case, there exists uncertainty about the regional distribution of impacts and abatement costs, that is about the distribution of the gains from cooperation. In the framework of this chapter, this relates to the question whether a country is a net emission exporter or importer.

The argument by Young (1994b) – that uncertainty about the distribution of the gains from cooperation can play a positive role in reaching agreement on emission reductions – follows immediately from the preference ordering. Let there be complete distributional uncertainty, that is the chance to be a net emission exporter or importer is equally $\pi = 0.5$. In this case, the strategy pair (r^h, r^h) maximizes not only the joint payoff but also for both countries their expected individual payoff because

$$0.5(a + x) > \max\{0.5(b + y), 0.5(c + z), 0\}. \tag{6.6}$$

Therefore, (r^h, r^h) would be the unique Nash equilibrium of the stage game and of the repeated game.

---

[3]The assumption of constant stage game payoffs may seem rather strong. However, in an abstract sense it serves to make the size of the punishment directly comparable to the stakes of the current cooperation problem. In this setting, the discount factor can be interpreted as the strength of punishment needed to sustain cooperation (see below). Similarly, differences in the severity of environmental problems could be taken account of by using different discount factors.

[4]This is, of course, not the only equilibrium. Indeed, given a sufficiently high discount factor, any feasible, individually rational payoff can be enforced by a subgame perfect equilibrium (see Fudenberg and Tirole 1991).

However, I have objected above that states often possess a fairly precise idea about the distributional effects even for relatively new international environmental problems. For example, the issue of transboundary acidification entered the international agenda with the accusation of some North European countries that they suffered serious environmental damages from emissions caused in the UK and Central Europe. Hence, countries had a clear picture about the main victims and polluters very much from the beginning.

Therefore, I assume in the following that both countries get to know whether they and the other country are net emission exporters or importers before choosing their action. Under what conditions can mutual cooperation be sustained as the solution of the repeated stage game? As the cooperative move r^h is a dominant strategy for the emission importing country, it suffices to look at the strategy choice of the emission exporting country. E's expected payoff for mutual cooperation $v_E^{r^h,r^h}$ in the infinitely repeated stage game is

$$v_E^{r^h,r^h} = x + \sum_{t=1}^{\infty} \rho^t(\pi_E a + (1 - \pi_E)x) = x + \frac{\rho(\pi_E a + (1 - \pi_E)x)}{1 - \rho}, \quad (6.7)$$

where ρ is the discount factor, a and x are E's expected stage game payoffs, and $\pi_E \in [0, 1]$ is country E's belief that it is in the position of an emission importer I in future rounds. Accordingly, the value for π_E reflects systematic differences in countries' belief that they are vulnerable to international environmental problems or, more generally, the perceived vulnerability to punishment, which also depends on the discount factor ρ. Similarly, assuming a different punishment strategy based on issue linkages, ρ would signify the importance of other issues that could be linked to the current environmental problem.

E's expected payoff for unilateral defection $v_E^{r^h,r^n}$ is

$$v_E^{r^h,r^n} = y + \sum_{t=1}^{\infty} \rho^t(\pi_E b + (1 - \pi_E)y) = y + \frac{\rho(\pi_E b + (1 - \pi_E)y)}{1 - \rho}. \quad (6.8)$$

The strategy pair (r^h, r^h) is a Nash equilibrium of the repeated stage game if $v_E^{r^h,r^h} \geq v_E^{r^h,r^n}$, which solves for

$$\rho \geq \frac{y - x}{\pi_E(a - b + y - x)}. \quad (6.9)$$

It is also subgame perfect (Selten 1965) because the punishment payoff (r^h, r^n) is the Nash equilibrium of the stage game.

From equation (6.9) it follows that cooperation is easier to achieve (a lower ρ is required) the smaller the gains from defection $(y - x)$, the greater the gains from mutual cooperation $(a - b)$, and the higher country E's belief π_E that it will be an emission importer in future rounds. Furthermore, from the assumption that (r^h, r^h) is the outcome with the highest expected joint payoff, it follows that $y - x < a - b$. Accordingly, for any payoffs that correspond to the preference relations as defined above and beliefs $\pi_E \geq 0.5$, there exists a discount factor $\rho < 1$ such that mutual cooperation can be sustained as a subgame perfect Nash equilibrium of the repeated stage game.

This result sounds encouraging: even though comprehensive international cooperation on a certain environmental problem is in the interest of only one of the countries, it can be achieved if a strong enough punishment mechanism is available. Prima facie this holds independent of the introduction of uncertainty into the analysis. However, in the next section a less optimistic scenario is presented for the case of international disagreement about the uncertainty pertaining to the environmental problem.

6.5 Repeated Interaction and Scientific Uncertainty

In most cases, objective probabilities for the damages from polluting emissions do not exist and, therefore, probabilities have to be formed subjectively. According to the common prior assumption – sometimes called the 'Harsanyi doctrine' – differences in subjective probability estimates of distinct individuals have to be explained by differences in information.[5] It has been assumed above that all countries have access to the same (uncertain) information. Hence, following the common prior assumption, they should come up with the same subjective probability assessment.

As regards international environmental problems that affect a variety of countries with different cultural and scientific backgrounds, this is not a reasonable assumption. This point has been emphasized by Funtowicz and Ravetz (1993), who argue that the complex and dynamic nature of international environmental problems seriously limits their pre-

---

[5]For a discussion of the common prior assumption see Aumann (1987).

dictability even with substantially improved mathematical models (see also Schellnhuber 1998). Hence, they conclude that there exists 'a plurality of legitimate perspectives' (Funtowicz and Ravetz 1993, 739), which should be taken into account in science as well as in the decision-making process.

Correspondingly, the extent of likely environmental damages from transboundary pollution is often fiercely debated and countries by no means agree on the probabilities of low and high damage scenarios. Beliefs about expected environmental damages associated with various policy measures will therefore vary among countries and they will hold different views about how much each country should reduce its emissions in the optimal cooperative solution. This puts the above trigger strategy – and any other punishment strategy which is based on the norm of cooperation – into a dilemma because different subjective probabilities can be mistaken as non-cooperative behavior. Punishment would be triggered too easily if cooperative behavior could only be monitored with noise.

To address this problem, I will interpret the above density function $f(\theta)$ as an aggregation of countries' subjective probabilities about the distribution of the random variable θ or, similarly, as the result of an emerging scientific consensus. It is then reasonable to assume that countries have a certain leeway when using this 'shared knowledge' to justify their action. This should be reflected in the trigger strategy. More specifically, let cooperation now be defined as the choice of an action that can be supported by at least one value from a certain percentile around the mean of the random variable θ as maximizing the expected joint payoff of the stage game.

A priori, it is not clear how much leeway in interpreting the state of knowledge should be conceded to the countries. At least, it can be assumed to decrease if the scientific knowledge about an environmental problem improves. For example, the admissible assessment of the damage scenario could be determined by the boundaries of the 90 per cent confidence interval around the best estimate, which move closer together as the variance (uncertainty) decreases. This resembles the approach chosen in the IPCC assessment reports to specify upper and lower bounds for likely climate change scenarios, for example an expected sea-level rise between 15 and 95 cm with a best estimate of 50 cm until 2100 (IPCC 1996a). In the following, I will work backwards and ask what leeway would be necessary to allow the emission exporting country to abstain from emission reductions with impunity, even though this strategy does not maximize the expected joint payoff of the stage game.

To get around the triggering of punishment, the emission exporting country must justify unilateral defection (r^h, r^n) by credibly arguing that it yields a higher expected joint payoff than mutual high reductions (r^h, r^h). This is the case if there exists a low damage scenario $\hat{\theta}$ within the admissible uncertainty range such that the expected joint benefits from E's high emission reductions are lower than the costs, that is if

$$\hat{\theta} \int_{q_i^{r^h, r^n}}^{q_i^{r^h, r^h}} d'_E(q_i) + d'_I(q_i)\, dq_i \leq \int_{e_i^{r^h}}^{e_i^{r^h}} -c'_i(e_i)\, de_i, \qquad (6.10)$$

what can be easily solved for $\hat{\theta}$.

Of course, the emission exporting country would use this leeway of interpreting the uncertain knowledge, as the resulting strategy corresponds to its distributional interests. Uncertainty serves as a welcome fig-leaf. Conversely, the emission importing country would still choose high reductions, as it is a dominant strategy.

In summary, the strategy pair (r^h, r^h) that maximizes the expected joint payoff of the stage game can only be achieved if inequality (6.9) holds and (6.10) is violated. This result hints at two important ways to improve the prospects of successful international cooperation: first, a higher punishment, which can be represented through a higher discount factor ρ; and second, a reduction of scientific uncertainties, represented by a higher $\hat{\theta}$ below which the punishment is triggered.

6.6   Scientific Uncertainty and Negotiations on Acid Rain – Quantitative Analysis

In November 1979, thirty-three states signed the Convention on Long-Range Transboundary Air Pollution (LRTAP) in Geneva. In subsequent protocols to the Convention, binding emission reductions have been agreed for a number of pollutants. Early concerns with transboundary pollution focused particularly on sulfur dioxide (SO_2). Accordingly, its emissions were the first to be regulated in the 1985 Helsinki Protocol, which required uniform reductions of at least 30 per cent relative to the 1980 level by 1993. Later, the reduction targets were strengthened in the 1994 Oslo Protocol, which specifies emission reductions based on the concept of critical loads (see also Section 6.7).

The simple game-theoretic model of the previous section can be applied to illustrate the role of model uncertainty in the negotiations of the first Sulphur Protocol. More precisely, I will quantitatively analyze whether some countries had the potential to justify their abstention from the Protocol with reference to scientific uncertainties, even if this was only a fig-leaf for their distributional interests. In the subsequent section, a qualitative analysis of the negotiation process will then corroborate to what extent this strategy has in fact played a role.

Data on SO_2 emissions, transport coefficients of transboundary emission flows and marginal abatement costs are available from the Cooperative Programme for Monitoring and Evaluation of Air Pollutants in Europe (EMEP) and the Regional Acidification Information and Simulation (RAINS) model. However, so far no damage cost estimates exist that are comparable across countries (Cough, Bailey, Biewald, Kuylenstierna, and Chadwick 1994). To obtain marginal damage costs, I will therefore follow the approach chosen by Mäler (1989, 1991) and assume that SO_2 emissions in Europe before the conclusion of the first Sulphur Protocol can be characterized as a Nash equilibrium of the non-cooperative game. It is then possible to work backwards and obtain marginal damage costs as they must equal marginal abatement costs in equilibrium.

This method can be defended by interpreting the thus derived marginal damage cost functions as 'the revealed preference of the governments and parliaments for reductions in emissions of sulphur' (Mäler 1991, 81). Although this procedure is not without problems, it seems justified here as the basic purpose of this section is a quantitative illustration of the theoretical argument outlined above, while the exact numerical results are of minor importance only.[6]

Negotiations of the first Sulphur Protocol have been dominated by countries either favoring uniform emission reductions of 30 per cent or arguing that presently no protocol with specified targets is needed. Similar to the previous section, I will therefore restrict the action space to these two options. Finally, solving the pollution game for one emission importing and one emission exporting country would entail the problem that the benefits of their emission reductions for other countries would be neglected, while they have to bear the full abatement costs. For this

---

[6]One problem is the sensitivity of the results with respect to the choice of the cheapest available abatement technology in the year of calibration (here 1985) because this determines marginal abatement costs and, by assumption, also marginal damage costs. Another problem is that this procedure assumes marginal damage costs to be constant. As I will only look at 30 per cent emission reductions, the latter point should not be that disturbing.

Table 6.2: Distributional interests regarding the first Sulphur Protocol

		non-signatories	
		$r^h = 30\%$	$r^n = 0\%$
signatories	$r^h = 30\%$	8537, −209	**5985, 1859**
	$r^n = 0\%$	2552, −2068	0, 0

reason, I will interpret the actors in the above model as two groups of countries, either objecting or favoring a protocol with 30 per cent emission reductions. As the first group, I will choose those countries that have not signed the first Sulphur Protocol, while the European signatories have been assigned to the second group.[7]

Payoffs can then be calculated according to Table 6.1 and equation (6.3), yielding the normal form representation of the stage game depicted in Table 6.2, where payoffs are expected annual net benefits in million DM.[8]

The preference relation is exactly as assumed in Table 6.1 of the theoretical section. The non-signatories, consisting mainly of countries that are either substantial net emission exporters or have a low ecological vulnerability, have no interest in a protocol. For the other countries, 30 per cent emission reductions is a dominant strategy, yielding the Nash equilibrium (r^h, r^n). Finally, mutual reductions of 30 per cent is the strategy combination that maximizes the expected joint payoff, and is therefore the cooperative solution according to the definition introduced above. This implies that one can use equations (6.9) and (6.10) to analyze the conditions under which mutual emission reductions can be achieved as

---

[7]The non-signatories group consists of: Greece, Ireland, Poland, Portugal, Spain, the United Kingdom and Yugoslavia; the signatories group of Austria, Belgium, Bulgaria, (former) Czechoslovakia, Denmark, Finland, France, (former) East Germany, (former) West Germany, Hungary, Italy, Luxembourg, the Netherlands, Norway, Sweden, Switzerland and the (former) Soviet Union. Romania and Turkey have been left out of the analysis due to data inconsistencies (see also Alcamo, Shaw, and Hordijk 1990, 93 on this point).

[8]Deposition reductions and transport coefficients have been calculated from the deposition budget matrix for oxidized sulfur in 1985 in Barrett and Seland (1995, Appendix E). Marginal abatement costs in 1985 and expected annual costs to achieve 30 per cent emission reductions by 1995 have been taken from the RAINS model. The year 1995 has been used as an approximation for the target year of the Protocol because the RAINS model does not contain abatement cost functions for 1993. Finally, version 5.1 of the RAINS model, whose development started in 1983, and not the more recent version 6.1 has been used, as it better reflects the knowledge – and hence the revealed preferences – of decision makers at the time when the first Sulphur Protocol was signed.

the subgame perfect equilibrium of the repeated game.

Using the same data as for the calculation of the stage game and setting the non-signatories' belief that they will be in the position of emission importers in future rounds $\pi_E = 0.5$, I find that the following two conditions have to hold:

- $\rho \geq 0.89$,

- a low damage scenario $\hat{\theta} \leq 0.90$ falls outside the range of credible scenarios.

The somewhat high discount factor ρ can be explained by the considerable short-term gains of unilateral defection for the non-signatories, which require high punishment to force them into cooperation. At the same time, the triggering strategy is designed such that the punishment depends on the difference between the joint payoff from mutual cooperation and the Nash equilibrium of the stage game, which is relatively low.

Of more interest in the context of this chapter is the result that cooperation breaks down if a low damage scenario $\hat{\theta} < 0.90$ is credible. Accordingly, non-signatories could hide their distributional interest behind the veil of uncertainty as long as they can credibly argue that environmental damages of SO_2 depositions are less than 90 per cent of expected damages.

It is rather difficult to quantify $\hat{\theta}$, in particular because a systematic damage cost evaluation has only recently become a priority issue in the LRTAP regime. Especially at the time before the conclusion of the first Sulphur Protocol no coherent estimates existed (see Chadwick and Hutton 1991). While there still remain considerable uncertainties, the knowledge has substantially improved since then – not the least through joint research efforts undertaken under the auspicious of LRTAP, for example by its working group on effects and associated task forces (UNECE 1992).

More precise assessments have been undertaken for the accuracy of sulfur transport models. A mathematical uncertainty analysis conducted at the International Institute for Applied Systems Analysis (IIASA) found that the uncertainty of total annual sulfur depositions is about 10 to 25 per cent (coefficient of variation) (Alcamo, Bartnicki, and Schöpp 1990, 167). Furthermore, the uncertainty of sulfur transport models has been reduced considerably in the course of time. For example, an early study by Eliassen (1978, 486) found total dry and wet deposition patterns only accurate to within ± 50 per cent (see also Alcamo, Bartnicki, and Schöpp 1990, 133). Quite in line with the central proposition of the chapter, this uncertainty was then used by the net exporting countries to dispute their responsibility for acidifying depositions occurring in Scandinavia (Wetstone and Rosencranz 1983, 136).

In summary, while there already existed a widespread consensus in the mid-1980s that substantial amounts of polluting emissions cross national borders and cause major environmental problems, the extent of damages was still very uncertain. This relatively weak state of knowledge provided a potential to the non-signatories to abstain from the first Sulphur Protocol. Furthermore, the significant improvement of the scientific knowledge indicates that this potential has declined during the course of time and might provide one reason why many countries from this group have signed the second Sulphur Protocol in 1994, even though it requires much higher emission reductions.[9] In the following section, I will analyze the empirical evidence that scientific uncertainty was really used as an argument in negotiations on transboundary acidification.

6.7   Scientific Uncertainty and Negotiations on Acid Rain – Qualitative Analysis

From the very beginning when the issue of transboundary acidification entered the agenda, the creation of mutually agreed-upon scientific knowledge has been a corner stone of international cooperation (Shaw 1993). The first substantial joint research effort was the 'Cooperative Technical Programme to Measure the Long-Range Transport of Air Pollutants', initiated in 1972 under the auspices of the OECD. The results (OECD 1977) offered the first independent international verification that in southern Norway and Sweden imported sulfur was primarily responsible for the acidification of lakes (Wetstone and Rosencranz 1983, 135). This served as the basis for the Convention on Long-Range Transboundary Air Pollution (LRTAP), which was signed shortly thereafter in November 1979 by thirty-three states. While the convention recognized that transboundary air pollution was a major problem, it did not

---

[9]This is not to deny the importance of other factors in explaining why countries that had abstained from the first Sulphur Protocol signed its successor. For example, the shift in the UK position is partly due to its discovery of acid rain as a national problem in the late 1980s, that is a shift in its distributional interests (Levy 1995, 63). However, to the extent that countries have agreed to reduction targets above those they would have pursued without international pressure, the improved scientific knowledge has certainly served to facilitate international cooperation.

contain any obligations to reduce polluting emissions.

However, subsequent proposals for a protocol on sulfur emissions contained costly reduction targets, and this strongly affected the distributional interests of individual states. While the net emission importing and ecologically vulnerable countries pushed for strict flat-rate reductions, the net emission exporting and less vulnerable countries were much less enthusiastic and often opposed binding reduction targets (Gehring 1994). The latter group, however, did not openly display their distributional interests but put forward other arguments to delay international action. One of them was the use of scientific uncertainty as a fig-leaf for their non-cooperative behavior (Boehmer-Christiansen 1988).[10]

This can be seen, for example, from the proceedings of the Multilateral Conference on the Environment, which took place in Munich from 24 to 27 June 1984, approximately one year before the adoption of the first Sulphur Protocol. Insufficient scientific knowledge was particularly emphasized by the USA and the UK, both of which were up-wind countries and did not perceive costly emission reductions to be in their national interest. Accordingly, the delegation of the UK stated:

> My Government's concern is to base action on a proper understanding of the factors that change and damage the environment. That is why we have consistently laid such stress on science. We see no point in making heroic efforts, at great costs, to control one out of many factors unless there is a reasonable expectation that such control will lead to real improvement in the environment.[11]

On the other side, the down-wind and ecologically vulnerable countries considered the knowledge as sufficient for acting. For example, the Finnish delegation stated:

> Continuous support to research is still needed both at national and international level. This cannot, however, be used as an excuse for postponing political decision making. Serious mistakes are made by those governments which do not act soon on the basis of the already available information.[12]

---

[10]Other issues used to justify abstention from the Protocol were the alleged unfair selection of the base year for the reduction targets (especially by the UK) and the lack of abatement technologies to achieve the required reduction targets (especially by Poland).

[11]Summary Record of the Multilateral Conference on the Environment, Statement by the Delegation of the United Kingdom, Annex 5.5, Munich, 24–27 June 1984.

[12]Ibid., Statement by the Delegation of Finland, Annex 5.12.

These statements nicely concur with the arguments in previous sections of this chapter that the assessment of scientific knowledge is strongly influenced by the different distributional interests of down-wind and up-wind countries. This is further corroborated by standardized interviews with policy makers, scientists and representatives of non-governmental organizations.

The following two questions have been asked of at least one representative from each of those groups in Finland (FI), Germany (DE), Hungary (HU), Italy, the Netherlands (NL), Norway (NO), Spain (ES), Sweden (SE), Switzerland (CH) and the United Kingdom (GB):[13]

- According to the view supported by government officials of your country, can the LRTAP-pollutant be regarded as a major cause of environmental damages in your own or in other European countries?

- According to the view supported by government officials of your country, as how reliable can the knowledge about the extent of transboundary emission be regarded?

In the answers, the following scale points could be assigned: '1' for very uncertain, '2' for rather uncertain, '3' for rather certain, and '4' for very certain. Accordingly, higher scores imply a higher degree of certainty. The same questions were asked at two time points at the stage of regime building: 1972, when the issue of transboundary acidification entered the international agenda, and 1978, one year before the adoption of the Convention on Long-Range Transboundary Air Pollution.

The results of the interviews are summarized in Figure 6.1. For the variable 'degree of certainty', a simple average of the answers to both questions and time points has been taken. For the variable 'national interests', I have used the ratio of imports to exports, assuming that countries' interests in international cooperation increase with imported emissions (potential benefits from cooperation) and decrease with exported emissions (potential reduction burdens from cooperation).

In accordance with the above exposition, Figure 6.1 shows that countries with a low interest in international cooperation emphasize the uncertainty of the knowledge about the environmental problem, and vice

[13]The interviews were undertaken as part of the project 'International Governmental Organizations and National Participation in Environmental Regimes', which was funded by the European Commission under Contract EV5V-CT94-0390. The assistance of country teams, which carried out the interviews, and of Caroline Huß, who administered the data, is gratefully acknowledged.

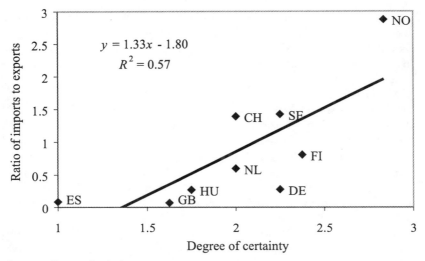

Source: Own calculations

Figure 6.1: National interests and the assessment of uncertainty

versa. Furthermore, given the choice of rather simplified indicators and the small number of cases, the R^2 of 0.57 is reasonably high.[14]

The second Sulphur Protocol of 1994 is based on the concept of 'critical loads', which are defined as 'a quantitative estimate of an exposure to one or more pollutants below which significant harmful effects on specified sensitive elements of the environment do not occur, according to present knowledge' (second Sulphur Protocol, Article 1.8). The emission reductions required to achieve critical loads have then been allocated among the parties on the basis of cost-efficiency scenarios calculated with the assistance of integrated assessment models, especially RAINS.[15] This means that the conventional politics-driven negotiation process, in which countries largely pursue their national interests, has

---

[14]Italy was excluded from the analysis as an outlier with a low ratio of imports to exports but a very high degree of certainty.

[15]However, countries' divergent willingness to undertake costly abatement measures was partly reflected in the use of national reduction plans as a baseline for the calculation of cost-efficient reduction scenarios. Furthermore, countries had some political bargaining leverage through the choice of the target year (2000, 2005, or 2010) and the reference scenario (finally, 60 per cent gap closure to achieve critical loads was chosen).

been partly replaced by a science-driven, computer-assisted approach (see Gehring 1994). This requires a far-reaching consensus about the scientific and technical basis and, in principle, makes the negotiation process even more susceptible to the use of scientific uncertainty as a fig-leaf to delay action.

Accordingly, disputes about critical loads data and integrated assessment models have played a major role in the negotiation process of the second Sulphur Protocol. For example, the Nordic countries, which favored strict emission reductions, determined particularly low critical loads that were challenged throughout the negotiations and somewhat adjusted later on (Gehring 1994, 182). In the beginning, some countries might even have favored the critical loads approach because they thought its associated uncertainties would make it a long-term enterprise that would hamper rather than accelerate the adoption of a new protocol. The quick progress in the development of critical loads maps left those countries trapped in their own delay tactics, from which they could not easily deviate without losing face.

Disputes also arose about the results of two integrated assessment models that had been developed by Swedish and British institutions as alternatives to the RAINS model. Not surprisingly, the Swedish CASM model (Coordinated Abatement Strategy Model) required the highest and the British ASAM model (Abatement Strategies Assessment Model) the lowest emission reductions from the UK (on the three models see UNECE 1993). However, neither of them could seriously challenge the use of the RAINS model, mainly because a large number of scientists from different countries was involved in its development at the International Institute for Applied Systems Analysis (IIASA). This shows that results from joint research projects were not so easy to dispute as national studies, thereby reducing the ability to hide behind the veil of uncertainty.

6.8   Concluding Remarks

The reduction of scientific uncertainties should lead to 'better' (in the Pareto sense) policy results because actors can more properly assess the costs and benefits of their action. This is certainly the strongest argument for national and in particular internationally coordinated joint research efforts, in which countries can benefit from sharing their knowledge.

In this chapter it has been argued that scientific uncertainty itself can have detrimental effects on the international negotiation process because it enables countries to defect from cooperation on grounds of insufficient knowledge. In contrast to the Harsanyi doctrine, it has been argued that decision makers in different countries may attach different subjective probabilities to the occurrence of damage scenarios, even if they possess exactly the same information. Punishment of non-cooperative behavior is then hampered by the problem of distinguishing between 'legitimate' deviations from the subjective probability assessment of other countries, for example those based on different cultural and scientific backgrounds, and a systematically biased interpretation of uncertain scientific knowledge to foster national interests. Therefore, science is not only a tool to assist political decision making, but itself becomes an object of international negotiation.

The empirical relevance of these arguments has been shown at the example of transboundary acidification, but disputes about scientific knowledge have been at least equally important in the climate change regime (Helm and Schellnhuber 1998; on the role of uncertainty in the ozone regime see Benedick 1998).

The Swedish scientist Svante Arrhenius had already argued in 1896 that a doubling of atmospheric CO_2 concentrations could induce the temperature to rise by $5°C$ (Arrhenius 1896), which comes surprisingly close to current estimates. However, his work was largely ignored, and when the issue was brought up again more than fifty years later, there was no consensus in the scientific community whether a greenhouse or an ice age scenario was the more likely prospect for the world. This dispute was largely settled at the end of the 1970s in favor of the global warming hypothesis, leading to an increased interest among the public and among political decision makers as well as strengthened international research efforts. Since then, there has been a close connection between negotiations for an international climate change regime and negotiations about consensual scientific knowledge.

Similar to the negotiations on transboundary acidification, some countries pointed to the gaps in scientific knowledge as a reason not to undertake 'premature' action, while others asserted that gaps in information should not be used as an excuse for worldwide inaction (see Rowlands 1995, 66–87). Furthermore, there has been a close correlation between countries' assessment of the scientific knowledge and their distributional interests. Countries which regarded an adaptation strategy as cheaper than a mitigation strategy or even hoped to benefit from climate change emphasized scientific uncertainties, most prominently the oil-exporting countries, the USA under the Bush administration and the Former Soviet Union. In contrast, low-lying island states were among the first to regard the scientific evidence as sufficient to warrant serious mitigation measures against climate change.

In the context of this dispute, the IPCC, which brought together some of the world's most preeminent scientists with the aim of formulating a consensual scientific view on climate change, plays a crucial role. The IPCC's first scientific assessment report of 1990 confirmed the global warming hypothesis and emphasized that this 'assessment is an authoritative statement of the views of the international scientific community' (IPCC 1990, iii). This was an important prerequisite for the Framework Convention on Climate Change to be signed one and a half years later.

The IPCC's second assessment report of 1995 played a similar role in the negotiations of the Kyoto Protocol. In the report, some bounds for likely effects of a doubling of atmospheric CO_2 concentrations relative to the pre-industrial level have been specified: most importantly an increase in global mean surface temperature between $1°$ and $3.5°C$, with a best estimate of $2°C$, and a sea-level rise between 15 and 95 cm, with a best estimate of 50 cm. Although the range of estimates is still substantial, it considerably limits countries' ability to reject serious mitigation measures on grounds of insufficient knowledge. Accordingly, agreement on the second assessment report was perhaps the most difficult issue at the second Conference of the Parties to the Climate Convention in Geneva, 1996. But after this hurdle was taken, disputes about the science of climate change played only a relatively minor role during the negotiations of the Kyoto Protocol and conflicts about the distribution of climate protection burdens are now more openly displayed.[16]

---

[16] An exception is greenhouse gas sinks, whose scientific basis was widely debated in Kyoto. However, this issue is closely related to the distribution of emission reduction burdens.

7. Dynamic Aspects and Threshold Effects

> A hypothesis or theory is clear, decisive, and positive, but
> it is believed by no one but the man who created it.
> Experimental findings, on the other hand, are messy,
> inexact things which are believed by everyone
> except the man who did that work.

Harlow Shapley (1885–1972)

7.1 Introduction

In the previous chapter, it was assumed that countries interact repeatedly with each other. This enabled them to react to other players' actions in earlier rounds, and to design punishment strategies which are conditioned on past behavior. However, repeated games do not allow for past play to influence the feasible actions or payoff functions in the current period.

Such a framework is suited for pollution flow problems like noise or the pollution of transboundary river courses. In contrast, for many international environmental problems damages are caused by the accumulated stock of pollutants, for example the CO_2 concentration in the atmosphere. This adds additional dynamic aspects to the analysis. First, one needs a description how the pollution stock accumulates over time as a function of emission levels and nature's absorption capacity for pollutants. Second, additional strategic considerations arise from the fact that past behavior now influences current payoffs via the pollution stock.

The other new theme introduced in this chapter is discontinuities in damage functions. It will be shown that for non-uniformly mixed pollutants like transboundary acidification, such thresholds can uniquely determine the solution of the non-cooperative game. For atmospheric pollution problems, however, they may lead to a situation of indeterminacy with infinitely many Nash equilibria. Furthermore, thresholds can serve as common policy goals (Haurie and Zaccour 1995), but they may also exacerbate free-rider behavior.

A priori, there is no need to introduce threshold effects and dynamics together. Indeed, the following analysis of thresholds mainly elaborates on the steady state, which is quite similar to a static framework, and I abstain from discussing complex dynamics (Gandolfo 1997). Accordingly, the main reason to merge these two topics has been space considerations.

Sections 7.2 and 7.3 introduce the two new aspects of this chapter – threshold effects in natural systems and pollution stock dynamics. In the following main part (Section 7.4), the dynamic transboundary pollution game with thresholds is discussed. In doing so, different cases are considered, in particular problems with uniformly or non-uniformly mixed pollutants and whether thresholds are binding in all countries or only in some countries.

7.2   Threshold Effects in Natural Systems

Threshold effects in natural systems have received little attention in the economic literature on international environmental cooperation (exceptions are Mäler 1992; Perrings and Pearce 1994; Mäler and de Zeeuw 1998). Two justifications for this are conceivable. First, it may be that no thresholds of considerable extent exist and, accordingly, damage costs of environmental pollution can essentially be described as a smooth function. Furthermore, even if there are thresholds, their location may be uncertain. A flat probability distribution over this location would then lead to a relatively smooth expected damage cost function, at least if the jump at the threshold is not 'too big'. Second, it may be that even strong thresholds have only minor effects on international cooperation and their explicit analysis would not lead to substantially new insights.

The focus in this chapter is on the second point – the effects of thresholds on the prospects of international cooperation. Before I turn to this issue, let me describe what I mean by thresholds and briefly discuss their empirical significance.

Figure 7.1 depicts the choice of optimal emission abatement for the simple case of one country experiencing a pollution flow problem. As usual, marginal abatement costs decrease continuously in emissions, but marginal damage costs are discontinuous at the threshold level of emissions $\hat{e}_i$. Furthermore, the threshold is binding in that it determines the optimal abatement level. In this case, the first-order conditions do not hold $(-c_i'(\hat{e}_i) > d_i'(\hat{e}_i))$ and optimality requires pushing emissions to the

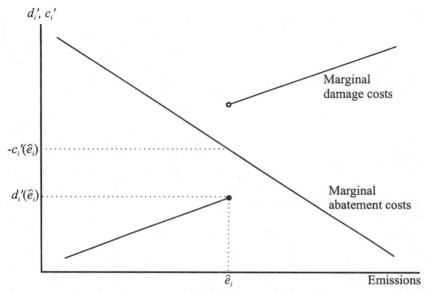

Figure 7.1: Optimal emission abatement with thresholds

point of discontinuity $\hat{e}_i$.[1]

Discontinuities in natural systems have been emphasized especially in the context of climate change (IPCC 1996b; Petschel-Held, Schellnhuber, Bruckner, Tóth, and Hasselmann 1999). One such example is the possible instability of the Atlantic thermohaline circulation, the so-called conveyor belt phenomenon delivering huge amounts of heat to the Northeast Atlantic and keeping Western and Northern Europe much warmer than they otherwise would be. A comparison of CO_2 emission projections and the associated estimated temperature increase with a stability criterion for the Atlantic thermohaline circulation yields that a permanent shut-down of the conveyor belt cannot be excluded (Stocker and Schmitter 1997). Possible implications of such a break down are a decrease in the annual mean air temperature in the northern North Atlantic by up to 20°C associated with winter temperatures lowered by more than

---

[1]In a probabilistic framework with uncertainty about the threshold location or the effectiveness of emission control policies, one would of course have to steer the system in safe distance from the threshold (Arrow and Fisher 1974; Perrings and Pearce 1994).

30°C. Consequently, the Norwegian Sea may be completely ice-covered in winter and the maximum sea-ice extent may even cover parts of the coasts of the British Isles (Schiller, Mikolajewicz, and Voss 1997). Other catastrophic climate change scenarios that might arise from a forcing of natural systems beyond certain thresholds include a run-away greenhouse effect, disintegration of the West Antarctic ice shield and dramatic changes in the South Asian monsoon patterns.

Accordingly, the principal idea that there are thresholds which should guide policy making has found its way into recent environmental treaties. A prominent example is the second Sulphur Protocol to combat acid rain in Europe, which strives to limit SO_2 depositions to the level of critical loads, below which significant harmful effects on specified sensitive elements of the environment do not occur (see Chapter 6). Another example is the Climate Convention's target of preventing dangerous anthropogenic interference with the climate system (see Chapter 2). Yet, while negotiators could agree on specific values for critical loads in the acid rain regime, no similar agreement on a threshold beyond which one would speak of a dangerous anthropogenic interference with the climate system exists. Nevertheless, the formulation of objectives in international environmental treaties often seems to be based on the idea of thresholds, which serve as focal points from which environmental protection targets are then derived.

In this context, it should be noted that thresholds need not be confined to jumps in natural systems but can also consist of values that are regarded as critical for other – including political – reasons. One example is the argument of the German Advisory Council on Global Change (WBGU 1996) that the temperature range of the late quaternary constitutes a threshold because most ecosystems as we know them today and other life-supporting environmental systems relied upon by humanity have evolved during this geological period. The doubling of the pre-industrial CO_2 concentration level is a further focal point in climate change negotiations, which is not backed by scientific evidence of a dramatic change in natural systems beyond this level.

For many other political and economic issues, it is also common to think in terms of thresholds, like a certain level of unemployment or a certain Dow-Jones level which are regarded as critical. One such example that has recently attracted a lot of attention are the 'Maastricht criteria' to become a member of the European monetary union. The target to reduce budget deficits and inflation rates below 3 per cent, in particular, shaped governments' financial policies to a substantial extent, even though there is no reason to believe that monetary stability is discontinuous at this particular level.

7.3 Dynamic Aspects of a Transboundary Pollution Game

Dynamic aspects of transboundary pollution games constitute the second new feature which is introduced in this chapter. This relates to the modeling of environmental damages as well as to the information structure of the game.

In particular, environmental damages in country i now arise from the accumulated stock (rather than the flow) of pollutants, denoted by s_i. With $\varphi_i(t)$ being the amount of pollutants which can be absorbed by the environment in country i during period t, this results in the equation of motion for the pollution stock

$$\dot{s}_i(t) = \sum_{j \in N} a_{ij} e_j(t) - \varphi_i(t), \qquad (7.1)$$

where $\dot{s}_i(t) = ds_i/dt$, $e_i(t)$ are emissions, a_{ij} is the share of emissions in country j which is relevant for environmental damages in country i and $N = \{1, 2, \ldots, n\}$ is the set of players or countries, indexed alternatively by i and j.[2]

For atmospheric pollution problems like climate change, no particular source receptor relation exists and only the global pollution stock matters. Accordingly, $a_{ij} = 1$ and $s_i(t)$ is identical for all $i \in N$ so that the equation of motion for the state variable is given by the difference between global emissions and global absorption:

$$\dot{s}(t) = \sum_{i \in N} (e_i(t) - \varphi_i(t)). \qquad (7.2)$$

I will continue to work with the more general formulation (7.1), which subsumes (7.2) as a special case.

Among the possible specifications of the absorption of pollutants $\varphi_i(t)$, two alternatives have been most widely used. For transboundary acidification it has been assumed that there exists a critical load, a fixed yearly

---

[2]The assumption that transport coefficients a_{ij} are time-independent is of course a simplification. For example, the direction and strength of winds that carry SO_2 particles may vary considerably over time. Therefore, one may think of a_{ij} as a long-run average, and such averages have indeed been used for the calculations in Chapter 6.

amount of pollutants $\hat{\varphi}_i(t)$, which can be removed by natural processes (Mäler 1992):

$$\varphi_i(t) = \hat{\varphi}_i(t) \qquad \text{if } s_i(t) \geq \varphi_i(t). \tag{7.3}$$

For climate change it is more appropriate to specify the decay as proportional to the global stock of pollutants:

$$\varphi(t) = \zeta s(t). \tag{7.4}$$

Here, $\zeta \in [0, 1]$ is the natural rate of decay, which is usually assumed to be independent of the pollution stock.

The second dynamic aspect relates to the additional strategic inter-action of decentralized decision makers that arises if the problem of in-ternational environmental cooperation is modeled as a differential game (Başar and Olsder 1994). Of central importance for the solution of such games is the specification of the information structure of the players. This is characterized by a set-valued function $\eta_i(t)$ that defines for each player $i \in N$ the information at time $t \in [0, T]$, where the time horizon of the game $[0, T]$ includes the case $T = \infty$. Two alternative specifications have received particular attention in the literature due to their relative simplicity. The first is the *open-loop* information structure, where the only relevant information is the initial state s_0 of the pollution stock:

$$\eta_i(t) = \{s_0\}, \qquad\qquad t \in [0, T]. \tag{7.5}$$

However, the implicit assumption that changes in the state variable s from the initial period cannot be observed seems rather restrictive. It might be appropriate for a military conflict model, where the state vari-able is the hidden stock of biological weapons. However, in international environmental problems the state of the environment and also polluting emissions of other countries can usually be monitored – at least to some extent.

This is taken into account by the *feedback* information structure, which assumes that each player observe the current state of the pollution stock:

$$\eta_i(t) = \{s(t)\}, \qquad\qquad t \in [0, T]. \tag{7.6}$$

This information structure is also relatively simple because one could imagine that players remember the complete history of the state – a structure that is called *closed-loop*:

$$\eta_i(t) = \{s(r), 0 \leq r \leq t\}, \qquad\qquad t \in [0, T]. \tag{7.7}$$

Although this structure is often the most realistic one and may also improve the prospects for mutually beneficial cooperation, it is usually rejected due to its complexity and because the greater information of players leads to informational non-uniqueness of equilibria (see Başar and Olsder 1994). Indeed, even the considerably simpler feedback structure can be solved analytically only for a small range of functions, in particular those with a linear dynamic system and a quadratic objective functional (see Section 7.5). Therefore, I will largely restrict the following analysis of a transboundary pollution game to an open-loop information structure, for which the solution techniques of optimal control theory can be used.[3]

7.4 Open-Loop Nash Equilibria of a Transboundary Pollution Game

As in previous chapters, production of the consumption good x_i causes pollutive emissions e_i, where

$$x_i = f_i(e_i) \qquad\qquad (f_i'(e_i) \geq 0,\ f_i''(e_i) \leq 0) \qquad (7.8)$$

represents the assumption that production is increasing in emissions but at a decreasing rate and no transfer payments are feasible. Utility u_i in period t increases in consumption and decreases in the pollution stock:

$$u_i = u_i(x_i), s_i) \quad (u_i'(x_i) \geq 0, u_i''(x_i) \leq 0, u_i'(s_i) \leq 0, u_i''(s_i) \leq 0). \quad (7.9)$$

Given an open-loop information structure, players observe only the initial state of the game and, accordingly, have no incentive to change their strategy during the game. Therefore, each country's decision can be framed as an optimal control problem in which it takes the strategies of the other countries as given.

My interest in this chapter is in those thresholds in the state variable which are prohibitive, meaning that countries want to secure their non-violation (see Figure 7.1 on page 145). The threshold can then be added

---

[3]For an introduction to optimal control theory see Chiang (1992), Kamien and Schwartz (1991), and for dynamic non-cooperative game theory Başar and Olsder (1994). There are by now a considerable number of applications to environmental economics, for example Forster (1980), Long (1992), Ploeg and de Zeeuw (1992) as well as Mäler and de Zeeuw (1998).

as a constraint to the optimal control problem.[4] Thus, each country $i \in N$ maximizes its discounted welfare stream, subject to the threshold level for the pollution stock $\hat{s}_i$ and taking the (open-loop Nash) strategies of the other countries as given. Substituting $x_i = f_i(e_i)$ one obtains[5]

$$\max_{e_i} \int_0^\infty e^{-rt} u_i(f_i(e_i), s_i) \, dt \quad \text{s.t.} \tag{7.10}$$

$$\dot{s}_i(t) = \sum_{j \in N} a_{ij} e_j(t) - \varphi_i(t) \tag{7.11}$$

$$\dot{s}_i(t) \leq 0 \quad \text{whenever } s_i(t) = \hat{s}_i(t) \tag{7.12}$$

$$s_i(0) = s_i^0 \ (s_i^0 \text{ given}), \tag{7.13}$$

$$e_i(t) \geq 0. \tag{7.14}$$

The Lagrangian of this problem – the constrained version of the Hamiltonian function $\mathcal{H}$ – is (time indices are suppressed for ease of notation)

$$\mathcal{L} = e^{-rt} u_i(f_i(e_i), s_i) + \lambda_i \left(\sum_{j \in N} a_{ij} e_j - \varphi_i \right) - \xi_i \left(\sum_{j \in N} a_{ij} e_j - \varphi_i \right). \tag{7.15}$$

Since the discount factor adds complexity to the derivatives, it is more convenient to work with the current-value Lagrangian

$$\mathcal{L}^c \equiv \mathcal{L} e^{rt} = u_i(f_i(e_i), s_i) + \mu_i \left(\sum_{j \in N} a_{ij} e_j - \varphi_i \right) - \gamma_i \left(\sum_{j \in N} a_{ij} e_j - \varphi_i \right), \tag{7.16}$$

where $\mu_i = \lambda_i e^{rt}$ and $\gamma_i = \xi_i e^{rt}$. Using Pontryagin's maximum principle (Pontryagin, Boltyanksii, Gamkrelidze, and Mischchenko 1962), the

---

[4]Alternative decision-making approaches in the presence of threshold effects have been proposed. For example, the tolerable windows approach abstains from identifying an optimal solution but rather determines the set of all solutions that do not violate certain conditions that are regarded as critical (Bruckner, Petschel-Held, Tóth, Fuessel, Helm, Leimbach, and Schellnhuber 1999; Schellnhuber 1999).

[5]If one simply added the state-space constraint $s_i(t) \leq \hat{s}_i(t)$ to the optimization problem (as in a static framework), this could lead to jumps in the costate variable at the point where the constraint becomes binding. The alternative formulation used here takes account of the fact that whenever the state-space constraint is satisfied with equality ($s_i(t) = \hat{s}_i(t)$) the pollution stock must not increase further ($\dot{s}_i(t) \leq 0$) (see Chiang 1992, 300).

following optimality conditions must be satisfied for all $i \in N$ in the open-loop Nash equilibrium (assuming interior solutions):

$$\frac{\partial \mathcal{L}^c}{\partial e_i} = -\frac{\partial u_i}{\partial f_i}\frac{\partial f_i}{\partial e_i} + (\mu_i - \gamma_i)a_{ii} = 0 \qquad (7.17)$$

$$\frac{\partial \mathcal{L}^c}{\partial \gamma_i} = \varphi_i - \sum_{j \in N} a_{ij}e_j \geq 0 \qquad \gamma_i \geq 0 \qquad \gamma_i \frac{\partial \mathcal{L}^c}{\partial \gamma_i} = 0 \quad (7.18)$$

$$s_i \leq \hat{s}_i \qquad \gamma_i(\hat{s}_i - s_i) = 0 \qquad (7.19)$$

$$\dot{\gamma}_i \leq 0 \qquad (= 0 \text{ when } s_i < \hat{s}_i) \qquad (7.20)$$

$$\dot{s}_i = \frac{\partial \mathcal{H}^c}{\partial \mu_i} = \sum_{j \in N} a_{ij}e_j - \varphi_i \qquad (7.21)$$

$$\dot{\mu}_i = -\frac{\partial \mathcal{L}^c}{\partial s_i} + r\mu_i = -\frac{\partial u_i}{\partial s_i} + \mu_i\left(\frac{\partial \varphi_i}{\partial s_i} + r\right) \qquad (7.22)$$

$$\lim_{t \to \infty} \lambda_i(t) = 0, \text{ which is equivalent to } \lim_{t \to \infty} \mu_i(t)e^{-rt} = 0 \quad (7.23)$$

$$\lim_{t \to \infty} \mathcal{L}(t) = 0, \text{ which is equivalent to } \lim_{t \to \infty} \mathcal{L}^c(t)e^{-rt} = 0. (7.24)$$

7.4.1 Non-Binding Constraints

If the constraint is not binding because the threshold has not been reached ($\gamma_i = 0$), the above equation system reduces to expressions (7.17), (7.21) and (7.22) plus the transversality conditions. According to optimality condition (7.17), each country should choose emissions such that its marginal social welfare of emissions is equal to the shadow price μ_i of the state variable – the change in welfare as a result of a one-unit change of the stock of pollution – weighted by the share of i's self-depositions a_{ii}.

Furthermore, with $\dot{\mu}_i = 0$ one can solve (7.22) for

$$\mu_i = \frac{\partial u_i/\partial s_i}{\partial \varphi_i/\partial s_i + r} \qquad (7.25)$$

and substitute this into (7.17) to get the optimality conditions in the steady state

$$\frac{\partial u_i}{\partial f_i}\frac{\partial f_i}{\partial e_i} = a_{ii}\frac{\partial u_i/\partial s_i}{\partial \varphi_i/\partial s_i + r}. \qquad (7.26)$$

Accordingly, optimal abatement efforts increase in national marginal damage costs and self-depositions a_{ii} – the latter being equal to 1 for atmospheric pollution problems. Similarly, they decrease with the natural rate of decay $\partial \varphi_i/\partial s_i$ and the discount rate r because both imply lower future damages of the current pollution stock. The only difference to the static version of a transboundary pollution game is indeed that marginal damage costs are now weighted by the natural decay rate and the discount rate.

Turning to the transversality conditions, equation (7.23) is satisfied because in the optimum $\mu_i(t)$ is finite according to (7.17) and by discounting a finite value tends towards 0 as t tends towards infinity. Similarly, the transversality condition (7.24) is satisfied due to the presence of the discount factor in the first term on the right-hand side of (7.15) and because λ_i has already been shown to tend towards 0. An analysis of the stability of the steady state can be found in Appendix 7.7.

7.4.2   Binding Constraints For Problems With Non-Uniformly Mixed Pollutants

Of more interest in the context of this chapter is the scenario where the constraint becomes binding in the course of time. In this case, the term $a_{ii}\gamma_i$ in equation (7.17) gives country i's additional abatement costs due to the threshold. This corresponds to the distance between $d_i'(\hat{e}_i)$ and $-c_i'(\hat{e}_i)$ in Figure 7.1.

The constraints may either be binding in all countries simultaneously ($\gamma_i \neq 0$ for all $i \in N$), or they may be binding in a subset of countries only. Turning to the first alternative, assume that there exists a unique non-negative emission vector such that $\dot{s}_i = 0$ for all $i \in N$.

Proposition 18 *Let $\varphi = (\varphi_i)_{i \in N}$ be a vector of the country-specific absorption of pollutants, $A = [a_{ij}]$ an $n \times n$ matrix of transport coefficients and $\mathbf{e} = (e_i)_{i \in N}$ an emission vector. If the constraint is binding in all countries ($\gamma_i \neq 0$ for all $i \in N$) and a unique (steady state) solution $A\mathbf{e} = \varphi$, $\mathbf{e} \geq 0$ exists, then this solution constitutes the unique Nash equilibrium.*

Proof. First, note that the solution $A\mathbf{e} = \varphi$, $\mathbf{e} \geq 0$ obviously constitutes a Nash equilibrium, meaning that no country can unilaterally improve its welfare: any unilateral emission increase would violate the threshold; and the marginal abatement costs of any emission decrease exceed the corresponding marginal damage costs by the assumption that the threshold is binding (see Figure 7.1). Second, by contradiction of the uniqueness of the Nash equilibrium assume that there would be a country in which depositions are either lower than or exceed the absorption capacity so that $\sum_{j \in N} a_{ij} e_j - \varphi_i \neq 0$. Following the previous argument, this country has an incentive to increase or decrease emissions until the level of depositions equals the absorption capacity – a contradiction. □

This means that thresholds can play a very important role in co-ordinating actors' behavior in the decentralized mode. Therefore, it is of interest to identify some general conditions under which a solution $Ae = \varphi$, $e \geq 0$ exists and, accordingly, Proposition 18 applies. An obvious condition is that the matrix of transport coefficients A must be non-singular. This is always the case if A has a dominant diagonal (see Takayama 1985, 381), that is if for every country the share of self-depositions is greater than the share of emission exports ($|a_{ii}| > \sum_{j \neq i} |a_{ji}|$ for all $i \in N$).

Obviously, A is singular for global environmental problems like climate change because only accumulated global emissions matter, so that all entries in A are equal to one. Therefore, the arguments in this section only apply to problems with a source receptor relationship for pollutants that can be represented by a non-singular emissions transport matrix. Given this assumption of non-singularity, the following two statements can be made.

Proposition 19 *Let A be a non-singular $n \times n$ matrix. If all countries are identical and $\gamma_i \neq 0$ for all $i \in N$, then a (steady state) solution $Ae = \varphi$, $e \geq 0$ exists and Proposition 18 applies. Furthermore, the unique Nash equilibrium is Pareto-optimal.*

Proof. By non-singularity of A, a unique solution to $Ae = \varphi$ exists. There can be no solution with $e_i < 0$ for all $i \in N$ because A and φ are non-negative by assumption. Accordingly, the vector e must have a positive entry for at least one $i \in N$ and by symmetry this implies $e_i \geq 0$ for all $i \in N$. Turning to the second part of Proposition 19, note that by symmetry there are only two ways in which the Pareto optimum can differ from the Nash equilibrium: either $Ae > \varphi$ or $Ae < \varphi$, that is depositions either exceed or are lower than the absorption in all countries. However, it is easy to see that none of these possibilities can be Pareto-optimal because aggregate welfare could be increased by more abatement efforts in the first case and by lowering abatement efforts in the second case. □

This equivalence of the Nash equilibrium and the Pareto-optimal solution is an interesting result because it would not have been obtained without the existence of binding thresholds and, thereby, shows that these can have important implications for the prospects of international cooperation. On the other hand, the assumption of identical countries seriously limits the practical relevance of this result.[6]

Another straightforward result arises for environmental problems that involve only two countries.

Proposition 20 *Let there be two countries, denoted i and j, and A is a non-singular $n \times n$ matrix. If A has a positive determinant, a solution $Ae = \varphi$, $e \geq 0$ exists if and only if $\varphi_i/\varphi_j > a_{ij}/a_{jj}$ for both countries. Conversely, if A has a negative determinant, a solution $Ae = \varphi$, $e \geq 0$ exists if and only if $\varphi_i/\varphi_j < a_{ij}/a_{jj}$.*

Proof. The inverse of the 2×2 transport matrix is

$$A^{-1} = \frac{1}{\det A} \begin{pmatrix} a_{jj} & -a_{ij} \\ -a_{ji} & a_{ii} \end{pmatrix}. \tag{7.27}$$

This yields the solution vector

$$\mathbf{e} = A^{-1}\varphi = \frac{1}{\det A} \begin{pmatrix} a_{jj}\varphi_i & -a_{ij}\varphi_j \\ -a_{ji}\varphi_i & a_{ii}\varphi_j \end{pmatrix}. \tag{7.28}$$

By non-singularity of A, $\det A \neq 0$. If $\det A > 0$, then $e > 0$ is satisfied if $a_{jj}\varphi_i - a_{ij}\varphi_j > 0$ for both countries, or, after rearrangement, if $\varphi_i/\varphi_j > a_{ij}/a_{jj}$. Similarly, if $\det A < 0$, all signs of the transport matrix change and $\mathbf{e} > 0$ is satisfied if $\varphi_i/\varphi_j > a_{ij}/a_{jj}$ for both countries. Note that $\det A = a_{ii}a_{jj} - a_{ij}a_{ji}$ and accordingly it is the share of self-depositions that determines which case applies. □

If the diagonal entries of A are higher than the off-diagonal entries – the case which is more relevant for transboundary pollution problems – a solution $Ae = \varphi$, $e \geq 0$ exists if the relation between critical loads in the own and the other country is greater than the relation between the other country's emission export coefficient and its self-deposition coefficient. Roughly, this means that a solution $Ae = \varphi$, $e \geq 0$ is more likely to exist if decisive thresholds in both countries are relatively similar and the greater the share of emissions that is deposited domestically.

---

[6]The assumption of identical countries is indeed essential for the equivalence of the Nash equilibrium and the Pareto optimum, and in contrast to the arguments in Mäler (1992, 74) it does not suffice that a solution $Ae = \varphi$, $e \geq 0$ exists. For example, if countries differ in that one has considerably lower abatement costs than the others, it may be efficient that this country shoulders a larger share of emission reductions even if high diagonal coefficients in the transport matrix A imply that depositions in this country would then be below the level of critical loads. Obviously, if all countries are identical, such a situation cannot occur.

This result is intuitively appealing because with a positive determinant both conditions emphasize the importance of domestic emissions in reaching critical loads, firstly because of the importance of self-depositions (high diagonal entries), and secondly because no country can hope to achieve its critical loads as a free rider, that is as a byproduct of another country's attempt to reach its much stricter critical loads. The analysis for a negative determinant works along the same lines.

It is straightforward to conjecture that similar arguments apply in the case of more than two countries and a solution $A\mathbf{e} = \varphi$, $\mathbf{e} \geq 0$ becomes more likely the more similar decisive thresholds and the higher the self-deposition coefficients. Unfortunately, a compact formulation as in Proposition 20 does not exist – at least apart from the trivial case where A is a diagonal matrix such that all off-diagonal elements are equal to zero. This, of course, would be the description of a purely domestic environmental problem because all transboundary emission coefficients are equal to zero.

Until now I have elaborated upon the case where a solution $A\mathbf{e} = \varphi$, $\mathbf{e} \geq 0$ exists. This is actually a necessary condition for the constraints to be binding simultaneously in all countries, because the latter requires that $\dot{\mathbf{s}} = A\mathbf{e} - \varphi = 0$ (assuming that thresholds are constant over time). Yet, this may easily be violated. Then, equation (7.17) shows that those countries in which the constraint is not binding ($\gamma_i = 0$) follow the same optimality calculations as if no threshold exists.

However, equation (7.17) describes a best response strategy that depends via the co-state variable μ_i on the pollution stock and, thereby, on the abatement efforts of the other countries. Binding constraints force countries to undertake additional emission reductions, leading to lower marginal damage costs and, accordingly, lower marginal abatement costs in those countries where constraints are not binding. In the extreme case of damage cost functions which are zero before the threshold and jump to infinity thereafter countries in which the constraint is not binding would undertake no abatement measures at all and get a complete free ride.

7.4.3 Binding Constraints for Problems With Uniformly Mixed Pollutants

In the previous section, I have focused on environmental problems with non-uniformly mixed pollutants which are characterized by a non-singular transport coefficients matrix. However, for atmospheric pollution problems like climate change and ozone depletion it is only the amount of accumulated emissions that matters for the severity of environmental damages, while the source of emissions is irrelevant.

In principle, the Nash equilibrium remains the same as given by the equation system (7.17) to (7.24), but all transport coefficients are now equal to one and the absorption capacity is given by $\varphi(t) = \zeta s(t)$. As a consequence, Proposition 18 and the corresponding corollaries no longer apply because they were based on the assumption of a non-singular transport matrix.

Furthermore, because damage costs are determined by the global pollution stock s, the constraints can be binding in all countries simultaneously only if the threshold $\hat{s}_i$ is the same across countries so that there exists a common policy goal. In the steady state which steers the system along the threshold, $\dot{s} = 0$ and accordingly $\sum_{i \in N} e_i = \varphi$. However, there are infinitely many emission vectors that satisfy this condition because only accumulated emissions matter, but not their distribution. This contrasts sharply with the possibly unique Nash equilibrium for the case of a non-singular transport matrix. To emphasize the contrast to the previous section, these results can be summarized as follows.

Proposition 21 *Let $(\hat{s}_i)_{i \in N}$ be a vector of country-specific thresholds. Given an atmospheric pollution problem, the condition $\hat{s}_i = \hat{s}_j$ for all pairs $i, j \in N$ is necessary for a solution $s_i = \hat{s}_i$ for all $i \in N$ to exist. Furthermore, every solution satisfying $s_i = \hat{s}_i$ constitutes a Nash equilibrium. Thus, if emissions are continuously divisible, there will be infinitely many Nash equilibria.*

It remains to consider the Nash equilibrium if constraints differ across countries. Following the same arguments as in the previous section, those countries where the constraint is not binding ($\gamma_i = 0$) will choose their marginal abatement costs to equal domestic marginal damage costs and thereby benefit from the emission reductions forced by the binding thresholds upon other countries. In the extreme case of damage functions that are zero before the threshold and rise to infinity thereafter, this will again give them a complete free ride.

However, as soon as there is more than one country in which the constraint is binding, there will be infinitely many Nash strategies on the part of those countries. Finally, if a country has a threshold which is substantially lower than in the other countries, and if this country is not able to secure this threshold by own abatement efforts, the threshold may well be violated. This might actually be the case for some low-lying island states that are threatened to be flooded by a rising sea level.

7.5 Feedback Nash Equilibria of a Transboundary Pollution Game

The informational limitations of the open-loop Nash equilibrium, which was applied as the solution concept in the preceding section, have already been mentioned. In contrast, feedback strategies specify an optimal plan for every value of the state variable at each point in time, rather than being conditioned only on the initial state.[7] Accordingly, whenever a new state is reached, this can be thought of as the starting point of a subgame of the original game. In a feedback strategy players optimize in every such subgame, hence it is subgame perfect.

The necessary conditions for a Nash equilibrium in feedback strategies are essentially the same as for open-loop strategies, but the equation of motion for the costate variable now becomes[8]

$$\dot{\mu}_i = -\frac{\partial \mathcal{H}_i^c}{\partial s_i} - \sum_{j \in N_{j \neq i}} \frac{\partial \mathcal{H}_i^c}{\partial e_j} \frac{\partial e_j^N}{\partial s_j} + r\mu_i, \qquad (7.29)$$

where the cross-term $(\partial \mathcal{H}_i^c / \partial e_j)(\partial e_j^N / \partial s_j)$ captures the effect that a player i now cares about the other players' response to changes in the state variable s.

This effect disappears in the open-loop case, because players do not observe changes in the state variable, and hence do not react to it. In feedback strategies, the additional term makes the equation of motion for the costate variable a partial differential equation, which can be solved analytically only in some exceptional cases like linear-quadratic differential games. These are characterized by a linear dynamic system and a quadratic objective functional. For more complex games, their justification rests on the hope that they constitute a reasonable second-order Taylor approximation. I will not pursue this line of research here further, but would like to point out two recent findings which are of some importance for international environmental cooperation.

Ploeg and de Zeeuw (1992) showed that in the open-loop Nash equilibrium countries choose lower pollution levels than in the feedback Nash

---

[7]The assumption that strategies depend only on time and the current state of the game is sometimes called the 'Markov restriction'.

[8]Often the analysis is restricted to stationary games, for which time t enters only in the discount factor, so that the problem is autonomous.

equilibrium. The reason for this is that if one country considers lowering its emissions, the state of the environment in other countries would improve as well. In the feedback case (but not in the open-loop case) these other countries would observe the improved state of the environment and relax their pollution control accordingly, a mechanism that prevents the choice of lower emissions from the very beginning. In equation (7.29), it is this effect which is captured by the cross-term $(\partial \mathcal{H}_i^c / \partial e_j)(\partial e_j^N / \partial s_j)$. Using more complex models, Cesar (1994, 141) as well as Mäler and de Zeeuw (1998) could not demonstrate this result analytically, but their numerical simulations confirm the considerably higher emission level in the feedback Nash equilibrium.

The second finding which may have important implications for assessing the prospects of international environmental cooperation concerns the common assumption of linear feedback strategies, which means that in the steady state actors choose emissions as a linear function of the pollution stock. Building on work by Tsutsui and Mino (1990), Dockner and Long (1993) have shown that allowing actors to adopt non-linear strategies has considerable effects on the solution of differential games. While the asymptotically stable feedback Nash equilibrium in linear strategies is unique for their model, there exists a large range of different equilibria in non-linear strategies. In particular, Dockner and Long (1993) show that for small enough discount rates there exists a feedback Nash equilibrium which approximates the Pareto-efficient welfare level. Once countries manage to embark on this strategy, it is self-enforcing and the free-rider problem can be overcome without binding international agreements.[9]

However, Dockner and Long (1993) restrict their analysis to the case of two identical countries. With a considerably greater number of actors which are characterized by substantial asymmetries as in the real world, agreement on Pareto-efficient strategies may be much more difficult to achieve.

7.6   Concluding Remarks

In this chapter, dynamic aspects of a transboundary pollution game that arise if damages are caused by the accumulated pollution stock rather than the pollution flow have been analyzed. Furthermore, implications

---

[9]The multiplicity of feedback Nash equilibria and their possible closeness to the Pareto-efficient outcome have also been emphasized by Dutta and Radner (1998).

of discontinuities in damage functions for the prospects of international cooperation were discussed.

On the negative side, incentives for free riding may increase if thresholds are binding only for some countries, as this group will be forced to undertake additional abatement efforts that can be exploited by other countries. On the positive side, universally binding thresholds may serve as common policy goals, and for the stylized case of identical countries the Nash equilibrium and the Pareto optimum are even equivalent.

Another important issue that has been raised is the possible indeterminacy of the outcome of the transboundary pollution game. For atmospheric pollution problems – but also for source receptor problems for which a steady state $A\mathbf{e} = \varphi$, $\mathbf{e} \geq 0$ is not feasible – this happens if thresholds are binding and countries adopt open-loop Nash strategies. Multiple equilibria can also arise without thresholds if countries adopt (non-linear) feedback strategies.

This assigns an important task to international environmental negotiations. They can provide a forum for countries to coordinate their strategies on one which comes close to a Pareto-efficient outcome, while avoiding those other equilibria which are considerably less efficient. In this sense, preplay communication or cheap talk can matter quite a lot.

However, finding a Pareto-efficient solution is only part of the problem. If transfer payments are feasible, this is compatible with completely different burden-sharing rules. In particular, for universally binding atmospheric pollution thresholds any allocation of abatement costs constitutes an open-loop Nash equilibrium so that little can be said about burden sharing from a game-theoretic analysis of strategic interactions.

How then do countries coordinate their policies if the non-cooperative mode fails? One possibility is that they switch to the fairness mode of cooperation, which establishes a close link to the first part of this book. There, fair burden sharing was introduced as a normative thought experiment. Now, it is argued that fairness criteria can serve as focal points (Schelling 1992; Sudgen 1995) to coordinate behavior if there are multiple Nash equilibria. This may also provide an explanation as to why the proposed solution that followed from the fair division analysis – the WESA mechanism – seems actually not so far away from observed behavior.

7.7   Appendix: Stability Analysis

For the case of non-binding constraints ($\gamma_i = 0$), the steady state can be characterized by $\dot{s}_i = 0$ and $\dot{\mu}_i = 0$ for all $i \in N$. However, to do so one would have to eliminate the variables e_j in equation (7.21). It turns out that it is more convenient to formulate the differential equations for the emission trajectories and eliminate instead the current value multipliers μ_i (see Long 1992 for climate change).

For convenience, assume that the arguments in the welfare function are additive separable and simplify notation by writing

$$u_i(f_i(e_i)) = -c_i(e_i). \tag{7.30}$$

As usual, $c_i(e_i)$ can be interpreted as the abatement costs to reduce emissions to level e_i. Accordingly, (7.17) can be written as

$$c_i'(e_i) = \mu_i a_{ii}. \tag{7.31}$$

Differentiating both sides with respect to t so as to derive the time evolution of marginal abatement costs yields

$$c_i''(e_i)\dot{e}_i = \dot{\mu}_i a_{ii}. \tag{7.32}$$

Together with (7.22), this results in the emission trajectories

$$\dot{e}_i = \frac{a_{ii}\left(\mu_i(\varphi_i'(s_i) + r) - u_i'(s_i)\right)}{c_i''(e_i)}. \tag{7.33}$$

Now, if $\varphi_i'(s_i) = 0$ (which is the case for a constant absorption $\varphi_i(t) = \hat{\varphi}_i$ as in acid rain) or if the absorption rate $\varphi_i'(s_i) = \zeta$ is the same for all countries (as is usually assumed for climate change) one can use equation (7.31) to get

$$\dot{e}_i = \frac{c_i'(e_i)(\zeta + r) - a_{ii}u_i'(s_i)}{c_i''(e_i)}. \tag{7.34}$$

Emission and state trajectories for global pollution problems follow straightforwardly by setting all transport coefficients a_{ii} equal to 1. Together with (7.21) there are $2n$ differential equations with $2n$ unknowns that determine the solution.

Calculus methods can be used to check the saddle-point stability of such a system of differential equations. Because the notation quickly becomes tedious, I restrict the following to the case of climate change ($\varphi(t) = \zeta s(t)$) and two countries. The Jacobian matrix at the steady state $(\bar{e}_1, \bar{e}_2, \bar{s})$ is given by

$$\mathcal{J}\mid_{(\bar{e}_1,\bar{e}_2,\bar{s})}=\frac{\partial(\dot{e}_1,\dot{e}_2,\dot{s})}{\partial(e_1,e_2,s)}=\begin{pmatrix}\frac{\partial\dot{e}_1}{\partial e_1}&\frac{\partial\dot{e}_1}{\partial e_2}&\frac{\partial\dot{e}_1}{\partial s}\\\frac{\partial\dot{e}_2}{\partial e_1}&\frac{\partial\dot{e}_2}{\partial e_2}&\frac{\partial\dot{e}_2}{\partial s}\\\frac{\partial\dot{s}}{\partial e_1}&\frac{\partial\dot{s}}{\partial e_2}&\frac{\partial\dot{s}}{\partial s}\end{pmatrix}. \tag{7.35}$$

As the numerator of equation (7.34) is equal to zero in the steady state, one gets

$$\frac{\partial\dot{e}_i}{\partial e_i}=\frac{(c_i''(e_i))^2(\zeta+r)}{(c_i''(e_i))^2}=\zeta+r \tag{7.36}$$

$$\frac{\partial\dot{e}_i}{\partial e_j}=0 \tag{7.37}$$

$$\frac{\partial\dot{e}_i}{\partial s}=-\frac{c_i''(e_i)u_i''(s)}{(c_i''(e_i))^2}=-\frac{u_i''(s)}{c_i''(e_i)} \tag{7.38}$$

$$\frac{\partial\dot{s}}{\partial e_i}=1 \tag{7.39}$$

$$\frac{\partial\dot{s}}{\partial s}=-\zeta \tag{7.40}$$

so that

$$\mathcal{J}\mid_{(\bar{e}_1,\bar{e}_2,\bar{s})}=\begin{pmatrix}\zeta+r&0&-\frac{u_1''(s)}{c_1''(e_1)}\\0&\zeta+r&-\frac{u_2''(s)}{c_2''(e_2)}\\1&1&-\zeta\end{pmatrix}. \tag{7.41}$$

Let ϱ_i denote an eigenvalue of $\mathcal{J}$. Because

$$\prod_i\varrho_i=\det\mathcal{J}=(\zeta+r)\left((\zeta+r)(-\zeta)+\frac{u_2''(s)}{c_2''(e_2)}\right)+\frac{u_1''(s)}{c_1''(e_1)}(\zeta+r)<0 \tag{7.42}$$

by $c_i''(e_i)>0$ and $u_i''(s)<0$, there exists a negative eigenvalue, implying saddle-point stability (see Levhari and Liviatan 1972; Long 1992). Note, however, that trace $\mathcal{J}>0$ so that by the modified Routh-Hurwitz's stability conditions the steady state is not asymptotically stable (see Berck and Sydsæter 1993). Thus stability arises only from the fact that one can use the control variable to put the system on the stable arm of the saddle.

8. Outlook

Dimidium facti,
qui coepit, habet.

Horace (65–8 BC)

To the Roman poet Horace we owe the above cited proverb 'who has started, has almost finished'. Having come nearly to the end of this book, one may very well reverse this. Although I hope to have shed some light on a number of important issues, new questions have arisen from there.

This need not be a bad sign. My ambition was not to treat a narrowly defined question in exhaustive detail, but to analyze the same object – international environmental cooperation – from different perspectives, focusing on different aspects and using different analytical tools from economics. I strongly believe that only such an approach, which emphasizes the diversity of explanatory models, can lead to a better understanding of the complexities of international environmental politics. Nevertheless, in this outlook I shall synthesize some results of the previous chapters and draw some general conclusions.

A central concept in economics is Pareto efficiency, and this figured prominently in the preceding chapters. Much of the analysis focused on the potential to overcome the 'tragedy of the international commons', which is associated with the pursuit of self-interest by sovereign but ecologically interdependent states. Here, it was shown that the prospects of agreeing on mutually beneficial cooperation, that is for Pareto improvements, are not as bleak as the simple Prisoner's Dilemma story suggests.

This is most clearly seen when we approach international environmental politics from the analytical perspective of cooperative game theory. If transfer payments are feasible, Pareto-efficient cooperation can be sustained as a core-stable solution, meaning that no individual state or coalition of states has an incentive to defect from global cooperation (Chapter 4). This holds for a wide range of alternative assumptions about the reaction towards defecting coalitions – including individual best-reply strategies or the abandonment of own emission mitigation efforts.

Viewed from the perspective of non-cooperative game theory, the picture is less clear. The results depend substantially on the particular model specifications and there are often multiple equilibria, which vary considerably in terms of their efficiency. Nevertheless, even here exists some scope for Pareto-efficient cooperation, arising from repeated games or issue linkages (Chapter 6), common policy goals in the presence of discontinuous damage functions and non-linear Markov strategies in dynamic games (Chapter 7).

A careful design of international agreements plays a crucial role for achieving this potential for cooperation. Widely discussed in this context are internationally tradable emission allowances, which may substantially increase the efficiency of accomplishing given reduction targets. These cost savings might then make agreement on more ambitious targets acceptable. However, the analysis in Chapter 5 showed the importance of taking into account the additional strategic considerations that arise at the international level. In contrast to national permit systems, there exists no central authority to determine the initial allocation of tradable allowances and this will be the outcome of negotiations among sovereign states. The opportunity to sell emission allowances introduces for some actors the unintended incentive to negotiate for more allowances than they would have done without trading.

Another issue of institutional design, which has been analyzed in some detail, is the importance of a commonly accepted scientific basis for international negotiations. Environmental problems are often very complex, and the problems for decision making that arise from associated uncertainties are pervasive. For transboundary environmental pollution, the strategic interaction of sovereign states adds a further facet to this problem. They may put forward scientific uncertainties as a pretext for doing little or nothing, even though this behavior actually rests on distributional interests like a low affectedness by the respective problem. The IPCC is an excellent example of an institution that helps to build a commonly accepted knowledge base, and in the repeated-game framework of Chapter 6 this proved crucial to increasing the efficiency of international cooperation.

Whereas Pareto efficiency is widely accepted as a desirable criterion, it is not very specific. There may be many points on the Pareto frontier. Indeed, if utility is transferable via monetary compensations, as has been assumed throughout much of the text, the set of Pareto-efficient solutions is infinite. This relates to the issue of burden sharing in international environmental cooperation that constituted another guiding question throughout the text.

Even at the level of national politics, disputes about the 'appropriate' value judgments on which to base the allocation of benefits and burdens to different parts of the society are paramount. At the international level, the problems are no smaller, especially with respect to climate change that will affect practically every country on earth, current as well as future generations, in a multitude of ways. Elaborating on the welfarist approach to decision making, Chapter 3 discussed some of the unavoidable value judgments and hinted at the difficulties of reaching an international consensus on them. Nevertheless, the importance of taking account of countries' respective capabilities that are associated with different income levels has emerged as something like a minimum requirement for any burden-sharing rule.

Acknowledging those difficulties, the fair division approach employed in Chapter 2 took a more modest stance. The equitable sharing of climate protection burdens was reduced to the problem of fairly dividing a common resource, the size of which was taken as given. Here, I have argued that some widely accepted fairness criteria can be formulated and that there exists an allocation mechanism which comes very close to satisfying all of them. An essential feature of this WESA mechanism is that low-emission countries should participate in reduction efforts to increase their global efficiency, but they should be compensated for their incremental abatement costs.

Interestingly, this result is fairly robust with respect to different initial allocations of entitlements to the common resource, on which much of the climate change literature has focused. Furthermore, because the low-emission countries are usually those with lower income levels, the principle that they should be fully compensated for their incremental abatement costs is principally in congruence with the more comprehensive welfarist perspective. This strengthens the appeal of the WESA mechanism as a policy recommendation coming out of a normative analysis of burden sharing.

Yet, even if this were widely accepted as a fair principle, there exists no central authority with the power to assure its implementation – despite the increasing number of voices arguing for a strengthening of international institutions. Therefore, burden sharing also has to be analyzed from a positive perspective – as the outcome of the strategic interaction of self-interested states. This poses certain restrictions on the polluter pays principle that underlies the WESA mechanism and many other proposals for fair burden sharing. However, in a cooperative game theory framework some room to implement fairness judgments remains, especially if the main polluters are among those that are most concerned about environmental problems. In particular, I suggested an allocation in the spirit of egalitarian equivalence that equalizes individual benefits measured as free environmental protection relative to either the Nash solution or the level of business-as-usual emissions.

It may be in order to conclude the text with some questions for further research. First, there certainly exists scope for model refinements. Among the most important issues is the incorporation of general equilibrium effects, which have been largely neglected throughout the analysis. However, this makes an analytical approach as pursued in this book substantially more difficult and often renders it intractable. In this respect, numerical simulation models and, in particular, computable general equilibrium models may prove very useful. These may also be used to calculate the implications of the various burden-sharing rules that have been discussed.

Second, in order better to assess the appropriateness of different models and the effects of various institutional arrangements on the general prospects for international cooperation, the link between theoretical and empirical work has to be strengthened. For the field of international environmental politics this is a particularly demanding task because econometric studies are seriously hampered by the low number of comparable cases. This is further aggravated by the problem of determining the counterfactual of what would have happened without a particular cooperation agreement.

Finally, the question of how to design institutions that most effectively exploit the potential for cooperation requires further attention. Beyond the analytical tools applied in this book, it may be fruitful to approach this issue from the perspective of evolutionary game theory. However, economics is not the only discipline that has to make a contribution to the question of institutional design. Therefore, it should do so in concert with other disciplines, such as political science, international law, and sociology.

Bibliography

Alcamo, J., J. Bartnicki, and W. Schöpp (1990). Long-range transport of sulfur and nitrogen compounds in Europe's atmosphere. In J. Alcamo, R. Shaw, and L. Hordijk (Eds.), *The Rains Model of Acidification: Science and Strategies in Europe*, pp. 115–178. Dordrecht: Kluwer Academic Publishers.

Alcamo, J., R. Shaw, and L. Hordijk (Eds.) (1990). *The Rains Model of Acidification: Science and Strategies in Europe*. Dordrecht: Kluwer Academic Publishers.

Arnsperger, C. (1994). Envy-freeness and distributive justice. *Journal of Economic Perspectives 8*(2), 155–186.

Arrhenius, S. (1896). On the influence of carbonic acid in the air upon the temperature on the ground. *Philosophical Magazine 41*, 237–276.

Arrow, K. J. (1951). *Social Choice and Individual Values*. New York: John Wiley and Sons.

Arrow, K. J. and A. C. Fisher (1974). Environmental preservation, uncertainty, and irreversibility. *Quarterly Journal of Economics 88*(2), 312–319.

Arrow, K. J. and R. Lind (1970). Uncertainty and the evaluation of public investment decisions. *American Economic Review 60*, 364–378.

Aumann, R. J. (1987). Correlated equilibrium as an expression of Bayesian rationality. *Econometrica 55*(1), 1–18.

Barrett, K. and Ø. Seland (1995). European transboundary acidifying air pollution: Ten years calculated fields and budgets to the end of the first Sulphur Protocol. EMEP/MSC-W Report 1/95, The Norwegian Meteorological Institute, Oslo.

Barrett, S. (1992). International environmental agreements as games. In R. Pethig (Ed.), *Conflicts and Cooperation in Managing Environmental Resources*, pp. 11–36. Berlin: Springer-Verlag.

Barrett, S. (1994). Self-enforcing international environmental agreements. *Oxford Economic Papers 46*, 878–894.

Barry, B. (1973). *The Liberal Theory of Justice*. Oxford: Clarendon Press.

Başar, T. and G. J. Olsder (1994). *Dynamic Noncooperative Game Theory* (2nd ed.). New York: Academic Press.

Baumol, W. J. (1986). *Superfairness: Applications and Theory*. Cambridge, Mass.: MIT Press.

Beckerman, W. and J. Pasek (1995). The equitable international allocation of tradable carbon emission permits. *Global Environmental Change 5*(5), 405–413.

Beitz, C. R. (1999). International liberalism and distributive justice. *World Politics 51*, 269–296.

Benedick, R. E. (1997). Backstage at the multilateral environmental negotiations. In F. Biermann, S. Büttner, and C. Helm (Eds.), *Zukunftsfähige Entwicklung. Herausforderungen an Wissenschaft und Politik*, pp. 235–255. Berlin: edition sigma.

Benedick, R. E. (1998). *Ozone Diplomacy. New Directions in Safeguarding the Planet* (2nd ed.). Cambridge, Mass.: Harvard University Press.

Bentham, J. (1789 [1988]). *The Principles of Morals and Legislation*. Amherst: Prometheus Books.

Berck, P. and K. Sydsæter (1993). *Economist's Mathematical Manual* (2nd ed.). Berlin: Springer.

Bergson, A. (1938). A reformulation of certain aspects of welfare economics. *Quarterly Journal of Economics 52*, 310–334.

Bernheim, B. D., B. Peleg, and M. D. Whinston (1987). Coalition-proof Nash equilibria: I. Concepts. *Journal of Economic Theory 42*, 1–12.

Bertram, G. (1992). Tradable emission permits and the control of greenhouse gases. *Journal of Development Studies 28*(3), 423–446.

Biermann, F. (1997). Financing environmental policies in the South: Experience from the multilateral ozone fund. *International Environmental Affairs 9*(3), 179–218.

Biermann, F. (1998). *Weltumweltpolitik zwischen Nord und Süd: Die neue Verhandlungsmacht der Entwicklungsländer*. Baden-Baden: Nomos.

Biermann, F. and U. E. Simonis (1998). A World Environment and Development Organisation: Functions, opportunities, issues. Policy Paper 9, Development and Peace Foundation, Bonn.

Boadway, R. and N. Bruce (1984). *Welfare Economics.* Oxford: Basil Blackwell.

Boehmer-Christiansen, S. (1988). Black mist and acid rain: Science as fig-leaf of policy. *The Political Quarterly 59*(2), 145–160.

Bohm, P. (1992). Distributional implications of allowing international trade in CO_2 emission quotas. *The Wold Economy 15*(1), 107–114.

Bohm, P. (1997). Are tradable carbon emission quotas internationally acceptable? An inquiry with diplomats as country representatives. Technical report, Nordic Council of Ministers, Copenhagen.

Bohm, P. and B. Larsen (1994). Fairness in a tradable-permit treaty for carbon emission reductions in Europe and the former Soviet Union. *Environmental & Resource Economics 3*(3), 219–239.

Bondareva, O. N. (1963). Some applications of linear programming methods to the theory of cooperative games [in Russian]. *Problemy Kibernetiki 10*, 119–139.

Brams, S. J. and A. D. Taylor (1996). *Fair Division: From Cake-Cutting to Dispute Resolution.* Cambridge, U.K.: Cambridge University Press.

Brennan, G. and J. Buchanan (1985). *The Reason of Rules: Constitutional Political Economy.* Cambridge, U.K.: Cambridge University Press.

Bruckner, T., G. Petschel-Held, F. L. Tóth, H. M. Fuessel, C. Helm, M. Leimbach, and H.-J. Schellnhuber (1999). Climate change decision-support and the tolerable windows approach. *Environmental Modeling and Assessment 4*(4), 217–234.

Buchholz, W. and K. A. Konrad (1995). Strategic transfers and private provision of public goods. *Journal of Public Economics 57*, 489–505.

Carraro, C. and D. Siniscalco (1993). Strategies for the international protection of the environment. *Journal of Public Economics 52*, 309–328.

Cesar, H. S. J. (1994). *Control and Game Models of the Greenhouse Effect: Economic Essays on the Comedy and Tragedy of the Commons.* Berlin: Springer.

Chadwick, M. and M. Hutton (Eds.) (1991). *Acid Deposition in Europe: Environmental Effects, Control Strategies and Policy Options.* York, U.K.: Stockholm Environment Institute.

Chander, P. (1993). Dynamic procedures and incentives in public good economies. *Econometrica 61*(6), 1341–1354.

Chander, P. and H. Tulkens (1995). A core-theoretic solution for the design of cooperative agreements on transfrontier pollution. *International Tax and Public Finance 2*, 279–293.

Chander, P. and H. Tulkens (1997). A core of an economy with multilateral environmental externalities. *International Journal of Game Theory 26*, 379–401.

Chiang, A. C. (1992). *Elements of Dynamic Optimization*. New York: McGraw-Hill.

Chichilnisky, G. and G. Heal (1994). Who should abate carbon emissions? An international viewpoint. *Economic Letters 44*, 443–449.

Chichilnisky, G., G. Heal, and D. Starrett (1993). International emission permits: Equity and efficiency. CEPR Publication 381, Columbia University and Stanford University.

Chichilnisky, G. and W. Thomson (1987). The Walrasian mechanism from equal division is not monotonic with respect to variations in the number of consumers. *Journal of Public Economics 32*, 119–124.

Chun, Y. (1986). The solidarity axiom for quasilinear social choice problems. *Social Choice and Welfare 3*, 297–310.

Cline, W. (1992). *The Economics of Global Warming*. Washington, D.C.: Institute for International Economics.

Convention on Long-Range Transboundary Air Pollution. Geneva, 13 November 1979, in force 16 March 1983. 18 ILM 1442 (1979).

Cooper, R. N. (1998). Toward a real global warming treaty. *Foreign Affairs* (March/April), 66–79.

Cough, C. A., P. D. Bailey, B. Biewald, J. C. I. Kuylenstierna, and M. J. Chadwick (1994). Environmentally targeted objectives for reducing acidification in Europe. *Energy Policy 22*(12), 1055–1066.

Crawford, V. P. (1979). A procedure for generating Pareto-efficient egalitarian-equivalent allocations. *Econometrica 47*(1), 49–60.

Dales, J. H. (1968). *Pollution, Property, and Prices*. Toronto: University of Toronto Press.

D'Aspremont, C. and J. Gabszewicz (1986). On stability of collusion. In G. Matthewson and J. E. Stiglitz (Eds.), *New Developments in the Analysis of Market Structure*, pp. 243–264. New York: Macmillan.

Debreu, G. and H. Scarf (1963). A limit theorem on the core of an economy. *International Economic Review 4*, 235–246.

Dockner, E. J. and N. V. Long (1993). International pollution control: Cooperative versus noncooperative strategies. *Journal of Environmental Economics and Management 24*(1), 13–29.

Dufwenberg, M. and G. Kirchsteiger (1998). A theory of sequential rationality. Research Papers in Economics 1, Stockholm University.

Dupont, C. (1994). Domestic politics and international negotiations: A sequential bargaining model. In P. Allan and C. Schmidt (Eds.), *Game Theory and International Relations: Preferences, Information and Empirical Evidence*, pp. 156–190. Cheltenham: Edward Elgar.

Dutta, P. K. and R. Radner (1998). A strategic analysis of global warming. Mimeo.

Dworkin, R. (1981a). What is equality? Part I: Equality of welfare. *Philosophy and Public Affairs 10*, 182–246.

Dworkin, R. (1981b). What is equality? Part II: Equality of resources. *Philosophy and Public Affairs 10*, 283–345.

Edmonds, J., M. Wise, and D. W. Barns (1995). Carbon coalitions: The cost and effectiveness of energy agreements to alter trajectories of atmospheric carbon dioxide emissions. *Energy Policy 23*(4/5), 309–335.

Egteren, H. v. and J. Tang (1997). Maximum victim benefit: A fair division process in transboundary pollution problems. *Environmental & Resource Economics 10*(4), 363–386.

Egteren, H. v. and M. Weber (1996). Marketable permits, market power and cheating. *Journal of Environmental Economics and Management 30*, 161–173.

Eliassen, A. (1978). The OECD study of long range transport of air pollutants: Long range transport modelling. *Atmospheric Environment 12*, 479–487.

Elster, J. (1991). Ethical individualism and presentism. University of Chicago, mimeo.

Eyckmans, J. (1997). *On the Incentives of Nations to Join International Environmental Agreements*. Ph.D. thesis, Katholieke Universiteit Leuven.

Falkinger, J., F. Hackl, and G. J. Pruckner (1997). A fair mechanism for efficient reduction of global CO_2-emissions. *Finanzarchiv 53*(3/4), 308–331.

Fankhauser, S., R. S. Tol, and D. W. Pearce (1997). The aggregation of climate change damages: A welfare theoretic approach. *Environmental & Resource Economics 10*, 249–266.

Fehr, N.-H. M. v. d. (1993). Tradable emission rights and strategic interaction. *Environmental & Resource Economics 3*, 129–151.

Finus, M. and B. Rundshagen (1998). Toward a positive theory of coalition formation and endogenous instrumental choice in global pollution control. *Public Choice 96*, 145–186.

Foley, D. K. (1967). Resource allocation in the public sector. *Yale Economic Essays 7*(1), 45–98.

Foley, D. K. (1970). Lindahl's solution and the core of an economy with public goods. *Econometrica 38*(1), 66–72.

Folmer, H., P. v. Mouche, and S. Ragland (1993). Interconnected games and international environmental problems. *Environmental & Resource Economics 3*(4), 313–335.

Forster, B. A. (1980). Optimal energy use in a polluted environment. *Journal of Environmental Economics and Management 7*(4), 321–333.

Frankel, J. and K. Rockett (1988). International macroeconomic policy coordination when policy makers do not agree on the true model. *American Economic Review 78*, 313–340.

Fudenberg, D. and J. Tirole (1991). *Game Theory*. Cambridge, Mass.: MIT Press.

Funaki, Y. and T. Yamato (1999). The core of an economy with a common pool resource: A partition function form approach. *International Journal of Game Theory 28*(2), 157–171.

Funtowicz, S. O. and J. R. Ravetz (1993). Science for the post-normal age. *Futures 25*(7), 739–755.

Gandolfo, G. (1997). *Economic Dynamics*. Berlin: Springer.

Gehring, T. (1994). *Dynamic International Regimes: Institutions for International Environmental Governance*. Frankfurt a.M.: Peter Lang.

Ghosh, P. (1993). Structuring the equity issue in climate change. In A. N. Achanta (Ed.), *The Climate Change Agenda: An Indian Perspective*, pp. 267–274. New Delhi: Tata Energy Research Institute.

Gibbons, R. (1992). *A Primer in Game Theory*. New York: Harvester Wheatsheaf.

Grubb, M. (1995). Seeking fair weathers: Ethics and the international debate on climate change. *International Affairs 71*(3), 463–496.

Grubb, M., J. Sebenius, A. Magalhaes, and S. Subak (1992). Sharing the burden. In I. M. Mintzer (Ed.), *Confronting Climate Change: Risks, Implications, and Responses*, pp. 305–322. Cambridge, U.K.: Cambridge University Press.

Hahn, R. W. (1984). Market power and transferable property rights. *Quarterly Journal of Economics 99*, 753–765.

Hanemann, W. M. (1994). Valuing the environment through contingent valuation. *Journal of Economic Perspectives 8*(4), 19–37.

Hanley, N. and C. L. Spash (1993). *Cost-Benefit Analysis and the Environment*. Cheltenham: Edward Elgar.

Hardin, G. (1968). The tragedy of the commons. *Science 162*, 1243–1248.

Harsanyi, J. C. (1955). Cardinal welfare, individualistic ethics and interpersonal comparison of utility. *Journal of Political Economy 63*, 309–321.

Haurie, A. and G. Zaccour (1995). Differential game models of global environmental management. In C. Carraro and J. A. Filar (Eds.), *Control and Game-Theoretic Methods for the Environment*, pp. 3–23. Boston: Birkhäuser.

Helm, C. (1995). *Sind Umweltschutz und Freihandel vereinbar? Ökologischer Reformbedarf des GATT/WTO-Regimes*. Berlin: Edition Sigma.

Helm, C. (1998). International cooperation behind the veil of uncertainty: The case of transboundary acidification. *Environmental & Resource Economics 12*(2), 185–201.

Helm, C., T. Bruckner, and F. L. Tóth (1999). Value judgments and the choice of climate protection strategies. *International Journal of Social Economics 26*(7/8/9), 974–998.

Helm, C. and H.-J. Schellnhuber (1998). Wissenschaftliche Aussagen zum Klimawandel: Zum politischen Umgang mit objektiv unsicheren Ergebnissen der Klimaforschung. In J. L. Lozán, H. Graßl, and P. Hupfer (Eds.), *Warnsignal Klima – Wissenschaftliche Fakten*, pp. 364–367. Berlin: Parey Buchverlag.

Helm, C. and D. Sprinz (1999). Measuring the effectiveness of international environmental regimes. PIK Report 52, Potsdam Institute for Climate Impact Research.

Hoel, M. (1992). International environmental conventions: The case of uniform reductions of emissions. *Environmental & Resource Economics 2*, 141–159.

Hoel, M. (1994). Efficient climate policy in the presence of free riders. *Journal of Environmental Economics and Management 27*, 259–274.

Ichiichi, T. (1981). Super-modularity: Applications to convex games and to the greedy algorithm for lp. *Journal of Economic Theory 25*, 283–286.

Iida, K. (1993). Analytical uncertainty and international cooperation: Theory and application to international economic policy coordination. *International Studies Quarterly 37*, 431–457.

IPCC (1990). *Climate Change: The IPCC Scientific Assessment*. Cambridge, U.K.: Cambridge University Press.

IPCC (1996a). *Climate Change 1995: Economic and Social Dimensions of Climate Change*. Cambridge, U.K.: Cambridge University Press.

IPCC (1996b). *Climate Change 1995: Impacts, Adaptations and Mitigation of Climate Change: Scientific-Technical Analyses*. Cambridge, U.K.: Cambridge University Press.

IPCC (1996c). *Climate Change 1995: The Science of Climate Change*. Cambridge, U.K.: Cambridge University Press.

Johansson, P.-O. (1993). *Cost-Benefit Analysis of Environmental Change*. Cambridge, U.K.: Cambridge University Press.

Kamien, M. I. and N. L. Schwartz (1991). *Dynamic Optimization* (2nd ed.). Amsterdam: North-Holland.

Kaneko, M. (1977). The ratio equilibria and the core of the voting game $G(N, W)$ in a public goods economy. *Econometrica 45*(7), 1589–1594.

Keohane, R. O. and M. E. Levy (Eds.) (1996). *Institutions for Environmental Aid: Pitfalls and Promise*. Cambridge, Mass.: MIT Press.

Klaassen, G. (1996). *Acid Rain and Environmental Degradation: The Economics of Emission Trading.* Cheltenham: Edward Elgar.

Kolm, S.-C. (1996). Playing fair with fairness: A comment to Arnsperger's 'envy-freeness and distributive justice'. *Journal of Economic Surveys 10*(2), 199–215.

Koutstaal, P. (1997). *Economic Policy and Climate Change: Tradable Permits for Reducing Carbon Emissions.* Cheltenham: Edward Elgar.

Krutilla, J. (1967). Conservation reconsidered. *American Economic Review 56*, 777–786.

Kverndokk, S. (1995). Tradable CO_2 emission permits: Initial distribution as a justice problem. *Environmental Values 4*, 129–148.

Kyoto Protocol to the United Nations Framework Convention on Climate Change. Kyoto, 10 December 1997. UN-Doc FCCC/CP/1997/L.7/Add.1 (1997).

Levhari, D. and N. Liviatan (1972). On stability in the saddle-point sense. *Journal of Economic Theory 4*, 88–93.

Levy, M. A. (1995). International cooperation to combat acid rain. In H. O. Bergesen and G. Parmann (Eds.), *Green Globe Yearbook of International Co-operation and Development*, pp. 59–68. Oxford: Oxford University Press.

Lind, R. C. (1997). Intertemporal equity, discounting, and economic efficiency in water policy evaluation. *Climatic Change 37*, 41–62.

Lindahl, E. (1919). *Die Gerechtigkeit der Besteuerung.* Lund: Gleerup [English translation: Just taxation – a positive solution. In R. A. Musgrave and A. T. Peacock (Eds.), *Classics in the Theory of Public Finance.* London: Macmillan, 1958].

Lipsey, R. G. and K. Lancaster (1956). The general theory of second best. *Review of Economic Studies 24*(7), 11–32.

Long, N. V. (1992). Pollution control: A differential game approach. *Annals of Operations Research 37*, 283–296.

Luce, R. D. and H. Raiffa (1957). *Games and Decisions.* New York: John Wiley and Sons.

Mäler, K.-G. (1989). The acid rain game. In H. Folmer and E. v. Ierland (Eds.), *Valuation Methods and Policy Making in Environmental Economics*, pp. 231–252. Amsterdam: Elsevier.

Mäler, K.-G. (1991). Incentives in international environmental problems. In H. Siebert (Ed.), *Environmental Scarcity. The Economic Dimension*, pp. 75–93. Tübingen: J.C.B. Mohr.

Mäler, K.-G. (1992). Critical loads and international environmental cooperation. In R. Pethig (Ed.), *Conflicts and Cooperation in Managing Environmental Resources*, pp. 71–81. Berlin: Springer.

Mäler, K.-G. and A. de Zeeuw (1998). The acid rain differential game. *Environmental & Resource Economics 12*, 167–184.

Mas-Colell, A. (1980). Remarks on the game-theoretic analysis of a simple distribution of surplus problem. *International Journal of Game Theory 9*(3), 125–140.

Mas-Colell, A. and J. Silvestre (1989). Cost sharing equilibria: A Lindahlian approach. *Journal of Economic Theory 47*, 239–256.

Mas-Colell, A., M. D. Whinston, and J. R. Green (1995). *Microeconomic Theory*. Oxford: Oxford University Press.

McGinnis, M. D. (1986). Issue linkage and the evolution of international cooperation. *Journal of Conflict Resolution 30*(1), 141–170.

Mirkowski, P. (1991). The when, the how and the why of mathematical expression in the history of economic analysis. *Journal of Economic Perspectives 5*(1), 97–112.

Montgomery, W. D. (1972). Markets in licences and efficient pollution control programs. *Journal of Economic Theory 5*, 395–418.

Morrow, J. D. (1994). Modelling the forms of international cooperation: Distribution versus information. *International Organization 48*(3), 387–423.

Moulin, H. (1987). Egalitarian-equivalent cost sharing of a public good. *Econometrica 55*(4), 963–976.

Moulin, H. (1990). Fair division under joint ownership. *Social Choice and Welfare 7*, 149–170.

Moulin, H. (1991). Welfare bounds in the fair division problem. *Journal of Economic Theory 54*(2), 321–337.

Moulin, H. (1992a). All sorry to disagree: A general principle for the provision of nonrival goods. *Scandinavian Journal of Economics 94*(1), 37–51.

Moulin, H. (1992b). An application of the Shapley value to fair division with money. *Econometrica 60*(6), 1331–1349.

Moulin, H. (1995). *Cooperative Microeconomics. A Game-theoretic Introduction.* Princeton, N.J.: Princeton University Press.

Moulin, H. and W. Thomson (1988). Can everyone benefit from growth? Two difficulties. *Journal of Mathematical Economics 17*, 339–345.

Murdoch, J. C. and T. Sandler (1997). The voluntary provision of a pure public good: The case of reduced CFC emissions and the Montreal Protocol. *Journal of Public Economics 63*, 331–349.

Murdoch, J. C., T. Sandler, and K. Sargent (1997). A tale of two collectives: Sulphur versus nitrogen oxides emission reduction in Europe. *Economica 64* (254), 281–301.

Myerson, R. B. (1991). *Game Theory: Analysis of Conflict.* Cambridge, Mass.: Harvard University Press.

Ng, Y.-K. (1997). A case for happiness, cardinalism, and interpersonal comparability. *Economic Journal 107*, 1848–1858.

Nordhaus, W. D. (1992). An optimal transition path for controlling greenhouse gases. *Science 258*, 1315–1319.

Nordhaus, W. D. and Z. Yang (1996). A regional dynamic general-equilibrium model of alternative climate-change strategies. *American Economic Review 86* (4), 741–765.

OECD (1977). *The OECD Programme on Long-range Transport of Air Pollutants.* Paris: OECD.

OECD (Ed.) (1992). *Climate Change: Designing a Tradeable Permit System.* Paris: OECD.

Osborne, M. J. and A. Rubinstein (1994). *A Course in Game Theory.* Cambridge, Mass.: MIT Press.

Ostrom, E. (1990). *Governing the Commons.* Cambridge, U.K.: Cambridge University Press.

Ott, H. E. (1998). The Kyoto Protocol: Unfinished business. *Environment 40* (6), 16–45.

Pazner, E. A. and D. Schmeidler (1978). Egalitarian equivalent allocations: A new concept of economic equity. *Quarterly Journal of Economics 92* (4), 671–687.

Perrings, C. and D. Pearce (1994). Threshold effects and incentives for the conservation of biodiversity. *Environmental & Resource Economics 4*, 13–28.

Petschel-Held, G., H.-J. Schellnhuber, T. Bruckner, F. L. Tóth, and K. Hasselmann (1999). The tolerable windows approach: Theoretical and methodological foundations. *Climatic Change 41*(3/4), 303–331.

Ploeg, F. v. d. and A. de Zeeuw (1992). International aspects of pollution control. *Environmental & Resource Economics 2*, 117–139.

Polinsky, M. (1980). Resolving nuisance disputes: The simple economics of injunctive and damage remedies. *Stanford Law Review 32*, 1075–1112.

Pontryagin, L. S., V. G. Boltyanksii, R. Gamkrelidze, and E. F. Mischchenko (1962). *The Mathematical Theory of Optimal Processes.* New York: John Wiley and Sons.

Portney, P. R. (1994). The contingent valuation debate: Why economists should care. *Journal of Economic Perspectives 8*(4), 3–17.

Protocol on Further Reduction of Sulphur Emissions. Oslo, 14 June 1994, in force.

Protocol on the Reduction of Sulphur Emissions or their Transboundary Fluxes by at least Thirty Per Cent. Helsinki, 8 July 1985, in force 2 September 1987. 27 ILM 707 (1987).

Rabin, M. (1993). Incorporating fairness into game theory and economics. *American Economic Review 83*(5), 1281–1302.

Rawls, J. (1971). *A Theory of Justice.* Cambridge, Mass.: Harvard University Press.

Rawls, J. (1993). The law of peoples. In S. Shute and S. Hurley (Eds.), *On Human Rights: The Oxford Amnesty Lectures 1993*, pp. 41–82. New York: Basic Books.

Rawls, J. (1999). *Law of Peoples.* Cambridge, Mass.: Harvard University Press.

Rayner, S., E. L. Malone, and M. Thompson (1999). Equity issues in integrated assessment. In F. L. Tóth (Ed.), *Fair Weather? Fairness and Equity Concerns in Climate Change*, pp. 11–43. London: Earthscan.

Roemer, J. (1986). The mismarriage of bargaining theory and distributive justice. *Ethics 97*, 88–110.

Rose, A. (1998). Global warming policy: Who decides what is fair? *Energy Policy 26*(1), 1–3.

Rose, A., B. Stevens, J. Edmonds, and M. Wise (1998). International equity and differentiation in global warming policy. *Environmental & Resource Economics 12*, 25–51.

Rosenthal, R. W. (1971). External economies and cores. *Journal of Economic Theory 3*, 182–188.

Rowlands, I. H. (1995). Explaining national climate change policies. *Global Environmental Change 5*(3), 235–249.

Samuelson, P. (1947). *Foundations of Economic Analysis*. Cambridge, U.K.: Cambridge University Press.

Scarf, H. E. (1971). On the existence of a cooperative solution for a general class of n-person games. *Journal of Economic Theory 3*, 169–181.

Schelling, T. (1992). *The Strategy of Conflict*. Cambridge, Mass.: Harvard University Press.

Schellnhuber, H.-J. (1998). Earth system analysis: The scope of the challenge. In H.-J. Schellnhuber and V. Wenzel (Eds.), *Earth System Analysis: Integrating Science for Sustainability*, pp. 3–195. Berlin: Springer.

Schellnhuber, H.-J. (1999). Earth system analysis and the second copernican revolution. *Nature 402*(6761), 19–23.

Schellnhuber, H.-J. and G. W. Yohe (1997). Comprehending the economic and social dimensions of climate change by integrated assessment. Proceedings of Conference of the World Climate Research Programme (WCPR).

Schiller, A., U. Mikolajewicz, and R. Voss (1997). The stability of the northern atlantic thermohaline circulation in a coupled ocean-atmosphere general circulation model. *Climate Dynamics 13*, 325–347.

Schwarze, R. and P. Zapfel (1998). Sulfur allowance trading and the regional clean air incentives market: How similar are the programs really? Discussion Paper 1998/06, Technical University Berlin.

Selten, R. (1965). Spieltheoretische Behandlung eines Oligopolmodells mit Nachfrageträgheit. *Zeitschrift für die gesamte Staatswissenschaft 121*, 301–324.

Sen, A. (1970). *Collective Choice and Social Welfare*. San Francisco: Holden Day.

Sen, A. (1987). *On Ethics and Economics.* Oxford: Blackwell.

Shackley, S. (1997). The IPCC: Consensual knowledge and global politics. *Global Environmental Change 7*(1), 77–79.

Shapley, L. S. (1953). A value for n-person games. In H. W. Kuhn and W. Tucker (Eds.), *Contributions to the Theory of Games II (Annals of Mathematical Studies, 28)*, pp. 307–317. Princeton, N.J.: Princeton University Press.

Shapley, L. S. (1967). On balanced sets and cores. *Naval Research Logistics Quarterly 14*, 453–460.

Shapley, L. S. (1971). Cores of convex games. *International Journal of Game Theory 1*, 11–26.

Shapley, L. S. and M. Shubik (1969). On the core of an economic system with externalities. *American Economic Review 59*, 678–684.

Shaw, R. W. (1993). Acid rain negotiations in North America and Europe: A study in contrast. In G. Sjöstedt (Ed.), *International Environmental Negotiations*, pp. 84–109. Newbury Park: Sage Publications.

Shubik, M. (1984). *A Game-Theoretic Approach to Political Economy.* Cambridge, Mass.: MIT Press.

Shue, H. (1995). Ethics, the environment and the changing international order. *International Affairs 71*(3), 453–461.

Simonis, U. E. (1996a). Internationally tradable emission certificates: Linking environmental protection and development. *Economics 53*, 96–110.

Simonis, U. E. (Ed.) (1996b). *Weltumweltpolitik: Grundriß und Bausteine eines neuen Politikfeldes.* Berlin: edition sigma.

Simonis, U. E. (1998). Das 'Kyoto-Protocol': Aufforderung zu einer innovativen Klimapolitik. FS II 98-403, Wissenschaftszentrum Berlin.

Smith, K. R. (1991). Allocating responsibility for global warming: The natural debt index. *Ambio 20*(2), 95–96.

Sprinz, D. and C. Helm (1999). The effect of global environmental regimes: A measurement concept. *International Political Science Review 20*(4), 359–369.

Starrett, D. A. (1973). A note on externalities and the core. *Econometrica 41*(1), 179–183.

Stavins, R. N. (1995). Transaction costs and tradeable permits. *Journal of Environmental Economics and Management 29*, 133–148.

Steinhaus, H. (1948). The problem of fair division. *Econometrica 16*, 101–104.

Stocker, T. F. and A. Schmitter (1997). Influence of CO_2 emission rates on the stability of the thermohaline circulation. *Nature 388*, 862–865.

Streeten, P. (1997). Contemporary economics: A critique. In F. Biermann, S. Büttner, and C. Helm (Eds.), *Zukunftsfähige Entwicklung. Herausforderungen an Wissenschaft und Politik*, pp. 33–52. Berlin: edition sigma.

Sudgen, R. (1995). A theory of focal points. *Economic Journal 105*, 533–550.

Summers, L. H. (1991). The scientific illusion of empirical macroeconomics. *Scandinavian Journal of Economics 93*, 129–148.

Takayama, A. (1985). *Mathematical Economics* (2nd ed.). Cambridge, U.K.: Cambridge University Press.

Thomson, W. (1983a). The fair division of a fixed supply among a growing population. *Mathematics of Operations Research 8*, 319–326.

Thomson, W. (1983b). Problems of fair division and the egalitarian solution. *Journal of Economic Theory 31*, 211–226.

Tietenberg, T. H. (1985). *Emissions Trading*. Washington, D.C.: Resources for the Future.

Tinbergen, J. (1946). *Redelijke Inkomensverdeling*. Haarlem: De Gulden Pers.

Tocqueville, A. d. (1860 [1969]). *Democracy in America*. New York: Anchor Books.

Tóth, F. L. (1995). Discounting in integrated assessment models. *Energy Policy 23*(4/5), 403–409.

Tóth, F. L. (Ed.) (1999). *Fair Weather? Fairness and Equity Concerns in Climate Change*. London: Earthscan.

Tsutsui, S. and K. Mino (1990). Nonlinear strategies in dynamic duopolistic competition and sticky prices. *Journal of Economic Theory 52*, 136–161.

UNCTAD (Ed.) (1992). *Combating Global Warming: Study on a Global System of Tradable Carbon Emission Entitlements*. Geneva: UNCTAD.

UNCTAD (1998). *Greenhouse Gas Emissions Trading: Defining the Principles, Modalities, Rules and Guidelines for Verification, Reporting & Accountability.* Geneva: UNCTAD.

UNECE (1992). Impacts of long-range transboundary air pollution. Air pollution studies No 8, ECE/EB.AIR/31, UNECE.

UNECE (1993). The state of transboundary air pollution: 1992 update. Air pollution studies No 9, ECE/EB.AIR/34, UNECE.

United Nations Framework Convention on Climate Change. New York, 9 May 1992, in force 21 March 1994. 31 ILM 849 (1992).

Uzawa, H. (1999). Global warming as a cooperative game. *Environmental Economics and Policy Studies 2*(1), 1–37.

Varian, H. R. (1974). Equity, envy, and efficiency. *Journal of Economic Theory 9*, 63–91.

Victor, D. G., N. Nakiçenovic, and N. Victor (1998). The Kyoto Protocol carbon bubble: Implications for Russia, Ukraine, and emission trading. IR-98-094, IIASA, Laxenburg.

Victor, D. G., K. Raustiala, and E. B. Skolnikoff (Eds.) (1998). *The Implementation and Effectiveness of International Environmental Commitments: Theory and Practice.* Cambridge, Mass.: MIT Press.

WBGU (1996). *World in Transition. Ways Towards Global Environmental Solutions.* Berlin: Springer.

Weber, R. J. (1988). Probabilistic values for games. In A. Roth (Ed.), *The Shapley Value.* Cambridge, U.K.: Cambridge University Press.

Wetstone, G. and A. Rosencranz (1983). *Acid Rain in Europe and North America: National Responses to an International Problem.* Washington D.C.: Environmental Law Institute.

Wickström, B.-A. (1992). Precedence, privilege, preferences, plus Pareto principle: Some examples on egalitarian ethics and economic efficiency. *Public Choice 73*, 101–115.

Yohe, G. and R. Wallace (1996). Near term mitigation policy for global change under uncertainty: Minimizing the expected cost of meeting unknown concentration thresholds. *Environmental Modeling and Assessment 1*(1/2), 47–57.

Young, H. P. (1994a). *Equity in Theory and Practice.* Princeton, N.J.: Princeton University Press.

Young, O. R. (1994b). *International Governance: Protecting the Environment in a Stateless Society*. Ithaca: Cornell University Press.

Young, O. R. (Ed.) (1997). *Global Governance: Drawing Insights from the Environmental Experience*. Cambridge, Mass.: MIT Press.

Zajac, E. E. (1995). *Political Economy of Fairness*. Cambridge, Mass.: MIT Press.

Index